About the Authors

Edward C. Baig writes the weekly "Personal Technology" column in *USA TODAY* and is a regular on *USA TODAY*'s "Talking Tech" podcasts. Ed is also the author of *Macs For Dummies,* 11th Edition (John Wiley & Sons), and the cowriter of *iPhone For Dummies.* Before joining *USA TODAY* as a columnist and reporter in 1999, Ed spent six years at *Business Week,* where he wrote and edited stories about consumer tech, personal finance, collectibles, travel, and wine tasting, among other topics. He received the Medill School of Journalism 1999 Financial Writers and Editors Award for contributions to the "*Business Week* Investor Guide to Online Investing." That followed a three-year stint at *U.S. News & World Report,* where Ed was the lead tech writer for the News You Can Use section but also dabbled in numerous other subjects.

Ed began his journalist career at *Fortune* magazine, gaining the best basic training imaginable during his early years as a fact checker and contributor to the Fortune 500. Through the dozen years he worked at the magazine, Ed covered leisure-time industries, penned features on the lucrative "dating" market and the effect of religion on corporate managers, and was heavily involved in the Most Admired Companies project. Ed also started up *Fortune*'s Products to Watch column, a venue for low- and high-tech items.

Bob LeVitus, often referred to as "Dr. Mac," has written or co-written over 65 popular computer books, with millions of copies in print. His titles include *OS X Mountain Lion For Dummies, iPhone For Dummies, Incredible iPad Apps For Dummies,* and *Microsoft Office 2011 For Mac For Dummies* for John Wiley & Sons; *Stupid Mac Tricks* and *Dr. Macintosh* for Addison-Wesley; and *The Little iTunes Book*, 3rd Edition, and *The Little iDVD Book*, 2nd Edition, for Peachpit Press.

Bob has also penned the popular "Dr. Mac" column for the *Houston Chronicle* for more than 15 years and has been published in pretty much every magazine that ever used the word *Mac* in its title. His achievements have been documented in major media around the world. (Yes, that was him juggling a keyboard in *USA TODAY* a few years back!)

Bob is known for his expertise, trademark humorous style, and ability to translate techie jargon into usable and fun advice for regular folks. Bob is also a prolific public speaker, presenting more than 100 Macworld Expo training sessions in the United States and abroad, keynote addresses in three countries, and Macintosh training seminars in many U.S. cities.

Dedications

I dedicate this book to my beautiful wife, Janie, for inspiring me in myriad ways every day I am with her. And to my incredible kids: my adorable little girl, Sydney (one of her first words was *iPod*); my little boy, Sammy (who is all smiles from the moment he wakes up in the morning); and my "canine" puppy daughter, Sadie (who thankfully hasn't chewed on the iPad yet). My kids are already hooked on the iPad — it's only a matter of time for the mini. This book is also dedicated to the memory of my "canine" son, Eddie Jr. I am madly in love with you all. — Ed Baig

Every book I've ever written and every book I will ever write is book is dedicated to my wife, Lisa, who taught me almost everything I know about almost everything I know except technology. They're also dedicated to my kids, Allison and Jacob, who love iPhones and iPads almost as much as I love them (my kids, not my gadgets). This book, however, is dedicated to my mom, Rhoda, who received her first iPad (an iPad mini, of course) for Chanukah and who will need this book a lot more than my wife or kids. Love ya, mom! — Bob LeVitus

Authors' Acknowledgments

Special thanks to everyone at Apple who helped us turn this book around so quickly: Katie Cotton, Natalie Kerris, Natalie Harrison, Teresa Brewer, Janette Barrios, Trudy Muller, Keri Walker, Jennifer Bowcock, Simon Pope, Christine Monaghan, Tom Neumayr, and everyone else who lent a hand from the mothership out in Cupertino. We couldn't have done it without you.

Big-time thanks to the gang at Wiley: Bob "Incredibly Laidback Under Pressure" Woerner, Kevin "The Ghost" Kirschner, Becky Whitney, Andy "The Boss" Cummings, and our incredible technical editor Dennis R. Cohen, whose suggestions and observations helped immensely (even the ones we ignored). Finally, thanks to everyone at Wiley we don't know by name. If you helped with this project in any way, you have our everlasting thanks.

Ed adds: Thanks to my agent, Matt Wagner, for again turning me into a *For Dummies* author. Matt had the right instincts to push the iPad franchise, even back when we were calling the first edition of this book *Project X For Dummies*. I'd also like to thank Geri Tucker, Nancy Blair, and all my *USA TODAY* friends and colleagues for your continuing support and encouragement of such projects. Thanks also go to Eli Blumenthal, who as an intern has gone above and beyond what is expected. Most of all, thanks to my loving family for understanding my nightly (and weekend) disappearances as we raced to get this project completed on time. You are quite simply the greatest.

And Bob says: Extra special thanks to Carole "Swifty" Jelen, who has been my literary agent for my entire career (over 20 years) and is still the best in the biz. I don't say this often enough, Carole, but you rock!

Publisher's Acknowledgments

We're proud of this book; please send us your comments at http://dummies.custhelp.com. For other comments, please contact our Customer Care Department within the U.S. at 877-762-2974, outside the U.S. at 317-572-3993, or fax 317-572-4002.

Some of the people who helped bring this book to market include the following:

Acquisitions and Editorial

Project Editor: Kevin Kirschner

Executive Editor: Bob Woerner

Copy Editor: Becky Whitney

Technical Editor: Dennis Cohen

Editorial Assistant: Annie Sullivan

Sr. Editorial Assistant: Cherie Case

Cover Photo: Background © Pavel Khorenyan/ iStockphoto. Image of iPad mini created by John Wiley & Sons, Inc.

Cartoons: Rich Tennant (www.the5thwave.com)

Composition Services

Senior Project Coordinator: Kristie Rees

Layout and Graphics: Joyce Haughey

Proofreaders: Melissa Cossell, BIM Indexing & Proofreading Services

Indexer: Potomac Indexing, LLC

Publishing and Editorial for Technology Dummies

   Richard Swadley, Vice President and Executive Group Publisher

   Andy Cummings, Vice President and Publisher

   Mary Bednarek, Executive Acquisitions Director

   Mary C. Corder, Editorial Director

Publishing for Consumer Dummies

   Kathleen Nebenhaus, Vice President and Executive Publisher

Composition Services

   Debbie Stailey, Director of Composition Services

Contents at a Glance

Table of Contents

Introduction

As Yogi Berra would say, "It was déjà vu all over again" — front-page treatment, top billing on network TV and cable, and diehards lining up for days in advance to ensure landing a highly lusted-after product from Apple. The product generating the remarkable buzz this time around is the iPad mini, the first iPad that doesn't sport a 10-inch screen (9.7 inches, to be precise). But this tiny titan packs a heck of a punch with its pocket- (or purse-) friendly 7.9-inch screen and the lowest price ever for an iPad. We hope you bought this book to find out how to get the most out of your remarkable device. Our goal is to deliver that information in a light and breezy fashion. We expect you to have fun using your iPad mini. We equally hope that you have fun spending time with us.

About This Book

We need to get one thing out of the way from the get-go: We think you're pretty darn smart for buying a *For Dummies* book. It says to us that you have the confidence and intelligence to know what you don't know. The *For Dummies* franchise is built around the core notion that everyone feels insecure about certain topics when tackling them for the first time, especially when those topics have to do with technology.

As with most Apple products, iPads are beautifully designed and intuitive to use. And though our editors may not want us to reveal this dirty little secret (especially on the first page, for goodness' sake), the truth is that you'll get pretty far by simply exploring the iPad's many functions and features on your own, without the help of this (or any other) book.

Okay, now that we've spilled the beans, we'll tell you why you shouldn't run back to the bookstore and request a refund. This book is chock-full of useful tips, advice, and other nuggets that should make your iPad experience all the more pleasurable. We'd even go so far as to say that you wouldn't find some of these nuggets anywhere else. So keep this book nearby and consult it often.

Conventions Used in This Book

First, we want to tell you how we go about our business. *iPad mini For Dummies* makes generous use of numbered steps, bullet lists, and pictures. Web addresses are shown in a special monofont typeface, `like this`. We also include a few sidebars with information that isn't required reading (not that any of this book is) but that we hope will provide a richer understanding of certain subjects. Overall, we aim to keep technical jargon to a minimum, under the guiding principle that, with rare exceptions, you need not know what any of it really means.

This book is written for people who use the iPad mini (though most of it applies to most iPad models). To avoid confusion and awkward sentences, though, we mostly refer to the iPad mini as an *iPad*. If we're talking about another model, we refer to it as a first-, second-, third-, or fourth-generation iPad, even though those aren't the official, Apple-sanctioned monikers.

Put another way, when you see the word *iPad,* we're talking about the iPad mini unless we say otherwise.

How This Book Is Organized

Here's something we imagine you've heard before: Most books have a beginning, a middle, and an end, and you do well to adhere to that linear structure — unless you're one of those knuckleheads out to ruin it for the rest of us by revealing that the butler did it.

Fortunately, there's no ending to spoil in a *For Dummies* book. Though you may want to digest this book from start to finish (and we hope you do), we don't penalize you for skipping ahead or jumping around. Having said that, we organized *iPad mini For Dummies* in the order we think makes the most sense, as follows.

Part I: Getting to Know Your iPad mini

In the introductory chapters of Part I, you tour the iPad mini inside and out, find out what all those buttons and other nonvirtual doodads do, and get some hands-on (or, more precisely, fingers-on) experience with the iPad's virtual multitouch display. And, of course, you'll see how easy it is to synchronize stuff on your Mac or PC — over USB or Wi-Fi — with your dynamic device.

Part II: The Internet iPad mini

Part II is all about getting connected with your iPad mini. Along the way, you discover how to surf the web with the Safari web browser, set up mail accounts, send and receive mail and iMessages, and work with maps.

Part III: The Multimedia iPad mini

Part III is where the fun truly begins. You discover how to use your iPad mini for music, video, movies, and photos, as well as how to buy and read iBooks from the iBookstore. It's also the part where you read all about the tablet's front and rear cameras.

Part IV: The iPad mini at Work

In this part, all you need to know about buying and using apps from the iTunes App Store is in Chapter 11. Then you'll get up close and personal with the Calendar and Contacts apps in Chapter 12. In Chapter 13, you spend some quality time with the Notes and Reminders apps as well as the Notification Center with a brief interlude paying tribute to social media. In Chapter 14, you meet Siri, your (mostly) intelligent assistant.

Part V: The Undiscovered iPad mini

In Part V, you find out how to apply your preferences using internal settings on the iPad mini, discover where to go for troubleshooting assistance if your iPad should misbehave, and find out about some must-have accessories you may want to consider.

Part VI: The Part of Tens

The Part of Tens is otherwise known as the *For Dummies* answer to David Letterman (both of which, as it happens, have close ties to Indianapolis). The lists in Part VI steer you to some of our favorite iPad apps as well as to some handy tips and shortcuts.

Icons Used in This Book

Little round pictures (or *icons*) appear in the left margins throughout this book. Consider these icons as miniature road signs, telling you something extra about the topic at hand or hammering home a point.

Here's what the five icons used in this book look like and mean.

These juicy morsels, shortcuts, and recommendations might make the task at hand faster or easier.

This icon emphasizes the stuff we think you ought to retain. You may even jot down a note to yourself on the iPad.

Put on your propeller beanie and insert your pocket protector; this text includes the truly geeky stuff. You can safely ignore this material, but if it weren't interesting or informative, we wouldn't have bothered to write it.

You wouldn't intentionally run a stop sign, would you? In the same fashion, ignoring warnings may be hazardous to your iPad and (by extension) your wallet. There, you now know how these warning icons work, for you have just received your first warning!

A New icon sits next to anything that's new or improved in iOS 6.

Where to Go from Here

Why, go straight to Chapter 1, of course (without passing Go).

In all seriousness, we wrote this book for you, so please let us know what you think. If we screwed up, confused you, left out something, or (heaven forbid) made you angry, drop us a note. If we hit you with one pun too many, it helps to know that also. Because writers are people too (believe it or not), we also encourage positive feedback if you think it's warranted. Kindly send an e-mail message to Ed at Baigdummies@gmail.com and to Bob at iPadLeVitus@boblevitus.com. We do our best to respond to reasonably polite e-mail in a timely fashion. Most of all, we thank you for buying our book. Please enjoy it along with your new iPad.

Note: At the time we wrote this book, all the information it contains was accurate for the Wi-Fi iPad mini and the Wi-Fi + Cellular iPad mini, version 6.0 of the iOS (operating system) used by the iPad, and version 10.7 of iTunes. Apple will likely introduce new iPad mini models and new versions of iOS and iTunes between book editions. If you've bought a new iPad mini and its hardware or user interface or the version of iTunes on your computer looks a little different, check out what Apple has to say at www.apple.com/ipad. You'll no doubt find updates on the company's latest releases. When a change is substantial, we may add an update or bonus information that you can download at this book's companion website: www.dummies.com/go/ipadfdupdates.

Part I
Getting to Know Your iPad mini

The 5th Wave   By Rich Tennant

iPad

"In fact it does come with a compass."

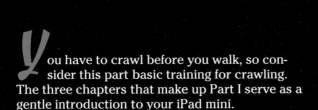

*Y*ou have to crawl before you walk, so consider this part basic training for crawling. The three chapters that make up Part I serve as a gentle introduction to your iPad mini.

We start out nice and easy in Chapter 1, with a big-picture overview, even letting you know what's in the box (if you haven't already peeked). Then we examine just some of the cool things your iPad mini can do. We finish things off with a quick-and-dirty tour of the hardware and the software so that you'll know where things are when you need them.

Next, after you're somewhat familiar with where things are and what they do, we move right along to a bunch of useful iPad skills, such as turning the darn thing on and off (which is very important) and locking and unlocking your iPad (which is also very important). Chapter 2 covers useful tips and tricks to help you master the iPad's unique multitouch interface so that you can use it effectively and efficiently.

Then, in Chapter 3, we explore the process of synchronization over USB and Wi-Fi and how to get data — contacts, appointments, movies, songs, podcasts, books, and so on — from your computer into your iPad, quickly and painlessly.

Unveiling the iPad mini

In This Chapter

▶ Looking at the iPad mini's brilliant disguises
▶ Touring the outside of the iPad mini
▶ Checking out the iPad mini's applications

Congratulations! You've selected one of the most incredible handheld devices we've ever seen. Of course, the iPad mini combines a killer audio and video iPod, an e-book reader, a powerful Internet communications device, a superb handheld gaming device, still and video cameras, and a platform for over 750,000 apps (at the time this book was written) — and probably a lot more by the time you read this chapter.

Apple has created four other iPad models; to avoid confusion, we refer to them as the first-, second-, third-, and fourth-generation iPads when we mention them in this book. We refer to the iPad mini as the iPad mini when necessary to differentiate it from other models, but we mostly refer to it as simply an iPad (because that's what it is).

In this chapter, we offer a gentle introduction to all the pieces that make up your iPad mini, plus overviews of its revolutionary hardware and software features.

Exploring the iPad mini's Big Picture

The iPad mini has many best-of-class features, but perhaps its most notable feature is its lack of a physical keyboard or stylus. Instead, it has a 7.9-inch, super-high-resolution touchscreen — 163 pixels per inch (ppi) — that you operate using a pointing device you're already intimately familiar with: your finger.

And what a display it is. It's true that some iPad models offer Retina displays with more ppi, but any way you look at it, the iPad mini's screen is still gorgeous.

Other things we love include the iPad mini's plethora of built-in sensors. It has an *accelerometer* to detect when you rotate the device from portrait to landscape mode and instantly adjust what's on the display accordingly.

The screen rotates — that is, unless the Screen Orientation Lock is engaged. We tell you more about this feature shortly.

A light sensor adjusts the display's brightness in response to the current ambient lighting conditions.

And your iPad mini has a three-axis gyro sensor that works in conjunction with the accelerometer and built-in compass. Although all iPads can sense their orientation and direction, the iPad mini senses such things even better and faster than some earlier models.

Last, but definitely not least, Siri — the spectacular, voice-controlled personal assistant — is happy to do almost anything you ask.

In the following sections, we're not simply marveling about the wonderful screen and sensors. Now it's time to take a brief look at the rest of the iPad's features, broken down by product category.

The iPad as an iPod

We agree with the late Steve Jobs on this one: The iPad is magical — and without a doubt, the best iPod Apple has ever produced. You can enjoy all your existing iPod content — music, audiobooks, audio and video podcasts, iTunes U courses, music videos, television shows, and movies — on the iPad's gorgeous, high-resolution color display, which is bigger, brighter, and richer than any iPod or iPhone display that came before it.

Here's the bottom line: If you can get the content — video, audio, or whatever — into iTunes on your Mac or PC, you can synchronize it and watch or listen to it on your iPad. And, of course, you can always buy or rent content on your iPad with the iTunes and iBooks apps.

Chapter 3 is all about syncing, but for now, just know that some video content may need to be converted to an iPad-compatible format (with proper resolution, frame rate, bit rate, and file format) to play on your iPad. If you try to sync an incompatible video file, iTunes alerts you that an issue exists.

If you see an error message about an incompatible video file, select the file in iTunes and choose Advanced↪Create iPad or Apple TV Version. When the conversion is finished, sync again. Chapter 8 covers video and video compatibility in more detail.

What's in the box

Somehow, we think you've already opened the handsome box that houses the iPad mini. But if you haven't, here's what you can expect to find inside:

- **Lightning–to–USB cable:** Use this handy cable to sync or charge your iPad. You can plug the USB connector into your Mac or PC to sync or plug it into the USB power adapter, which we describe next.

  Note: If you connect the USB cable to USB ports on your keyboard, USB hub, display, or another external device, or even to the USB ports on an older Mac or PC, you may be able to sync, but more than likely can't charge the battery. For the most part, only your computer's built-in USB ports (and only recent-vintage computers, at that) have enough juice to recharge the battery. If you use an external USB port, you probably see a `Not Charging` message next to the Battery icon at the top of the screen.

  A powered USB hub, one that plugs into an AC outlet, will *probably* recharge your iPad. Some USB hubs don't provide enough juice to recharge an iPad, but others do. If you have a powered hub, try it. If you see the `Not Charging` message, your hub's not juicy enough.

- **USB power adapter:** Use this adapter to recharge your iPad from a standard AC power outlet.

- **Some Apple logo decals:** Of course.

- **iPad instruction sheet:** Unfortunately (or fortunately, if you're the author of a book

about using the iPad), this little one-page, two-sided "manual" offers precious little useful information beyond "Learn more about iPad features at `www.apple.com/ipadmini`."

- **iPad Info sheet:** Well, it must be important, because it says so right on the cover. You can find basic safety warnings, a bunch of legalese, warranty information, and info on how to dispose of or recycle the iPad. *What! You're getting rid of it already?* A few other pieces of advice: Don't drop the iPad if you can help it, keep the thing dry, and — as with all handheld electronic devices — give full attention to the road while driving (or walking, for that matter).

- **iPad mini:** You were starting to worry. Yes, the iPad mini itself is also in the box.

What's not in the box is a stereo headset. If you want to use a headset for music, video, games, or anything else, you have to find one elsewhere. Might we suggest that you find one that includes a built-in microphone. If you have an iPhone or iPod touch, the headset that comes with it will work just fine. Although the iPad doesn't come with the Voice Memos app that comes with the iPhone, it can record to many of the apps that are available in the App Store, such as the free iTalk Recorder app from Griffin Technology or the $0.99 Voice Memos for iPad app from KendiTech, Inc. A headset with a microphone also serves you well for FaceTime video chats, telephone calls with the free Skype app, and for working with Siri or translating speech-to-text.

And here's another tip at no extra cost: The free HandBrake application (`http://handbrake.fr`) often provides better results than iTunes when converting movie files to an iPad-friendly format. It has a preset for the iPad, so it's simple to use, and it can often convert movie files that iTunes chokes on.

The iPad as an Internet communications device

But wait — there's more! The iPad mini is not only a stellar iPod but also a full-featured Internet communications device with — we're about to drop some industry jargon on you — a rich HTML e-mail client that's compatible with most POP and IMAP mail services, with support for Microsoft Exchange ActiveSync. (For more on this topic, see Chapter 5.) Also onboard is a world-class web browser (Safari) that, unlike on many mobile devices, makes web surfing fun and easy on the eyes. Chapter 4 explains how to surf the web using Safari.

Another cool Internet feature is *Maps,* a killer mapping application that's much improved in iOS 6. By using GPS (Wi-Fi + Cellular models) and triangulation, the iPad mini can determine your location, let you view maps and satellite imagery, and obtain driving directions and traffic information regardless of where you happen to be. (See Chapter 6 for the scoop on Maps.) You can also find businesses, such as gas stations, pizza restaurants, hospitals, and Apple Stores, with only a few taps.

We daresay that the Internet experience on an iPad is far superior to the Internet experience on any other handheld device.

The iPad as an e-book reader

Download the free iBooks app and/or any of the excellent (and free) third-party e-book readers such as the Kindle and Nook apps, and you'll discover a whole new way of finding and reading books. The iBookstore and Newsstand app, covered in Chapter 10, are chock-full of good reading at prices that are lower than a printed copy. Better still, when you read an e-book, you're helping the environment and saving trees. Furthermore, some (if not many) titles include audio, video, or graphical content not available in the printed editions. Plus, a great number of really good books are absolutely free. And best of all, you can carry your entire library in one hand. If you've never read a book on your iPad, give it a try. We think you'll like (or love) it.

The iPad as a multimedia powerhouse

The spectacular screen makes watching videos and movies an extreme pleasure. And, if you add an adapter cable, as discussed in Chapter 17, it's also great for watching video on your HDTV (or even on a non-HD TV), with support for output resolutions up to 1080p.

You don't even need an adapter cable if you have a $99 Apple TV, a marvelous little device that lets you stream audio and video to your HDTV wirelessly.

And because your iPad mini features not one but two cameras, the included FaceTime video-chatting app takes the iPad mini's multimedia acumen to new heights. Chapter 8 gets you started with FaceTime and Apple TV.

The iPad as a platform for third-party apps

The App Store offers more than 700,000 apps for the iPhone, iPad, and iPod touch at the time of this writing, in categories that include games, business, education, entertainment, healthcare and fitness, music, photography, productivity, travel, sports, and many more. The cool thing is that most of them, even ones designed for the iPhone or iPod touch, also run flawlessly on the iPad.

Of those 700,000+ apps, more than 275,000 of them are designed specifically for the iPad's larger (than an iPhone) screen, with more arriving daily.

Chapter 11 helps you fill your iPad with all the cool apps your heart desires. We share our favorite free and for-sale apps in Chapters 18 and 19, respectively.

What do you need in order to use an iPad?

To actually *use* your iPad mini, only a few simple things are required. Here's a list of everything you need:

- An iPad
- An Apple ID (assuming that you want to acquire apps, videos, music, iBooks, podcasts, and so on, which you almost certainly do)
- Internet access — broadband wireless Internet access is recommended

In previous editions of this book, we say that you *need* a computer with iTunes to sync your iPad. We've since amended our advice. Since all iPads made today let you activate, set up, update, back up, and restore your iPad mini wirelessly without a computer, you don't technically *need* one to use your iPad. But it's still nice to have a computer; many tasks are faster and easier on a computer with iTunes than on your iPad.

If you decide to introduce your iPad to your computer (and we think you should), here's what's required for syncing (which we discuss at length in Chapter 3):

- A Mac with a USB 2.0 or 3.0 port, Mac OS X version 10.6.8 or later, and iTunes 10.6 or later
- A PC with a USB 2.0 or 3.0 port; Windows 8, Windows 7, Windows Vista, or Windows XP Home or Professional Edition with Service Pack 3 or later; and iTunes 10.7 or later (free download at www.itunes.com/download)

Touring the iPad Exterior

The iPad mini is a harmonious combination of hardware and software. In the following sections, we take a brief look at the hardware — what's on the outside.

On the top

On the top of your iPad mini, you find the headphone jack, microphone, and Sleep/Wake button, as shown in Figure 1-1 and described in this list:

- **Sleep/Wake button:** This button is used to put your iPad's screen to sleep or to wake it up. It's also how you turn your iPad on or off. To put it to sleep or wake it up, just press the button. To turn it on or off, press and hold the button for a few seconds.

   Your iPad's battery runs down faster when your iPad is awake, so we suggest that you make a habit of putting it to sleep when you're not using it.

   When your iPad is sleeping, nothing happens if you touch its screen. To wake it up, merely press the button again or press the Home button on the front of the device (as described in a moment).

   If you have an iPad mini Smart Cover (or a third-party case that uses the Smart Cover mechanism), you can simply open the cover to wake your iPad and close the cover to put it to sleep.

Figure 1-1: The top side of the iPad mini.

Find out in Chapter 15 how to make your iPad go to sleep automatically after a period of inactivity.

✓ **Headphone jack:** This jack lets you plug in a headset. You can use the Apple headsets or headphones that came with your iPhone or iPod. Or you can use pretty much any headphones (or headset) that plug into a 3.5-mm stereo headphone jack.

Throughout this book, we use the words *headphones, earphones,* and *headset* interchangeably. Strictly speaking, a headset includes a microphone so that you can talk (or record) as well as listen; headphones or earphones are for listening only. Either type works with your iPad.

✓ **Microphone:** The tiny dot in the middle of the top edge of your iPad mini is a pretty good microphone.

On the bottom

On the bottom of your iPad are the speaker and dock connector, as shown in Figure 1-2:

✓ **Speakers:** The speakers play stereo audio — music or video soundtracks — if no headset is plugged in.

Figure 1-2: The bottom of the iPad mini.

✔ **Lightning connector:** This connector has three purposes:

- *Recharge your iPad's battery:* Simply connect one end of the included Lightning–connector–to–USB cable to the iPad and the other end to the USB power adapter or a suitable USB port on your Mac, PC, or powered USB hub.

- *Synchronize your iPad:* Connect one end of the same cable to the Lightning connector and the other end to a USB port on your Mac or PC.

- *Connect your iPad to cameras or televisions using an adapter:* Such connectors include the Lightning–to–USB Camera Adapter ($29) or the other adapter cables discussed in Chapter 15.

In the "What's in the box" sidebar, earlier in this chapter, read the note about using the USB ports on anything other than your Mac or PC, including keyboards, displays, and hubs.

On the right side

On the right side of your iPad are the Volume Up/Down control and the Mute switch, as shown in Figure 1-3:

✔ **Mute switch:** When the switch is set to Silent mode — the down position, with an orange dot visible on the switch — your iPad doesn't make any sound when you receive new mail or an alert pops up on the screen. Note that the Mute switch doesn't silence what we think of as *expected* sounds, which are sounds you expect to hear in a particular app. Therefore, it doesn't silence the iTunes or Videos apps, nor does it mute games and other apps that emit noises. About the only thing the Mute switch mutes are unexpected sounds, such as those associated with notifications from apps or the iPad operating system (iOS).

If the switch doesn't mute notification sounds when engaged (that is, you can see the little orange dot on the switch), look for a little Screen Orientation icon (shown in the margin) to the left of the Battery icon near the top of your screen.

When you flick the Mute switch, you may see this icon, for two possible reasons. The most likely reason is that you've selected the Lock Rotation option in the Settings app's General pane.

✔ **Volume Up/Down control:** The Volume Up/Down control is a single button that's just below the Mute switch. The upper part of the button increases the volume; the lower part decreases it.

The Camera app uses the Volume Up button as a shutter release button as an alternative to the onscreen shutter release button. Press either one to shoot a picture or start/stop video recording.

Figure 1-3: The right side has two buttons.

On the front and back

On the front and back of your iPad mini, you find the following items (labeled in Figure 1-4):

✔ **Touchscreen:** You find out how to use the iPad's gorgeous, high-resolution, color touchscreen in Chapter 2. All we have to say at this time is . . . try not to drool all over it.

✔ **Home button:** No matter what you're doing, you can press the Home button at any time to display the Home screen (refer to Figure 1-4).

- **Front camera:** The front camera is serviceable and delivers video that's decent enough for video chats, but not so hot for still photos.

- **Application buttons:** Each of the 20 buttons (icons) shown on the screen (refer to Figure 1-4) launches an included iPad application. You read more about these applications later in this chapter and throughout the rest of the book.

- **Rear camera:** The camera on the back of the iPad mini is much better than the one in front. It records superb HD video at 1080p and takes excellent still photos.

Figure 1-4: The front and back of the iPad — either way, a study in elegant simplicity.

Status bar

The status bar, which is at the top of the screen, displays tiny icons that provide a variety of information about the current state of your iPad:

✔ **Airplane mode:** Airplane mode should be enabled when you fly. It turns off all of the wireless features of your iPad — the cellular, 4G, 3G, GPRS (General Packet Radio Service), and EDGE (Enhanced Datarate for GSM Evolution) networks; Wi-Fi; and Bluetooth — so you can enjoy music, video, games, photos, or any app that doesn't require an Internet connection while you're in the air.

Tap the Settings app and then tap the Airplane Mode switch to say *On*. The icon shown in the margin appears on the left side of your status bar whenever Airplane mode is enabled.

Disable Airplane mode when the plane is at the gate before takeoff or after landing so that you can send or receive e-mail and iMessages.

There's no need to enable Airplane mode on flights that offer onboard Wi-Fi. On such flights, it's perfectly safe to use your iPad's Wi-Fi while you're in the air (but not until the captain says so).

✔ **LTE (Wi-Fi + Cellular models only):** This icon lets you know that your carrier's 4G LTE network is available and your iPad can use it to connect to the Internet.

✔ **3G (Wi-Fi + Cellular models only):** This icon informs you that the high-speed 3G data network from your wireless carrier (that's AT&T or Verizon in the United States) is available and that your iPad is connected to the Internet via 3G. (Wondering what 3G, 4G, and these other data networks are? Check out the nearby sidebar, "Comparing Wi-Fi, 4G, LTE, 3G, GPRS, and EDGE.")

✔ **GPRS (Wi-Fi + Cellular models only):** This icon says that your wireless carrier's GPRS data network is available and that your iPad can use it to connect to the Internet.

✔ **EDGE (Wi-Fi + Cellular models only):** This icon tells you that your wireless carrier's EDGE network is available and you can use it to connect to the Internet.

✔ **Wi-Fi:** If you see the Wi-Fi icon, your iPad is connected to the Internet over a Wi-Fi network. The more semicircular lines you see (up to three), the stronger the Wi-Fi signal. If you have only one or two semicircles of Wi-Fi strength, try moving around a bit. If you don't see the Wi-Fi icon on the status bar, Internet access with Wi-Fi isn't available.

Comparing Wi-Fi, LTE, 3G, GPRS, and EDGE

Wireless (that is, cellular) carriers may offer one or more data networks relevant to the iPad as of this writing. Your iPad can take advantage of them all. The speediest are the LTE networks, which the carriers are rolling out as fast as they can. The second-fastest network is 3G, and the older, even slower data networks are EDGE and GPRS. Your iPad starts by trying to connect via Wi-Fi. If that doesn't work, it tries to connect via LTE. If that fails, it tries the slower 3G, EDGE, or GPRS networks, displaying the appropriate icon on the status bar.

Most Wi-Fi networks, however, are faster than even the fastest LTE cellular data network — and much faster than 3G, EDGE, or GPRS. So, because all iPads can connect to a Wi-Fi network if one is available, they do so, even when an LTE, 3G, GPRS, or EDGE network is also available.

Last but not least, if you don't see one of these icons — LTE, 3G, GPRS, EDGE, or Wi-Fi — you don't have Internet access. Chapter 2 offers more details about these different networks.

> ✓ **Personal Hotspot (Wi-Fi + Cellular models only):** You see this icon when you're sharing your Internet connection with computers or other devices over Wi-Fi. Personal Hotspot may not be available in all areas or from all carriers, and additional fees may apply. Contact your wireless carrier for more information.

> ✓ **Syncing:** This icon appears on the status bar when your iPad is syncing with iTunes on your Mac or PC.

> ✓ **Activity:** This icon tells you that a network or another activity is occurring, such as over-the-air synchronization, sending or receiving e-mail, or loading a web page. Some third-party applications also use this icon to indicate network or other activity.

> ✓ **VPN:** This icon shows that you're connected to a virtual private network (VPN).

> ✓ **Lock:** This icon tells you when your iPad is locked. See Chapter 2 for information on locking and unlocking your iPad.

> ✓ **Screen Orientation Lock:** This icon appears when the Screen Orientation Lock is engaged.

> ✓ **Location Services:** This icon appears when an app (such as Maps; see Chapter 6 for more about the improved Maps app) is using Location Services (GPS) to establish your physical location (or at least to establish the physical location of your iPad).

✔ **Do Not Disturb:** This icon appears whenever Do Not Disturb is enabled, silencing incoming FaceTime calls and alerts. See Chapter 15 for details on Do Not Disturb.

✔ **Play:** This icon informs you that a song is now playing. You find out more about playing songs in Chapter 7.

✔ **Bluetooth:** This icon indicates the current state of your iPad's Bluetooth connection. If you see this icon on the status bar, Bluetooth is on, and a device (such as a wireless headset or keyboard) is connected. If the icon is gray, Bluetooth is turned on, but no device is connected. If the icon is white, Bluetooth is on, and at least one device is connected. If you don't see a Bluetooth icon, Bluetooth is turned off. Chapter 15 goes into more detail about Bluetooth.

✔ **Battery:** This icon reflects the level of your battery's charge. It's completely filled when your iPad mini isn't connected to a power source and its battery is fully charged (as shown in the margin). The icon then empties as your battery becomes depleted. It shows when you're connected to a power source, and when the battery is fully charged or is charging. You see an onscreen message when the charge drops to 20 percent or below and another message when it reaches 10 percent.

Discovering the Delectable Home Screen and Dock Icons

The iPad mini Home screen displays 20 icons. Because the rest of this book covers each and every one of these babies in full and loving detail, we provide merely brief descriptions here.

To get to your Home screen, tap the Home button. If your iPad is asleep when you tap, the unlock screen appears. After your iPad is unlocked, you see whichever page was on the screen when it went to sleep. If that happens to have been the Home screen, you're golden. If it wasn't, merely tap the Home button again to summon your iPad's Home screen.

In the following sections, we tell you briefly about the icons preloaded on your iPad's first Home screen page, as well as the icons you find on the Dock that are always accessible from every Home screen.

Home is where the screen is

If you haven't rearranged your icons, you see the following applications on your Home screen, starting at the upper-left corner:

✔ **Messages:** This app provides a unified messaging service dubbed iMessage to iPads, iPhones, iPod touches, and Macs. You can exchange unlimited free text or multimedia messages with any other device running iOS 5 or later (the iPad, iPhone, and iPod touch) or Mac OS X Mountain Lion.

Chapter 5 mentions all the intriguing details of managing messages using this mesmerizing messaging app.

✔ **FaceTime:** Participate in FaceTime video chats, as you discover in Chapter 8.

✔ **Photos:** The iPad's terrific photo manager keeps getting better. It lets you view photos synced from your computer, saved from an e-mail or web page, or saved from one of the myriad third-party apps that let you save your handiwork in the Photos app. You can zoom in or out, create slide shows, e-mail photos to friends, crop, do a bit of image editing, and much more. And it's where you'll find the Camera Roll album with photos, and videos you've shot with your iPad camera, screen shots, as well as pictures saved in Safari, Mail, and Messages. You can even look at pictures from another camera or SD card (using the optional $29 Lightning–to–USB Camera Adapter), To get started, see Chapter 9.

✔ **Camera:** This app is for shooting pictures or videos with your iPad's front- or rear-facing camera. You find out more in Chapters 8 (videos) and 9 (camera).

✔ **Maps:** This application is among our favorites. View street maps or satellite imagery of locations around the globe, or ask for directions, traffic conditions, or even the location of a nearby pizza joint. You can find your way around the Maps app with the handy tips you find in Chapter 6.

✔ **Clock:** The Clock app includes alarm clocks, timers, and more. You hear more about this nifty new app in Chapter 13.

✔ **Photo Booth:** This one is a lot like those old-time photo booths, but you don't have to feed it money. You discover details about Photo Booth in Chapter 9.

✔ **Calendar:** No matter what calendar program you prefer on your Mac or PC (as long as it's iCal, Calendar, Microsoft Entourage, or Microsoft Outlook or online calendars such as Google or iCloud), you can synchronize events and alerts between your computer and your iPad. Create an event on one device, and the event is automatically synchronized with the other device the next time the two devices are connected. Neat stuff.

✔ **Contacts:** This handy little app contains information about the people you know. Like the Calendar app, it synchronizes with the Contacts app on your Mac or PC (as long as you keep your contacts in Address Book,

Contacts, Microsoft Entourage, or Microsoft Outlook), and you can synchronize contacts between your computer and your iPad. If you create a contact on one device, the contact is automatically synchronized with the other device the next time your devices are connected. Chapter 12 explains how to start using the Calendar and Contacts apps.

- **Notes:** This program enables you to type notes while you're out and about. You can send the notes to yourself or to anyone else by e-mail, or you can save them on your iPad until you need them. For help as you start using Notes, flip to Chapter 13.

- **Reminders:** This app may be the only to-do list you ever need. It integrates with iCal, Calendar, Outlook, and iCloud, so to-do items and reminders sync automatically with your other devices, both mobile and desktop. You'll hear much more about this great app, but you have to visit Chapter 13.

- **Newsstand:** This relatively new app is where you find iPad editions for magazines and newspapers that you subscribe to. You shop for periodical apps at the App Store and then purchase subscriptions and individual issues as in-app purchases. You can read more about Newsstand in Chapter 10.

- **iTunes:** Tap this puppy to purchase music, movies, TV shows, audiobooks, and more. You find more info about iTunes (and the Music app) in Chapter 7.

- **App Store:** This icon enables you to connect to and search the iTunes App Store for iPad applications that you can purchase or download for free over a Wi-Fi or cellular data network connection. Chapter 11 is your guide to buying and using apps from the App Store.

- **Game Center:** This is the Apple social-networking app for game enthusiasts. Compare achievements, boast of your conquests and high scores, or challenge your friends to battle. You hear more about social networking and Game Center in Chapter 13.

- **Settings:** This is where you change settings for your iPad and its apps. D'oh! With so many different settings in the Settings app, you'll be happy to hear that Chapter 15 is dedicated exclusively to Settings.

Sittin' on the Dock of the iPad

At the bottom of the iPad screen, four icons sit in a special shelf-like area called the *Dock*.

The quality that makes the icons on your Dock special is that they're available on every Home screen page.

By default, the Dock icons are

- **Safari:** Safari is your web browser. If you're a Mac user, you know that already. If you're a Windows user who hasn't already discovered the wonderful Safari for Windows, think Internet Explorer on steroids. Chapter 4 shows you how to start using Safari on your iPad.

- **Mail:** This application lets you send and receive e-mail with most POP3 and IMAP e-mail systems and, if you work for a company that grants permission, Microsoft Exchange, too. Chapter 5 helps you start e-mailing everyone you know from your iPad.

- **Videos:** This handy app is the repository for your movies, TV shows, and music videos. You add videos via iTunes on your Mac or PC or by purchasing them from the iTunes Store using the iTunes app on your iPad. Check out Chapter 8 to find out more.

- **Music:** Last but not least, this icon unleashes all the power of an iPod right on your iPad so that you can listen to music or podcasts. You discover how it works in Chapter 7.

Apple puts four icons on the Dock, but it can hold up to six. Feel free to add or remove icons from the Dock until it feels right to you. To rearrange, add, or delete icons from the Dock, press and hold the icon until all the icons wiggle. Then drag the icon to wherever you want it. Press the Home button to save your arrangement.

Let us mention one last feature: the totally useful Notification Center. We wanted to mention it even though it doesn't have an icon of its own. You hear much more about it in Chapter 13; to see it now (we know you can't wait), swipe your iPad screen from top to bottom to make it appear. Then swipe from bottom to top to put it away again.

2

iPad mini Basic Training

In This Chapter

▶ Getting going

▶ Setting up the mini

▶ Locking your iPad

▶ Mastering multitouch

▶ Cutting, copying, and pasting

▶ Multitasking with your iPad

▶ Printing with your iPad

▶ Spotlighting search

*B*y now, you may know that the original larger iPads are very different from other computers. So it goes for the iPad mini.

These slate-style machines are rewriting the rulebook for mainstream computing. How so? For starters, iPads don't come with a mouse or any other kind of pointing device. They lack traditional computing ports or connectors, such as USB. And they have no physical or built-in keyboards.

iPads even differ from other so-called tablet PCs, some of which feature a pen or stylus and let you write in digital ink. As we point out (pun intended) in Chapter 1, the iPad relies on an input device that you always have with you: your finger.

Tablet computers of one form or another have been around since the last century. They just never captured the fancy of Main Street. Apple's very own Newton, an ill-fated, 1990s personal digital assistant, was among the machines that barely made a dent in the market.

What's past is past, of course, and technology, not to mention Apple itself, has come a long way since Newton. And suffice it to say that, moving forward, tablets (led by the iPad brigade, of course) promise to enjoy a much rosier outlook. Indeed, since the iPad burst onto the scene, numerous tech titans (as well as smaller companies) have introduced their own touch-enabled tablets, many that rely on the Google Android mobile operating system, some on versions of Microsoft's Windows operating system, and a few on other operating systems. Some solid machines are among them, but the iPad remains the market leader and a true pioneer in the space.

If you got caught up in the initial mania surrounding the iPad, you probably plotted for weeks about how to land one. After all, the iPad, like its close cousin the iPhone, rapidly emerged as the hippest computer you could find. (We consider you hip just because you're reading this book.) You had to plot in advance to get the subsequent versions as well. We suspect that you've strategized on getting the iPad mini, too.

Speaking of the iPhone, if you own one or its close relative, the Apple iPod touch, you already have a gigantic start in figuring out how to master the iPad multitouch method of navigating the interface with your fingers. You have our permission to skim the rest of this chapter, but we urge you to stick around anyway because some things on the iPad work in subtly different ways than on the iPhone or iPod touch. If you're a total novice, don't fret. Nothing about multitouch is painful.

Getting Started on Getting Started

As with its larger sibling, you don't *need* a computer (and the connection to iTunes and whatever program you use to store your contacts) to use an iPad mini. You see, the current flavor of the iOS operating system, version 6 as this book went to press, lets you activate, set up, and apply iOS updates to an iPad wirelessly, without having to connect it to a computer. (Chapter 3 has complete details.)

But even though you don't, technically, *need* a computer, we think you'll prefer using your iPad with one rather than without one. So we don't recommend using your iPad totally unplugged unless you really don't have a computer available to use.

In our experience, many tasks — such as iOS software updates and rearranging application icons, to name just a couple — are faster and easier to do using iTunes on a Mac or PC than on the iPad.

Now, here are the four things you need in order to use your iPad (and yes, after thinking about it, we put a computer on the list):

- **A computer:** This can be either a Macintosh running Mac OS X version 10.5.8 or later, or a PC running Windows 8, Windows 7, Windows Vista, or Windows XP Home or Professional Edition with Service Pack 3 or later. That's the official word from Apple anyway. We got the original iPad to make nice with a Dell laptop that had Windows XP Pro and SP2, and we've known XP Home systems that play nicely as well.

  The iCloud service has higher requirements: Mac OS X Mountain Lion, Lion (10.7), or higher for Macs; or Windows Vista or Windows 7 and 8 for PCs. Flip to Chapter 3 for details about iCloud.

- **iTunes software:** More specifically, you need version 10.6 or later of iTunes — emphasis on the *later* because by the time you read this, it probably will be later.

  That is, unless you're a fan of the popular TV show *Mad Men* and can't remember what decade you're living in. All kidding aside, Apple constantly tweaks iTunes to make it better. You can go to `www.itunes.com/download` to fetch a copy. Or, launch your current version of iTunes and then choose iTunes (Help in Windows)⟳Check for Updates.

  For the uninitiated, *iTunes* is the nifty Apple jukebox software that owners of iPods and iPhones, not to mention PCs and Macs, use to manage music, videos, apps, and more. iTunes is at the core of the iPad as well because an iPod is built into the iPad. You can use iTunes to synchronize a bunch of stuff from your Mac or PC to and from an iPad, including (but not limited to) apps, photos, movies, TV shows, podcasts, iTunes U lectures, and of course, music.

  Syncing is such a vital part of this process that we devote an entire chapter (Chapter 3) to the topic.

- **An Apple ID account:** Read Chapter 7 for details on how to set up an account, but, like most things Apple, the process isn't difficult. You'll want an account to download content from iTunes or the App Store or to take advantage of iCloud.

- **Internet access:** Your iPad can connect to the Internet in one of two ways: Wi-Fi or cellular (if you bought an iPad mini with the capabilities of tapping into 3G or 4G networks when available). You can connect your iPad to cyberspace via Wi-Fi in your home, office, school, favorite coffeehouse, or bookstore, or in numerous other spots.

  At press time, 3G (third-generation) and 4G (fourth-generation) wireless data connections were available from many carriers in countries too numerous to mention; in the United States, you can choose between AT&T, Sprint, and Verizon Wireless. These wireless carriers are still building the zippier *4G* (fourth-generation) networks across the USA, with Verizon in the lead with the fastest variety, called *LTE* — shorthand for Long Term Evolution. While AT&T plays catch-up on LTE, the latest iPad on AT&T makes nice with other pretty fast networks, including something known as *HSPA+*. Sprint is a relative LTE newbie as of this writing, so its network isn't nearly as far-reaching.

Unlike the cellphone contract you may have with AT&T, Sprint, or Verizon (or most every other cellular carrier), no long-term service commitment is required to connect your iPad to the network.

As this book goes to press, data rates (no contract required) are "reasonably" priced as long as you don't stream or download a lot of movies or watch tons of videos while connected over 3G or 4G:

- *AT&T:* $14.99 a month for 250 megabytes (MB), 3GB for $30, and 5GB for $50

- *Sprint:* $14.99 a month for 300 MB, 3GB for $34.99, and 6GB for $49.99

- *Verizon:* $20 for 1GB, $30 a month for 2GB, $50 for 5GB, $80 for 10GB

Putting this in perspective, 2GB of cellular service is more than enough for lower-bandwidth tasks such as web surfing and checking your e-mail. If, on the other hand, you like to slurp down prodigious amounts of video over the 3G or 4G network, your monthly allotment will disappear in mere days and you'll find yourself in penalty mode, which costs $10 a gigabyte for the carriers as this book went to press. Keep in mind that with 4G, you're likely to consume more data in a hurry, as Ed regrettably found out in the message shown in Figure 2-1.

Figure 2-1: Data goes "Poof!" awfully fast under 4G.

Find a Wi-Fi network if you want to buy, rent, or watch movies.

Turning On and Setting Up the iPad mini

Apple has taken the time to partially charge your iPad mini, so you get some measure of instant gratification. After taking your iPad out of the box, press and hold the Sleep/Wake button on the upper-right edge. (See Chapter 1 for the location of all the buttons.) The first thing you likely see is the Set Up iPad screen. If the iPad was set up on your behalf at the Apple Store instead — and if you have the time when you make your purchase, by all means, take the folks in the store up on the opportunity — you see the famous Apple logo, followed less than a minute or so later by the white letters spelling out *IPAD* on top of a gray background.

From then on, you proceed with setup on your own, but don't worry; it's a simple process. On the next several screens, you get to choose your language and country, select whether to enable location services, and select your wireless network: Wi-Fi or (depending on your model) Wi-Fi + Cellular.

You also can set up the tablet as a new iPad, or restore it from either an iCloud Backup or iTunes Backup. For the purpose of this chapter, we assume you're setting up a new iPad.

If that's the case, you can sign in with an Apple ID if you already have one, or you can create a new one (for free).

You have a few more choices to make during setup before you can truly start enjoying your new iPad: You can choose whether to set up Apple's iCloud Internet service or to bypass this service. Using iCloud means you can store your photos, apps, contacts, calendars, and more on the Internet and have your friends at Apple wirelessly *push* (send) them to your device. And you can back up all your goodies to the cloud. But you can bypass iCloud altogether, if you prefer otherwise, and back up to your computer.

You also must decide during setup whether to turn on the Siri feature. *Siri* is a chatty voice assistant who might help you get a dinner reservation or suggest that you grab an umbrella because rain is in the forecast. Siri came to the iPad with iOS 6 after making a name for herself on the iPhone 4S. To call her into duty — yes, it's a female voice — press and hold the Home button. Selecting Siri means sharing your voice input and contacts with Apple because that's how your request is processed. Though you find a Siri setting only on the third-generation iPad (and later models) and on the iPad mini, turning on Siri also turns on *dictation,* or the ability to use your voice in lieu of banging away on a keyboard.

You can also choose whether to automatically send diagnostics and usage data to Apple to help them help others down the road. Apple won't hold it against you if you decline — neither will we.

A few other things are worth mentioning here: During the setup process, Apple offers to turn on a feature called Find My iPad, a really clever way to possibly uncover a lost or stolen device. It's a good idea to take up Apple on its invitation because we've used the closely related Find My iPhone feature on more than one occasion to find a wayward smartphone. But if you're not sure, you can at least reserve judgment until Chapter 15, in which we show you how to turn it on in the Settings app.

More options are presented during setup. You get to decide whether (and how) people can reach you via the FaceTime video chat service we elaborate on in Chapter 8. Based on your Apple ID, Apple lists the e-mail addresses that folks can use when they want to initiate a FaceTime call. But if you don't like the addresses listed, you can deselect them there.

Meantime, to silence the iPad, or rather to merely turn it off, press and hold the Sleep/Wake button again until a red arrow appears at the top of the screen. Then drag the arrow from the left to the right with your finger. Tap Cancel at the bottom of the screen if you change your mind.

Locking the iPad mini

Carrying a naked cellphone in your pocket or a handbag is begging for trouble. Unless the phone has a locking mechanism, you may inadvertently dial a phone number.

You don't have to worry about dialing your boss at 4 a.m. on an iPad — it's not a phone, after all (though apps such as Line2 or Skype can turn it into one). But you still have these sound reasons to lock your iPad:

- ✔ You won't inadvertently turn it on.
- ✔ You keep prying eyes at bay.
- ✔ You spare the battery some juice.

Apple makes locking the iPad a cinch.

In fact, you don't need to do anything to lock the iPad mini; it happens automatically as long as you don't touch the screen for a minute or two. As you find out in Chapter 15, you can also set the amount of time your iPad must be idle before it automatically locks.

Can't wait? To lock the iPad immediately, press the Sleep/Wake button.

If you have an optional Smart Cover for the iPad mini (or, we presume, any of the third-party equivalents that are sure to emerge), opening and closing the cover locks and unlocks your iPad, but the Smart Cover has the added advantage of awakening your iPad without your dragging the slider (though you may still have to enter a passcode).

Unlocking the iPad is easy, too. Here's how:

1. **Press the Sleep/Wake button or the Home button on the front of the screen.**

   Either way, the onscreen slider appears.

2. **Drag the slider to the right with your finger.**

3. **Enter a passcode if you need to.**

   See Chapter 15 to find out how to password-protect your iPad.

Mastering the Multitouch Interface

With few exceptions, until the iPhone and iPad came along, most every computer known to mankind has had a physical mouse and a typewriter-style QWERTY keyboard to help you accomplish most of the things you can do on a computer. (The term *QWERTY* is derived from the first six letters on any standard typewriter — you remember those? — or computer keyboard.)

The iPad mini, like the bigger iPad and the iPhone, dispenses with a physical mouse and keyboard, which seemed like such a revolutionary step just a few years ago. By now, a virtual keyboard doesn't seem novel.

Neither does the fact that the iPads (and iPhone and iPod touch) remove the standard physical buttons in favor of a *multitouch display*. This beautiful and responsive finger-controlled screen is at the heart of the many things you do on the iPad mini.

In the following sections, you discover how to move around the multitouch interface with ease. Later, we'll hone in on how to make the most of the keyboard.

Training your digits

Rice Krispies have *Snap! Crackle! Pop!* Apple's response for the iPad is *Tap! Flick! Pinch!* (Yikes — another ad comparison!) And don't forget *Drag!*

Fortunately, tapping, flicking, pinching, and dragging aren't challenging gestures, so you can master many of the iPad's features in no time:

  ✓ **Tap:** Tapping serves multiple purposes. Tap an icon to open an application from the Home screen. Tap to start playing a song or to choose the photo album you want to see. Sometimes, you *double-tap* (tapping twice in rapid succession), which has the effect of zooming in (or out) of web pages, maps, and e-mails.

- **Flick:** Flicking is just what it sounds like — a flick of the finger on the screen lets you quickly scroll lists of songs, e-mails, and picture thumbnails. Tap the screen to stop scrolling, or merely wait for the scrolling list to stop.

- **Pinch/spread:** Place two fingers on the edges of a web page, map, or picture and then spread your fingers apart to enlarge the images. Or, pinch your fingers together to make the map or picture smaller. Pinching and spreading (or what we call *unpinching*) are cool gestures that are easy to master and sure to wow an audience.

- **Drag:** Here's where you slowly press your finger against the touchscreen without lifting it. You might drag to move around a web page or map that's too large for the iPad's display area.

- **Drag downward from the top of the screen:** This special gesture displays the Notification Center (which you find out about in Chapter 13). Press your finger at the top of the screen and drag downward.

- **Four- or five-finger swipes and pinches:** To quickly reveal the multitasking bar (see the later section, "Multitasking"), use four or five fingers to swipe upward. Swipe left or right with four or five fingers to switch between recently used apps. Finally, pinch using four or five fingers to jump to your Home screen. The four- or five-finger swipes and pinches require you to enable Multitasking Gestures in the Settings app's General pane.

Navigating beyond the Home screen

The Home screen we discuss in Chapter 1 is not the only screen of icons on your tablet. After you start adding apps from the iTunes App Store (which you discover in Chapter 11), you may see two or more tiny dots among the Safari, Mail, Videos, and Music icons and the row of icons directly above them, plus a tiny Spotlight search magnifying glass to the left of the dots. Those dots denote additional screens, each containing up to 20 additional icons, not counting the 4 to 6 separate icons that are docked at the bottom of each of these Home screens. (You can have fewer than 4 docked icons at the bottom, but we can't think of a decent reason why you'd want to ditch any of them. In any case, more on these in a moment.)

Here's what you need to know about navigating among the screens:

- To navigate between screens, flick your finger from right to left or left to right across the middle of the screen, or tap directly on the dots. The number of dots you see represents the current number of screens on your iPad. The dot that's all white denotes the screen you're viewing.

You can also drag your finger in either horizontal direction to see a different screen. Unlike flicking — you may prefer the term *swiping* — dragging your finger means keeping it pressed against the screen until you reach your desired page.

✔ Swipe — don't tap — or you'll probably open one of the application icons instead of switching screens.

✔ Press the Home button to jump back to the Home screen.

✔ The Dock — that is, the Safari, Mail, Videos, and Music icons in the bottom row — stays put as you switch screens. In other words, only the first 20 icons on the screen change when you move from one screen to another.

You can add one or two more icons to the Dock if you so choose. Or, move one of the four default icons into the main area of the Home screen to make space available for additional app icons you may use more often, as described later in this chapter.

Select, cut, copy, and paste

Being able to select and then copy and paste from one place on a computer to another has seemingly been a divine right since Moses, and that's the case on the Apple tablet as well. You can copy and paste (and cut) with pizzazz.

On the iPad, you might copy text or a URL from the web and paste it into an e-mail or a note. Or, you might copy a bunch of pictures or video into an e-mail.

Say that you're jotting down ideas in the Notes application that you'll eventually copy into an e-mail. Here's how to exploit the copy-and-paste feature, using this scenario as an example:

1. **Double-tap a word to select it.**

2. **Tap Select to select the adjacent word, or tap Select All to grab everything.**

   You can also drag the blue *grab points* (handles) to select a larger block of text or to contract the text you've already selected (refer to Figure 2-2). This may take a little practice.

3. **After you select the text, tap Copy. If you want to delete the text block, tap Cut instead.**

4. **Open the Mail program (see Chapter 5) and start composing a message.**

5. **When you decide where to insert the text you just copied, tap the cursor.**

   Up pop commands to Select, Select All, and Paste, as shown in Figure 2-3.

6. Tap Paste to paste the text into the message.

Grab handles

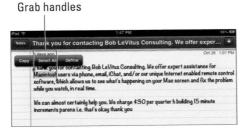 

Figure 2-2: Drag the grab handles to select text.   Figure 2-3: Tap Paste to make text appear from nowhere.

Here's the pizzazz part. If you made a mistake when you were cutting, pasting, or typing, shake the iPad mini. Doing so undoes the last edit (provided that you tap the Undo Typing option when it appears).

If you happen to select a word with a typo, you'll have the option — in addition to Cut, Copy, and Paste — to replace it. Tap Replace and the iPad may show you possible replacement words. For example, replacement words for *test* might be *fest, rest,* or *text.* Tap the word to substitute it for the word you originally typed.

Multitasking

Multitasking lets you run numerous apps in the background simultaneously and easily switch from one app to another. The following examples illustrate what multitasking enables you to do on your iPad mini:

- ✔ **Third-party app:** Slacker Personal Radio, for example, continues to play music while you surf the web, peek at pictures, or check e-mail. Without multitasking, Slacker would shut down the moment you opened another app.

- ✔ **Navigation app:** It can update your position while you're listening to, say, Pandora Internet radio. From time to time, the navigation app will pipe in with turn-by-turn directions, lowering the volume of the music so that you can hear the instructions.

- ✔ **Photo website:** If the image uploading process is taking longer than you want, you can switch to another app, confident that the images will continue to upload behind the scenes.

- ✔ **Evernote app:** We've been able to leave voice notes in this app while checking out a web page.

To switch among multitasking applications, do one of the following:

- ✔ **Double-tap the Home button.** A bar appears at the bottom of the screen, as shown in Figure 2-4. The bar, sometimes called the multitasking tray or Recents list, holds icons for applications that are *suspended* (running in the background). Swipe from right to left on the bar to see more apps; tap an app's icon and it appears just as it was the last time it was used.

Figure 2-4: A bar for recently used apps.

- ✔ **Use the four- or five-finger gesture.** Using four or five fingertips, you can swipe upward to reveal the multitasking bar, swipe left or right to switch between apps, or pinch to return to the Home screen. This is one of our favorite features.

You can also do the following when the multitasking bar is displayed:

- ✔ **Access convenient controls instantly.** Swipe the bar from left to right, and your iPad displays controls for iPod audio (Volume, Play/Pause, Next/Previous Track), Brightness, and Screen Rotation Lock (or Mute, if you have the button on the side set to Screen Rotation Lock).

  Here you also find the control for streaming content to devices such as Apple's AirPort Express base station and Apple TV, or AirPlay-enabled, third-party devices made by Denon, Marantz, B&W, JBL, Sonos, and iHome, to name a few.

- ✔ **Remove an app from the multitasking bar.** When you remove an app, it's no longer running in the background (suspended). Press and hold your finger against any app on the bar until all the apps start to wiggle. Then, to remove the app, tap the red circle with the minus sign, which appears in the upper-left corner of apps on the bar when they wiggle. Poof — the app's gone. If you're noticing that some of your apps have been crashing, try closing some or all of the apps running in the background to free up system resources.

Multitasking on the iPad differs from multitasking on a Mac or PC. You can't display more than one screen at a time. Moreover, there's some philosophical debate about whether this feature is multitasking, fast task switching, or some combination. Rather than getting bogged down in the semantics, we're just glad that multitasking, or whatever you want to call it, is available.

Organizing icons into folders

Finding the single app that you want to use among apps spread out over 11 screens may seem like a daunting task. But Apple felt your pain and added a handy organizational tool — the folder. The Folders feature lets you create folder icons, each with up to 20 icons for apps.

To create a folder, follow these steps:

1. **Press your finger against an icon until all the icons on the screen wiggle.**

2. **Decide which apps you want to move to a folder, and then drag the icon for the first app on top of the second app.**

   The two apps now share living quarters inside a newly created folder. Apple names the folder according to the category of apps inside the folder.

3. **(Optional) Change the folder name by tapping the X on the bar where the folder name appears and typing a new name.**

To launch an app that's inside a folder, tap that folder's icon and then tap the icon for the app that you want to open.

You can drag apps into and out of any folder as long as there's room for them — and, for that matter, drag apps to any Home screen. You can also drag apps on or off the Dock.

When you drag all the apps from a folder, the folder disappears automatically.

Printing

Apple didn't include built-in printer functionality with the original iPad. A variety of third-party apps helped fill the bill to some degree, but still the faithful waited for Apple to come up with a solution. The AirPrint feature that subsequently arrived provided just such a remedy — to a point. You can print wirelessly from the iPad to an AirPrint-capable printer, made by the likes of HP, Epson, Canon, and others. We hope that Apple will support Bluetooth wireless printing, but that hasn't happened as of this writing. AirPrint works with Mail, Photos, Safari, and iBooks (PDF files). You can also print from apps in Apple's optional iWork software suite, as well as from third-party apps with built-in printing.

To print on third-party printers, check out apps, such as HandyPrint, Printopia 2, or Print n Touch.

Although AirPrint printers need no special software, they have to be connected to the same Wi-Fi network as the iPad.

To print, follow these steps:

1. **Tap the Print command, which appears in different places depending on the app you're using.**

2. **Tap Select Printer to select a printer, which the iPad locates in short order.**

3. **Depending on the printer, specify the number of copies you want to print, the number of double-sided copies, and a range of pages to print.**

4. **When you're happy with your settings, tap Print.**

If you display the multitasking bar while a print job is under way, the Print Center app icon appears on the multitasking bar along with all your other recently used apps. A red badge indicates how many documents are in the print queue, along with the currently printing document.

Searching for content on your iPad

Using the Safari browser (see Chapter 4), you can search the web via the Google, Yahoo!, or Bing search engines.

But you can also search for people and programs across your iPad mini and within specific applications. We show you how to search within apps in the various chapters dedicated to Mail, Contacts, Calendar, and Music.

Searching across the iPad, meanwhile, is based on the powerful Spotlight feature that's familiar to Mac owners. Here's how it works:

1. **To access Spotlight, flick to the left of the main Home screen (or, as we mention earlier in this chapter, press the Home button from the main Home screen).**

2. **Tap the bar at the top of the screen that slides into view, and enter your search query using the virtual keyboard.**

   The iPad spits out results the moment you type a single character, and the list narrows as you type additional characters.

   The results are pretty darn thorough. Say that you entered **Ring** as your search term, as shown in Figure 2-5. Contacts whose last names have *Ring* in them show up, along with friends who might do a trapeze act in the Ringling Bros. circus. All the

Figure 2-5: Putting the Spotlight on search.

songs on your iPad by Ringo Starr show up, too, as do such song titles as Tony Bennett's "When Do The Bells Ring for Me," if that happens to be in your library. The same goes for apps, videos, audiobooks, events, and notes containing the word *Ring*.

3. Tap any listing to jump to the contact, ditty, or application you seek.

In Settings (see Chapter 15), you can specify the order of search results so that apps come first, contacts second, songs third, and so on.

The Incredible, Intelligent, and Virtual iPad Keyboard

As you know by now, instead of a physical keyboard, several "soft" (or "virtual") English-language or (depending upon what you chose during setup) foreign-language keyboard layouts slide up from the bottom of the iPad screen, including variations on the alphabetical keyboard, the numeric and punctuation keyboard, and the more-punctuation-and-symbols keyboard.

Indeed, the beauty of a software keyboard is that you see only the keys that are pertinent to the task at hand. The layout you see depends on the application. The keyboards in Safari differ from the keyboards in Notes. For example, although having a dedicated .com key on the Safari keyboard makes perfect sense, having such a key in the Notes keyboard isn't essential. Figure 2-6 displays the difference between the Notes (top) and Safari (bottom) keyboards.

Figure 2-6: The bottom row of keys on the Notes (top) and Safari (bottom) keyboards.

Before you consider how to *use* the keyboard, we want to share a bit of the philosophy behind its so-called *intelligence*. Knowing what makes this keyboard smart can help you make it even smarter when you use it:

- ✔ It has a built-in English dictionary that even includes words from today's popular culture. It has dictionaries in other languages, too, automatically activated when you use a given international keyboard, as described in the sidebar "A keyboard for all borders," later in this chapter.

- ✔ It adds your contacts to its dictionary automatically.

- ✔ It uses complex analysis algorithms to predict the word you're trying to type.

- ✔ It suggests corrections as you type. It then offers you the suggested word just below the misspelled word. When you decline a suggestion and the word you typed is *not* in the iPad dictionary, the mini adds that word to its dictionary and offers it as a suggestion if you mistype a similar word in the future.

Decline incorrect suggestions (by tapping the characters you typed as opposed to the suggested words that appear beneath what you've typed). This helps your intelligent keyboard become even smarter.

✔ It reduces the number of mistakes you make as you type by intelligently and dynamically resizing the touch zones for certain keys. You can't see it, but it is increasing the zones for keys it predicts might come next and decreasing the zones for keys that are unlikely or impossible to come next.

Discovering the special-use keys

The iPad keyboard contains several keys that don't actually type a character. Here's the scoop on each of these keys:

✔ **Shift:** If you're using the alphabetical keyboard, the Shift key (arrow pointing up) switches between uppercase and lowercase letters. You can tap the key to change the case, or hold down Shift and slide to the letter you want to capitalize.

✔ **Caps Lock:** To turn on Caps Lock and type in all caps, you first need to enable Caps Lock (if it's not already enabled). You do that by tapping the Settings icon (usually found on the first Home screen) and tapping General➪Keyboard. Tap the Enable Caps Lock item to turn it on. After the Caps Lock setting is enabled, double-tap the Shift key to turn on Caps Lock. (The Shift key turns blue whenever Caps Lock is on.) Tap the Shift key again to turn off Caps Lock. To disable Caps Lock, just reverse the process by turning off the Enable Caps Lock setting (tap Settings➪General➪Keyboard).

Enable the Split Keyboard option (tap Settings➪General➪Keyboard), and you can split the keyboard in a most thumb-typist-friendly manner, as shown in Figure 2-7. When you're ready to split your keyboard, press the Typewriter key, and tap Split from the menu.

Figure 2-7: Press and hold the Typewriter key to split (top) and merge (bottom) the keyboard.

✔ **#+= or 123:** If you're using keyboards that show only numbers and symbols, the traditional Shift key is replaced by a key labeled #+= or 123 (sometimes shown as .?123). Pressing that key toggles between keyboards that have only symbols and numbers.

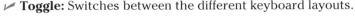

✔ **Toggle:** Switches between the different keyboard layouts.

✔ **International Keyboards:** This option shows up only if you've turned on an international keyboard, as explained in the nearby sidebar "A keyboard for all borders."

✔ **Delete:** Tapping this key, otherwise known as Backspace, erases the character immediately to the left of the cursor.

✔ **Return:** Move the cursor to the beginning of the next line.

✔ **Hide Keyboard:** Tap to hide the keyboard. Tap the screen in the appropriate app to bring back the keyboard.

✔ **Dictation:** Tap the Microphone key and start talking. As you speak, a larger key with a Microphone icon on it appears above the Dictation key, and the iPad listens to what you have to say. Tap the key again and the iPad attempts to convert your words into text. You can use this dictation feature in many of the instances in which you can summon the keyboard, including the built-in Notes and Mail apps, as well as any third-party apps you have on your mini. See Chapter 14 for more on dictation.

When you use dictation, the things you say are recorded and sent to Apple to convert your words into text. Just make sure to proofread what you've said because the process isn't foolproof. Apple also collects other information, including your first name and nickname, names and nicknames of folks in your Contacts list, song names in iTunes, and more. Apple says this helps the dictation feature perform its duties. If any of this freaks you out, however, tap Settings⇨General⇨Keyboard and slide the Dictation switch to Off. You can also restrict the use of dictation in Settings, as explained in Chapter 15.

If you have an iPhone or iPod touch, it's worth noting that keyboards on the iPad mini more closely resemble the keyboard layout of a traditional computer rather than those smaller-model devices. That is, the Delete key is in the upper-right corner, the Return key is just below it, and the Shift keys are on either side. This similarity to traditional keyboard layouts certainly improves the odds of successful touch-typing.

Finger-typing on the virtual keyboards

The virtual keyboards in Apple's multitouch interface just might be considered a stroke of genius. And they just might as equally drive you nuts.

If you're patient and trusting, in a week or so you'll get the hang of finger-typing — which is vital to moving forward, of course, because you rely on a virtual keyboard to tap a text field, enter notes, type the names of new contacts, and so on.

A keyboard for all borders

Apple is expanding the iPad's reach globally with international keyboard layouts on the tablet for dozens of languages. To access a keyboard that isn't customized for Americanized English, tap Settings⇨General⇨Keyboard⇨International Keyboards⇨Add New Keyboard. Then flick through the list to select any keyboard you want to use. (Alternatively, tap Settings⇨General⇨International⇨Keyboards.) Up pops the list shown in the figure, with custom keyboards for German, Japanese, Portuguese, and so on. Apple even supplies three versions of French (including keyboards geared to Canadian and Swiss customers) and several keyboards for Chinese. Heck, you can even find a U.K. version of English. Within Settings, you can choose software and hardware keyboard layouts.

Have a multilingual household? You can select as many of these international keyboards as you might need by tapping the language in the list. Of course, you can call upon only one language at a time. So when you're in an application that summons a keyboard, tap the International Keyboard button sandwiched between the .?123 key and spacebar (or the Microphone key if Dictation/Siri is turned on; refer to Figure 2-6) until the keyboard you want to call on for the occasion shows up. Tap again to pick the next keyboard in the corresponding list of international keyboards that you turned on in Settings. If you keep tapping, you come back to your original English keyboard.

To remove a keyboard that you've already added to your list, tap the Edit button in the upper-right corner of the screen and then tap the red circle with the white horizontal line that appears next to the language to which you want to say *adios*.

One more note about the Chinese keyboards: You can use handwriting character recognition for simplified and traditional Chinese, as shown here. Just drag your finger in the box provided. We make apologies in advance for not knowing what the displayed characters here mean. (We neither speak nor read Chinese.)

As we note earlier in this chapter, Apple has built intelligence into its virtual keyboard, so it can correct typing mistakes on the fly and take a stab at predicting what you're about to type next. The keyboard isn't exactly Nostradamus, but it does an excellent job of coming up with the words you have in mind.

As you start typing on the virtual keyboard, we think you'll find the following tips extremely helpful:

✔ **See what letter you're typing.** As you press your finger against a letter or number on the screen, the individual key you press darkens until you lift your finger, as shown in Figure 2-8. That way, you know you've struck the correct letter or number.

✔ **Slide to the correct letter if you tap the wrong one.** No need to worry if you touched the wrong key. You can slide your finger to the correct key because the letter isn't recorded until you release your finger.

✔ **Tap and hold to access special accent marks, alternative punctuation, or URL endings.** Sending a message to an overseas pal? Keep your finger pressed against a letter, and a row of keys showing variations on the character for foreign alphabets pops up, as shown in Figure 2-9. This row lets you add the appropriate accent mark. Just slide your finger until you're pressing the key with the relevant accent mark and then lift your finger.

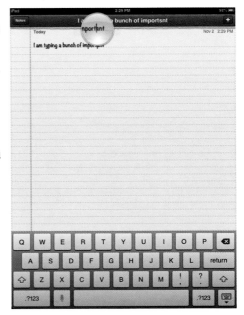

Figure 2-8: The ABCs of virtual typing.

Meanwhile, if you press and hold the .com key in Safari, it offers you the choice of .com, .net, .edu, or .org, with additional options if you also use international keyboards — pretty slick stuff.

✔ **Tap the spacebar to accept a suggested word, or tap the suggested word to decline the suggestion.** Alas, mistakes are common at first. Say that you meant to type a sentence in the Notes application that reads, "I am typing an important. . . ." But because of the way your fingers struck the virtual keys, you actually entered "I am typing an *importsnt. . . .*" Fortunately, Apple knows that the *a* you meant to press is next to the *s* that showed up on the keyboard, just as *t* and *y* and *e* and *r* are side by side. So the software determines that *important* was indeed the word you had in mind and places it in red under the suspect word. To accept the suggested word, merely tap the spacebar. And if for some reason you meant to type *importsnt* instead, tap the suggested word (*important,* in this example) to decline it.

If you don't appreciate this feature, you can turn off Auto-Correction in Settings. See Chapter 15 for details; see Chapter 20 for Auto-Correction tricks.

Figure 2-9: Accenting your letters.

Because Apple knows what you're up to, the virtual keyboard is fine-tuned for the task at hand. This is especially true when you need to enter numbers, punctuation, or symbols. The following tips help you find common special characters or special keys that we know you'll want to use:

- ✔ **Finding keys for web addresses:** If you're entering a web address in the Safari web browser (see Chapter 4), the keyboard includes the dedicated period, forward slash, and .com keys.

- ✔ **Putting the @ in an e-mail address:** If you're composing an e-mail message (see Chapter 5), a dedicated @ key pops up on the keyboard.

- ✔ **Switching from letters to numbers:** When you're typing notes or sending e-mail and you want to type a number, symbol, or punctuation mark, tap the 123 key to bring up an alternative virtual keyboard. Tap the ABC key to return to the first keyboard. This toggle isn't hard to get used to, but you may find it irritating.

- ✔ **Adding apostrophes:** If you press and hold the Exclamation Mark/ Comma key, a pop-up offers the apostrophe.

TIP

We already mentioned that the iPad mini, unlike some tablets from the past (and a few in the present), eschews a pen or stylus. But there are occasions when you might want to call upon a digital pen, and products from third-party companies such as Wacom fill the bill. Wacom sells the Bamboo Stylus for around $20 to $30, a potentially useful tool for those with fingers that are too broad, oily, or greasy or who sketch, draw, or jot notes.

Editing mistakes

We think typing with abandon, without getting hung up over mistyped characters, is a good idea. The self-correcting keyboard can fix many errors (and occasionally introduce errors of its own). That said, plenty of typos are likely to turn up, especially in the beginning, and you have to correct them manually.

Figure 2-10: Magnifying errors while typing in Notes.

TIP

A neat trick for doing so is to hold your finger against the screen to bring up the magnifying glass, as shown in Figure 2-10. Use the magnifying glass to position the pointer on the spot where you need to make the correction. Then use the Delete key (also called Backspace) to delete the error, and press whatever keys you need to type the correct text.

3

The Kitchen Sync: Getting Stuff to and from Your iPad mini

In This Chapter

▶ Setting up an iPad mini, computer-free

▶ Starting your first sync

▶ Disconnecting during a sync

▶ Synchronizing contacts, calendars, e-mail accounts, and bookmarks

▶ Synchronizing music, podcasts, videos, photos, books, and applications

▶ Getting your head around iCloud

*W*e have good news and . . . more good news. The good news is that you can easily set up your iPad mini so that your contacts, appointments, events, mail settings, bookmarks, books, music, movies, TV shows, podcasts, photos, and applications are synchronized between your computer and your iPad (or other i-devices). And the more good news is that after you set it up, your contacts, appointments, and events can be kept up to date automatically in multiple places — on your computer(s), iPad(s), iPhone(s), and iPod touch(es).

Here's more good news: Whenever you make a change in one place, it's reflected almost immediately in all the other places it occurs. So, if you add or change an appointment, an event, or a contact on your iPad while you're out and about, the information automatically updates on your computers and i-devices. If no Wi-Fi or cellular network is available at the time, the update syncs the next time your iPad encounters a wireless network, all with no further effort on your part.

This communication between your iPad and computer is called *syncing* (short for *synchronizing*). Don't worry: It's easy, and we walk you through the entire process in this chapter.

But wait. We have even more good news. Items that you choose to manage on your computer, such as movies, TV shows, podcasts, and e-mail account settings, are synchronized only one way — from your computer to your iPad, which is the way it should be.

In this chapter, you find out how to sync all the digital data your iPad can handle. And because iOS 6 lets you set up your iPad computer-free (so you're not *required* to sync your iPad with a computer running iTunes), you also find out how to sync both with and without using iTunes and your computer. But some things are easier with a computer than without.

The information in this chapter is based on iTunes version 10.7 and iOS 6.0, which were the latest and greatest when these words were written. If your screens don't look exactly like ours, you probably need to do either of the following:

- **Upgrade to iTunes 10.7 or higher:** Launch iTunes (on your Mac or PC) and choose iTunes⇨Check for Updates.

- **Upgrade your iPad to iOS 6 or higher:** Click the Check for Update button on the Summary tab for your iPad, as you see later, in Figure 3-2, and follow the instructions for updating your iPad operating system (if necessary). Or tap Settings⇨General⇨Software Update.

By the way, both upgrades are free, and both offer useful new features and have significant advantages over their predecessors.

Because Apple updates iTunes and iOS often, having the latest and greatest version is a double-edged sword. So sometimes you'll see something in this book that looks different on your iPad because you're using a *newer* version of the iOS than we had when we wrote this. If you discover one of these and you're certain you're using the latest-and-greatest versions of both iTunes and iOS, drop us a note so we can fix it; our e-mail addresses appear at the end of this book's introduction.

Setting Up an iPad Computer-Free

In this section, you find out how to set up and use an iPad without involving a computer.

Unless your iPad is brand-spanking-new and fresh out of the box, chances are good that you've performed the steps that follow. We cover them here because if you choose to use your iPad computer-free, these steps comprise the entire setup process.

Even so, we urge you to read this whole chapter, even if you're firmly committed to running computer-free. As you see in the next few pages, some tasks that are easy using iTunes on your Mac or PC are difficult or impossible on a stand-alone, PC-free iPad.

That said, here are the steps you take to set up a new, fresh-out-of-the-box iPad without connecting it to a Mac or PC:

1. **Turn on the iPad or wake it if it's sleeping.**

   An arrow appears near the bottom of the screen, flashing messages in many languages. We're pretty sure they all say Slide to Set Up, because that's what the English rendition says.

2. **Swipe the Slide to Set Up arrow to the right.**

   The first thing you see on your shiny new (or freshly restored) iPad is the Wi-Fi screen.

3. **Tap to choose a Wi-Fi network, provide a password (if necessary), and then tap the blue Join button.**

   A check mark appears next to the network you select.

   Note that you *can* skip this step by tapping the Next button without selecting a Wi-Fi network, but we suggest you select a network now, if you can. (If you do wait to set up your Wi-Fi network, turn to Chapter 15 to find out how to do so via Settings.)

4. **Tap the Next button in the upper-right corner to advance to the Location Services screen.**

5. **Tap to enable or disable Location Services.**

   Location Services is your iPad's way of knowing where, precisely, you are geographically. The Maps app, for example, which is covered in Chapter 6, relies on Location Services to determine where in the world you are.

   You can turn Location Services on or off globally or for individual apps in Settings, as you discover in Chapter 15.

6. **Tap the Next button in the upper-right corner to advance to the Set Up iPad screen.**

   Your choices are Set Up As a New iPad, Restore from iCloud Backup, and Restore from iTunes Backup.

   See Chapter 16 for the scoop on restoring from iCloud or iTunes backups.

7. **Tap Set Up As a New iPad.**

   A check mark appears next to your selection.

8. **Tap the Next button in the upper-right corner to advance to the Apple ID screen.**

9. **Tap Sign In with an Apple ID, or tap Create a Free Apple ID.**

   If you have an Apple ID, sign in with it here; if you don't have one, tap the Create a Free Apple ID button. If you tap Skip This Step and proceed without supplying an Apple ID, you can't take advantage of the myriad excellent and free features described in this and other chapters. Obtain an Apple ID if you don't already have one, because you need it to take advantage of iCloud. See the end of this chapter for an introduction to this service.

   Note that if you skip this step now, you can sign in later by tapping Settings⇨iCloud⇨Account.

10. **When the Terms and Conditions screen appears, read it thoroughly and then tap the blue Agree button in the lower-right corner to acknowledge that you agree to the terms and conditions. Then tap Agree again when the Terms and Conditions alert appears.**

    What happens if you disagree? You don't want to know. And, of course, you won't be able to use your iPad.

11. **Tap the Next button in the upper-right corner to advance to the Set Up iCloud screen.**

12. **Tap either Use iCloud or Don't Use iCloud.**

    A check mark appears next to your selection.

    There's more info about iCloud at the end of this chapter, or tap the What Is iCloud link on this screen for the party line from Apple.

    Don't worry: If you choose not to enable iCloud now, you can enable it at any time in the Settings app, as described in Chapter 15.

13. **Tap the Next button in the upper-right corner to advance to the iCloud Backup screen.**

14. **Tap either Back Up to iCloud or Back Up to My Computer.**

    A check mark appears next to your selection. See Chapter 16 for the scoop on iCloud and iTunes backups (including instructions for restoring from them).

15. **Tap the Next button in the upper-right corner to advance to the Find My iPad screen.**

16. **Tap either Use Find My iPad or Don't Use Find My iPad.**

    A check mark appears next to your selection.

    If you misplace your iPad, you can use Find My iPad to display its current location on a map. You can also choose to display a message or play a sound, lock the screen, or erase contents on your missing iPad.

    Find My iPad won't find your iPad if the battery is drained, the iPad is turned off, or no network connection (Wi-Fi or cellular) is available.

17. **Tap the Next button in the upper-right corner to advance to the Siri screen.**

18. **Tap either Use Siri or Don't Use Siri.**

    A check mark appears next to your selection.

    Your iPad mini offers the extremely desirable option, at least in our humble opinion, of using your voice to control your iPad as well as the capability to dictate (speech-to-text) text in any app that displays an onscreen keyboard.

    You can find out more about using Siri and dictation in Chapter 14, but for now, let us just say that we love this feature and we use it when appropriate (which is often).

    If you choose not to enable Siri at this time, you can switch on this feature at any time in the Settings app's General pane.

19. **Tap the Next button in the upper-right corner to advance to the Diagnostics screen.**

20. **Tap Automatically Send or Don't Send to either send or not send anonymous diagnostic and usage data to Apple.**

    A check mark appears next to your selection.

21. **Tap the Next button in the upper-right corner to advance to the Thank You screen.**

22. **Tap Start Using iPad to, well, start using your iPad.**

    Your iPad's Home screen appears in all its glory.

If you're using a computer-free iPad, that's the end of the story. Rather than use iTunes on your Mac or PC as described in the next section, you have to make do with the available options in specific apps and in the Settings app (covered extensively in Chapter 15).

Note that these are the same steps you would follow after restoring your iPad to factory condition, as described in Chapter 16.

Syncing with iTunes

Synchronizing your iPad with iTunes on a Mac or PC provides three main advantages over computer-free iPad use.

- ✓ **Media management:** iTunes helps you manage your media — music, movies, apps, and so on — more easily than managing it directly on your iPad.

- ✓ **Content management:** Managing your iPad's contents with iTunes provides numerous options that you won't find anywhere on your iPad.

- ✓ **App and Home screen management:** Managing your iPad's apps and Home screen layouts is much easier in iTunes than on your iPad.

Synchronizing your iPad with your computer is a lot like syncing an iPod or iPhone with your computer. If you're an iPod or iPhone user, the process is a piece of cake. But it's not too difficult, even for those who've never used an iPod, an iPhone, or iTunes. Follow these steps:

1. **Start by connecting your iPad to your computer with the USB cable that comes supplied with your iPad.**

   When you connect your iPad to your computer, iTunes should launch automatically. If it doesn't, chances are that you plugged the cable into a USB port on your keyboard, monitor, or hub. Try plugging it into one of the USB ports on your computer instead. Why? Because USB ports on your computer supply more power to a connected device than do USB ports on a keyboard, monitor, or most hubs. Also, the iPad requires a lot of that power — even more than an iPod or an iPhone.

   You may see an alert asking whether you want iTunes to open automatically when you connect this iPad. Click Yes or No, depending on your preference. You have the opportunity to change this setting, later if you like, so don't give it too much thought.

   If iTunes still doesn't launch automatically, try launching it manually.

   If you prefer to sync wirelessly (although it can be noticeably slower), just launch iTunes manually.

2. **Select your iPad in the iTunes sidebar on the left side of the iTunes window.**

   You see the Set Up Your iPad pane, as shown in Figure 3-1. If you've already set up and named your iPad, you can skip Steps 3 and 4 and click the Summary pane to set up your options.

    If you don't see an iPad in the sidebar, and you're sure that it's connected to a USB port on your computer (not the keyboard, monitor, or hub), restart your computer. If you're syncing wirelessly, your iPad and computer must be on the same Wi-Fi network, and your iPad must be plugged into a power source.

3. **Name your iPad by typing a name in the Name text box.**

   We've named this one *Bob L's iPad 16 (3d-gen)*.

4. **Decide whether you want iTunes to automatically synchronize the items shown in Figure 3-1 with your iPad every time you connect it to your computer:**

   - *If you want iTunes to do any of these things automatically,* select the check box next to the appropriate option so that it displays a check mark, click the Done button, and continue with the "Synchronizing Your Media" section, later in this chapter.

• *If you want to synchronize manually,* make sure that all three check boxes are deselected (refer to Figure 3-1), and click Done. The "Synchronizing Your Data" section, later in this chapter, tells you all about how to configure your contacts, calendars, bookmarks, notes, e-mail accounts, and applications manually; the "Synchronizing Your Media" section shows you how to sync apps, music, and so on.

You don't have to decide now. If you're not sure, leave all three check boxes deselected for now. It's easy to enable one or all three at any time.

We've chosen to not select any of the three check boxes so that we can show you how to manually set up each type of sync in the upcoming sections.

After you click the Done button (it applies to you only if you've just performed Steps 3 and 4), the Summary pane appears.

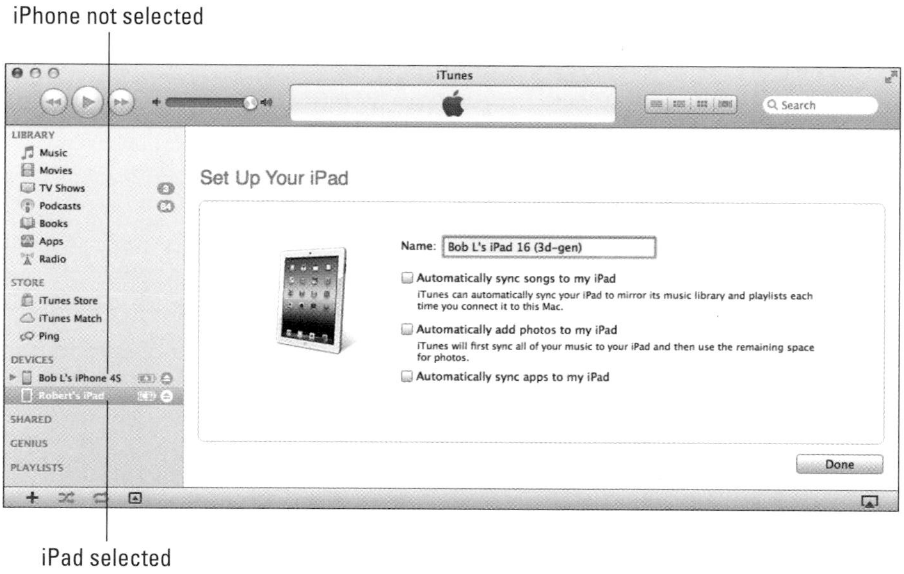

iPhone not selected

Set Up Your iPad

Name: Bob L's iPad 16 (3d-gen)

☐ Automatically sync songs to my iPad
iTunes can automatically sync your iPad to mirror its music library and playlists each time you connect it to this Mac.

☐ Automatically add photos to my iPad
iTunes will first sync all of your music to your iPad and then use the remaining space for photos.

☐ Automatically sync apps to my iPad

Done

iPad selected

Figure 3-1: This is the first thing you see in iTunes.

If the Summary pane doesn't appear, make sure that your iPad is still selected in the sidebar on the left side of the iTunes window and then click the Summary button near the top of the window, as shown in Figure 3-2.

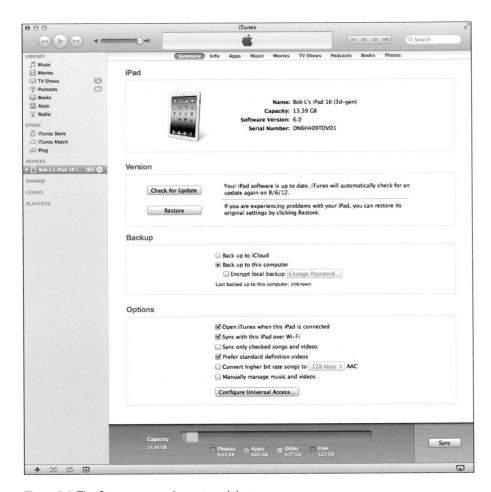

Figure 3-2: The Summary pane is pretty painless.

iPad backup

Whether you know it or not, your iPad backs up your settings, app data, and other information on your iPad whenever you connect to a computer and use iTunes to

- Sync with your iPad mini
- Update your iPad mini
- Restore your iPad mini

Every time you sync your iPad and computer, most (but not all) of your iPad content — including (but not limited to) photos in the Camera Roll, text messages, notes, contact favorites, sound settings, and more — is backed up to either your computer's hard drive or to iCloud before the sync begins. Most of your media — including songs, TV shows, and movies — *isn't* backed up in this process. This shouldn't be a problem; these files are usually restored when you sync with iTunes again.

Backups are saved automatically and stored on your computer by default, or you can choose to back up to iCloud by clicking the appropriate button in the iTunes Summary pane.

To switch to backing up to iCloud using iTunes on your computer, follow these steps:

1. **Connect the iPad to the computer.**

   If iTunes doesn't launch automatically when you connect the iPad, launch it now.

2. **Select your iPad in the sidebar on the left side of iTunes.**

3. **Click the Summary tab.**

4. **Click Back Up to iCloud or Back Up to This Computer.**

   If you choose to back up to your computer, you can encrypt your backup with a password by selecting the Encrypt iPad Backup check box.

If anything goes wonky or you get a new iPad, you can restore most (if not all) of your settings and files that aren't synced with iCloud or iTunes on your computer. Or, if you've backed up an iPhone or iPod touch or another iPad, you can restore the new iPad from the older device's backup.

If you're using an iPad computer-free, here's how to enable backing up to iCloud from your iPad, which we strongly suggest you do without further delay:

1. **Tap Settings⇨iCloud⇨Storage & Backup.**

2. **Tap iCloud Backup to switch it on.**

Choosing this option means your iPad no longer backs up automatically if you connect it to a computer.

If you are a computer-free iPad user, you don't care, because you never connect your iPad to a computer. But if you sync your iPad with your computer, like many folks do, give some thought to which option suits your needs. Restoring from a computer backup requires physical or Wi-Fi access to that computer, but you don't need Internet access. Restoring from iCloud requires Internet access and can happen anywhere on Earth that has it.

One last thing to look at on the Backup section: If you want to password-protect your iPad backups (your iPad creates a backup of its contents automatically every time you sync), be sure to also select the Encrypt iPad Backup check box from the Backup area.

Backups are good; pick one or the other and move on.

iPad options

From the Summary pane, you can set any options that you want from the Options area:

- **Open iTunes When This iPad Is Connected check box:** Select this option if you want iTunes to launch automatically whenever you connect your iPad to your computer.

  Why might you choose not to enable this option? If you intend to connect your iPad to your computer to charge it, for example, you might not want iTunes to launch every time you connect it.

  If you choose to enable it, iTunes launches and synchronizes automatically every time you connect your iPad.

  Don't worry about this too much right now. As usual, if you change your mind, you can always come back to the Summary pane and deselect the Open iTunes When This iPad Is Connected check box.

  If you select the Open iTunes When This iPad Is Connected check box but you don't want your iPad to sync automatically every time it's connected, launch iTunes and choose iTunes➪Preferences (Mac) or Edit➪Preferences (PC). Click the Devices tab at the top of the window and select the Prevent iPods, iPhones, and iPads from Syncing Automatically check box. This method prevents your iPad from syncing automatically even if the Open iTunes When This iPad Is Connected option is selected. If you choose this option, you can sync your iPad by clicking either the Sync or Apply button that appears in the lower-right corner of the iTunes window when your iPad is selected in the sidebar. (It says *Sync* in Figure 3-2.)

- **Sync with This iPad Over Wi-Fi:** If you want to sync automatically over your Wi-Fi connection, select this check box.

- **Sync Only Checked Songs and Video:** If you want to sync only items that have check marks to the left of their names in your iTunes library, select this check box.

✔ **Prefer Standard Definition Videos:** If you want high-definition videos you import to be automatically converted into smaller, standard-definition video files when you transfer them to your iPad, select this check box.

Standard-definition video files are significantly smaller than high-definition video files. You'll hardly notice the difference when you watch the video on your iPad mini (though you'll almost certainly notice on a third-or fourth-generation iPad with a Retina display), but you can have more video files on your iPad mini, because they take up less space.

The conversion from HD to standard definition takes a *long* time, so be prepared for very long sync times when you sync new HD video and you have this option selected.

If you plan to use Apple's Lightning Digital AV Adapter ($49) or Apple TV ($99) to display movies on an HDTV, consider going with high-definition. Although the files will be bigger and your iPad mini will hold fewer videos, the HD versions look spectacular on a big-screen TV. There's more info on these accessories in Chapter 17.

✔ **Convert Higher Bit Rate Songs to 128 Kbps AAC:** If you want songs with bit rates higher than 128 Kbps converted into smaller 128-Kbps AAC files when you transfer them to your iPad, select this check box.

A *higher* bit rate means that the song will have better sound quality but use a lot of storage space. Songs that you buy at the iTunes Store or on Amazon, for example, have bit rates of around 256 Kbps. So, a 4-minute song with a 256 Kbps bit rate is around 8MB; convert it to 128 Kbps AAC and it's roughly half that size (that is, around 4MB), while sounding almost as good.

Most people don't notice much (if any) difference in audio quality when listening to music on most consumer audio gear. So unless you have your iPad hooked up to a great amplifier and superb speakers or headphones, you probably won't hear much difference — though your iPad can hold roughly twice as much music if you choose this option. Put another way, we're picky about our audio, and we both select this option to allow us to carry more music around with us on our iPads. And neither of us has noticed much impact on sound quality with the headphones or speakers we use with our iPads.

✔ **Manually Manage Music and Videos:** To turn off automatic syncing in the Music and Video panes, select this check box.

One more thing: If you decide to select the Prevent iPods, iPhones, and iPads from Syncing Automatically check box in the iTunes Preferences (that's iTunes⇨Preferences on a Mac and Edit⇨Preferences on a PC) on the Devices tab, you can still synchronize manually by clicking the Sync or Apply button in the lower-right corner of the window.

Why the Sync *or* Apply button? Glad you asked. If you've changed *any* sync settings since the last time you synchronized, the Sync button instead says *Apply*. When you click that button — regardless of its name — your iPad will start to sync.

Disconnecting the iPad

When the iPad is syncing with your computer, you see the Eject icon to the right of its name in the sidebar turn into a Sync icon, as shown in Figure 3-3, and spin around.

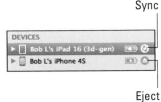

At the same time, a message appears at the top of the iTunes window to inform you that your iPad is syncing, as shown in Figure 3-4.

When the sync is finished, the wheel in Figure 3-3 stops spinning and morphs back into an Eject icon, and the message in Figure 3-4 disappears.

Figure 3-3: The Eject icon (Bob L's iPhone 4S) turns into a Sync icon (Bob L's iPad 16), during a sync.

If you disconnect your iPad before the sync finishes, all or part of the sync may fail. Though it isn't usually a problem, it's safer to cancel the sync and let it finish gracefully than to yank the cable out while a sync is in progress. So don't do that, okay?

Click to cancel sync.

Figure 3-4: Click the *x* to cancel a sync.

To cancel a sync properly and *safely,* disconnect your iPad from your Mac or PC and click the little *x* to the right of the sync message in iTunes (refer to Figure 3-4).

Synchronizing Your Data

Did you choose to set up data synchronization manually by not selecting any of the three check boxes in the Set Up Your iPad pane, as shown in Figure 3-1? If so, your next order of business is to tell iTunes what data you want to synchronize between your iPad and your computer. You do this by selecting your iPad in the sidebar on the left side of the iTunes screen. Then click the Info button, which is to the right of the Summary button.

The Info pane has five sections: Contacts, Calendars, Mail Accounts, Other, and Advanced.

On some displays, you may see only one or two sections at any time and have to scroll up or down to see the others.

One last thing: To use your iPad with your Google or Yahoo! account, you must first create an account on your iPad, as described in Chapter 5. After you've created a Yahoo! or Google account on your iPad, you can enable contact or calendar syncing with it in the Settings app's Mail, Contacts, Calendars section.

Contacts

In Figure 3-5, note that the section is named Sync Contacts because this image was captured on a Mac. Contacts (formerly known as Address Book) is the Mac application that syncs with your iPad's Contacts app.

Figure 3-5: Want to synchronize your contacts? This is where you set up things.

If you use a PC, you see a drop-down list that gives you the choices of Outlook, Google Contacts, Windows Address Book, or Yahoo! Address Book. Don't worry — the process works the same on either platform.

The iPad syncs with the following address book programs:

- ✔ **Mac:** Address Book and Contacts
- ✔ **PC:** Outlook or Windows Address Book
- ✔ **Mac and PC:** Yahoo! Address Book and Google Contacts

You can sync contacts with multiple applications.

Here's what each option does:

- ✔ **All Contacts:** One method is to synchronize all your contacts (refer to Figure 3-5). This synchronizes every contact in your Mac or PC address book with your iPad's Contacts app.

- ✔ **Selected Groups:** You can synchronize any or all groups of contacts you've created in your computer's address book program. Just select the appropriate check boxes in the Selected Groups list, and only those groups will be synchronized.

If you sync with your employer's Microsoft Exchange calendar and contacts, any personal contacts or calendars already on your iPad will be wiped out.

Calendars

The Calendars section of the Info pane determines how synchronization is handled for your appointments, events, and reminders. You can synchronize all your calendars, as shown in Figure 3-6. Or you can synchronize any or all individual calendars you've created in your computer's calendar program. Just select the appropriate check boxes.

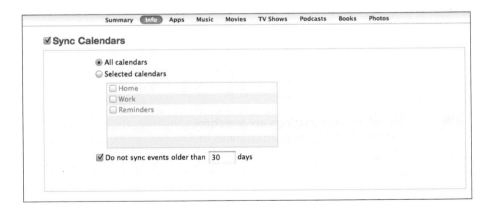

Figure 3-6: Setting up syncing for calendar events.

The iPad syncs with the following calendar programs:

- ✔ **Mac:** iCal or Calendar
- ✔ **PC:** Microsoft Outlook 2003, 2007, and 2010
- ✔ **Mac and PC:** Google and Yahoo! Calendars

You can sync calendars with multiple applications.

Mail Accounts

You can sync account settings for your e-mail accounts in the Mail Accounts section of the Info pane. You can synchronize all your e-mail accounts (if you have more than one), or you can synchronize individual accounts, as shown in Figure 3-7. Just select the appropriate check boxes.

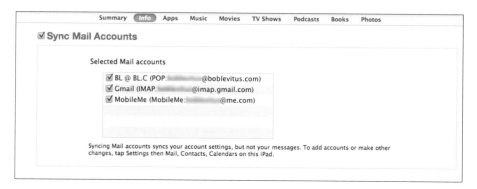

Figure 3-7: Transfer e-mail account settings to your iPad.

The iPad syncs with the following mail programs:

- **Mac:** Mail
- **PC:** Microsoft Outlook 2003, 2007, and 2010
- **Mac and PC:** Gmail and Yahoo! Mail

E-mail account settings are synchronized only one way: from your computer to your iPad. If you make changes to any e-mail account settings on your iPad, the changes aren't synchronized back to the e-mail account on your computer. Trust us: This is a good feature, and we're glad Apple did it this way.

By the way, the password for your e-mail account may or may not be saved on your computer. If you sync an e-mail account and the iPad asks for a password when you send or receive mail, do this: Tap Settings on the Home screen, tap Mail, tap your e-mail account's name, and then type your password in the appropriate field.

Other

The Other section has a single item: Sync Safari Bookmarks.

Select the Sync Safari Bookmarks check box if you want to sync your Safari bookmarks; don't select it if you don't.

Just so you know, the iPad syncs bookmarks with the following web browsers:

- ✔ **Mac:** Safari
- ✔ **PC:** Microsoft Internet Explorer and Safari

Advanced

Every so often, the contacts, calendars, mail accounts, or bookmarks on your iPad get so screwed up that the easiest way to fix things is to erase that information on your iPad and replace it with information from your computer.

If that's the case, go to the Advanced section of the Info pane and click to select the appropriate check boxes, as shown in Figure 3-8. Then, the next time you sync, that information on your iPad is replaced with information from your computer.

Figure 3-8: Replace the information on your iPad with the information on your computer.

 Because the Advanced section is at the bottom of the Info pane and you have to scroll down to see it, you can easily forget that the section is there. Although you probably won't need to use this feature often (if ever), if you do need it, you'll be happy that you remembered it's there.

Synchronizing Your Media

If you chose to let iTunes manage synchronizing your data automatically, welcome. This section looks at how you get your media — your music, podcasts, videos, and photos — from your computer to your iPad.

 Podcasts and videos (but not photos) from your computer are synced only one-way: from your computer to your iPad. If you delete a podcast or a video that got onto your iPad via syncing, the podcast or video won't be deleted from your computer when you sync.

That said, if you buy or download any of the following items on your iPad, the item *will* be copied back to your computer automatically when you sync:

- ✔ Songs
- ✔ Podcasts
- ✔ Videos
- ✔ iBooks, e-books, and audiobooks
- ✔ Apps
- ✔ Playlists that you create on your iPad

And if you save pictures from e-mail messages, the iPad camera, web pages (by pressing and holding on an image and then tapping the Save Image button), or screen shots (which can be created by pressing the Home and Sleep/Wake buttons simultaneously), these too can be synced.

Taking a screen shot creates a photo of what's on your screen. It's a handy tool, and it's what we used to generate almost every figure in this book.

You use the Apps, Tones, Music, Podcasts, Movies, TV Shows, iTunes U, Books, and Photos panes to specify the media that you want to copy from your computer to your iPad. The following sections explain the options you find in each pane.

To view any of these panes, make sure that your iPad is still selected in the sidebar and then click the appropriate button near the top of the window.

The following sections focus only on syncing. If you need help acquiring apps, music, movies, podcasts, or anything else for your iPad, this book contains chapters dedicated to each of these topics. Flip to the most applicable chapter for help.

The last step in each section is "Click the Sync or Apply button in the lower-right corner of the window." You have to do this only when selecting that item for the first time and if you make any changes to the item afterward.

Apps

If you've downloaded or purchased any iPad apps from the iTunes App Store (see Chapter 11), set your automatic syncing options as follows:

1. **Click the Apps button, and then select the Sync Apps check box.**

2. **Choose the individual apps you want to transfer to your iPad by selecting their check boxes.**

   For your convenience, a pop-up menu lets you sort your applications by kind, name, category, date, or size. Or you can type a word or phrase into the Search field (the oval with the magnifying glass in the upper-right corner of the iTunes window) to search for a specific app.

If you also use an iPhone or iPod touch, choose Show Only iPad Apps in the pop-up menu to hide iPhone and iPod touch apps that aren't optimized for your iPad.

3. **(Optional) Rearrange app icons in iTunes by dragging them where you want them to appear on your iPad (see Figure 3-9).**

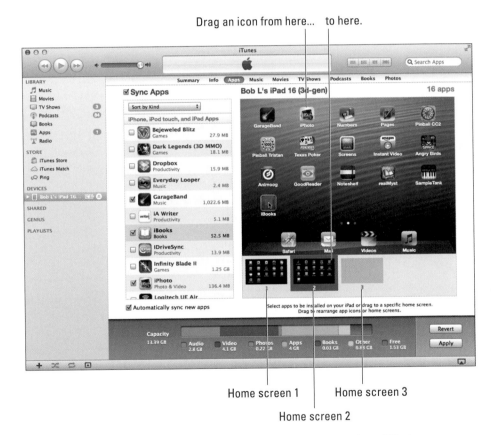

Figure 3-9: Dragging the iPhoto icon from the list of iPhone, iPod touch, and iPad apps to Home screen 2.

Your iPad comes supplied with 4 apps at the bottom of the screen in the Dock, plus 16 apps on its Home screen. As you acquire new apps, your iPad creates additional Home screens automatically — up to 10 of them — to display the overflow.

In iTunes, you can see the number of screens on the right (three Home screens are shown in Figure 3-9; no apps are on Home screen 3 yet).

On your iPad, look for a series of little dots above the Dock. These indicate the number of Home screens; so in Figure 3-9, three dots mean three Home screens. Note that the middle (second) dot is lit up in white, to indicate which Home screen you're viewing (Home screen 2 in Figure 3-9).

iTunes also displays little Home screen proxies below the big Home screen (numbered 1, 2, and 3); note that Home screen 2 is highlighted in blue.

You can even drag app icons from one Home screen to another, if you like: Drag an icon onto the Home screen proxy and it's moved to that Home screen. Click any proxy to rearrange the icons on that page.

If you have a lot of apps, you're sure to love this feature (which was introduced in iTunes 9) as much as we do. But if you don't care which apps go where, just select the check boxes for the apps you want on the iPad.

4. **Click the Sync or Apply button in the lower-right corner of the window.**

   Your apps are synced, and your icons are rearranged on your iPad just the way you arranged them in iTunes.

Note that apps are so darn cool we've given them an entire chapter of their own — namely, Chapter 11, where you discover how to find, rearrange, review, and delete apps and much, much more. Plus, two entire chapters in Part VI are dedicated to cool apps.

Music, music videos, and voice memos

To transfer music to your iPad, follow these steps:

1. **Click the Music button, and then select the Sync Music check box in the Music pane.**

2. **Select the Entire Music Library radio button or the Selected Playlists, Artists, Albums, and Genres radio button.**

   If you choose the latter, select the check boxes next to particular playlists, artists, albums, and genres you want to transfer. You can also choose to include music videos or voice memos, or both, by selecting the appropriate check boxes at the top of the pane (see Figure 3-10).

| Summary | Info | Apps | Music | Movies | TV Shows | Podcasts | Books | Photos |

☑ **Sync Music**   479 songs

○ Entire music library
◉ Selected playlists, artists, albums, and genres

☑ Include music videos
☑ Include voice memos
☐ Automatically fill free space with songs

Playlists

☐ ⚙ 90's Music
☑ ⚙ Classical Music
☐ ⚙ Music Videos
☐ ⚙ My Top Rated
☑ ⚙ Recently Added
☑ ⚙ Recently Played
☐ ⚙ Top 25 Most Played

Artists

☑ Beatles
☑ David Bowie
☑ Rolling Stones

Genres

☑ British Invasion
☐ Other
☐ Pop
☑ Rock

Albums

☐ Beatles – White Album Cd 1
☐ Beatles – White Album Cd 2
☐ Beatles – With The Beatles
☐ Beatles – Yellow Submarine
☐ David Bowie – 20th Century Boy

Figure 3-10: Use the Music pane to copy music, music videos, and voice memos from your computer to your iPad.

If you select the Automatically Fill Free Space with Songs check box, iTunes fills any free space on your iPad with music.

If you choose this option, you may find yourself with too little free space on your iPad to take new photos or movies, download new apps, or save documents you create on your iPad.

If you have more music in your iTunes Library than your iPad will hold, you're going to love iTunes Match, Apple's $25-a-year service for storing your music in iCloud, a service you hear much more about in Chapter 7.

3. **Click either the Sync or Apply button in the lower-right corner of the window.**

   Your music, music videos, and voice memos are synced.

Music, podcasts, and especially videos are notorious for chewing up massive amounts of storage space on your iPad. If you try to sync too much media, you see error messages warning you that you don't have enough room on your iPad for everything you tried to sync. Forewarned is forearmed. To avoid these errors, select playlists, artists, and/or genres that total less than the free space on your iPad.

How much free space does your iPad have? Glad you asked. Look near the bottom of the iTunes window while your iPad is selected (refer to Figure 3-9).

You see a chart that shows the contents of your iPad, color-coded for your convenience. See Chapter 20 for a tip on working with this graph.

Movies

To transfer movies to your iPad, follow these steps:

1. **Click the Movies button and select the Sync Movies check box.**

2. **Choose an option from the pop-up menu for movies that you want to include automatically, as shown in Figure 3-11, or select the check box for each movie you want to sync.**

   Regardless of the choices you make in the pop-up menu, you can always select individual movies by selecting their check boxes.

3. **Click the Sync or Apply button in the lower-right corner of the window.**

   Your movies are synced.

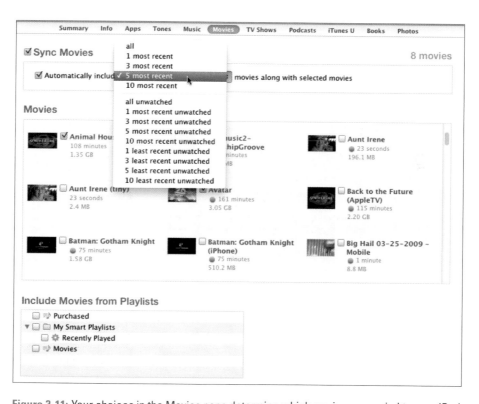

Figure 3-11: Your choices in the Movies pane determine which movies are copied to your iPad.

TV shows

The procedure for syncing TV shows is slightly different from the procedure for syncing movies. Here's how it works:

1. **Click the TV Shows button and select the Sync TV Shows check box to enable TV show syncing.**

2. **Choose how many episodes to include from the pop-up menu in the upper-left corner, as shown in Figure 3-12.**

3. **In the upper-right corner, choose whether you want all shows or only selected shows from the pop-up menu. (Again, refer to Figure 3-12.)**

4. **If you want to also include individual episodes or episodes on playlists, select the appropriate check boxes in the Episodes section (which is labeled *South Park Episodes* in Figure 3-12) and the Include Episodes from the Playlists section of the TV Shows pane.**

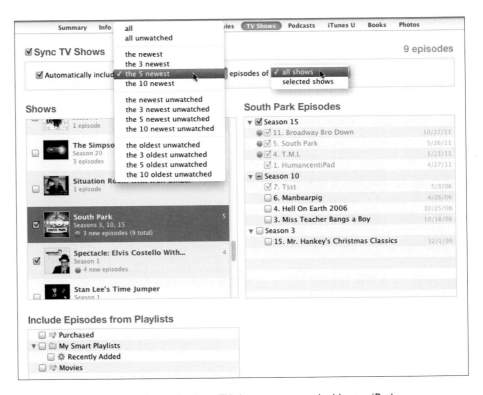

Figure 3-12: These menus determine how TV shows are synced with your iPad.

5. **Click the Sync or Apply button in the lower-right corner of the window.**

   Your TV shows are synced.

   Regardless of the choices you make in the pop-up menus, you can always select individual episodes by selecting their check boxes.

Podcasts

To transfer podcasts to your iPad, follow these steps:

1. **Click the Podcasts button and select the Sync Podcasts check box in the Podcasts pane.**

   Two pop-up menus allow you to specify which episodes and which podcasts you want to sync.

2. **Select how many episodes of a podcast you want to sync in the pop-up menu on the left.**

3. **Choose whether to sync all podcasts or only selected podcasts from the pop-up menu in the upper-right corner.**

4. **If you have podcast episodes on playlists, you can include them by selecting the appropriate check boxes under Include Episodes from Playlists.**

5. **Click the Sync or Apply button in the lower-right corner of the window.**

   Your podcasts are synced.

   Regardless of the choices you make from the pop-up menus, you can always select individual episodes by selecting their check boxes.

iTunes U

To sync educational content from iTunes U, follow these steps:

1. **Click the iTunes U button and select the Sync iTunes U check box to enable iTunes U syncing.**

2. **Choose how many items to include using the first pop-up menu.**

3. **Choose whether you want all collections or only selected collections from the second pop-up menu.**

4. **If you want to also include individual items on playlists, select the appropriate check boxes in the Collections and Items sections of the iTunes U pane.**

5. **Click the Sync or Apply button in the lower-right corner of the window.**

Your iTunes U episodes are synced.

Regardless of the choices you make in the pop-up menus, you can always select individual items by selecting their check boxes.

Books

To sync e-books and audiobooks, follow these steps:

1. **Click the Books button and select the Sync Books check box to enable book syncing.**

Two pop-up menus at the top of the Books section may make it easier to manage your book collection. The first pop-up lets you see only books or only PDF Files, or both. The second lets you sort your books by either title or author.

2. **Choose All Books or Selected Books by selecting the appropriate radio button.**

3. **If you chose Selected Books, select the check boxes of the books you want to sync.**

4. **Scroll down the page a little and select the Sync Audiobooks check box to enable audiobook syncing.**

5. **Choose All Audiobooks or Selected Audiobooks.**

6. **If you chose Selected Audiobooks, select the check boxes of the audiobooks you want to sync.**

If the book is divided into parts, you can select check boxes for the individual parts, if you want.

7. **Click the Sync or Apply button in the lower-right corner of the window.**

Your books and audiobooks are synced.

Photos

The iPad syncs photos with the following programs:

- ✔ **Mac:** iPhoto 9.2 or later or Aperture 3 or later
- ✔ **PC:** Adobe Photoshop Elements 8 or later

You can also sync photos with any folder on your computer that contains images. To sync photos, follow these steps:

1. **Click the Photos button and select the Sync Photos From check box.**

2. **Choose an application or a folder from the pop-up menu (which says iPhoto in Figure 3-13).**

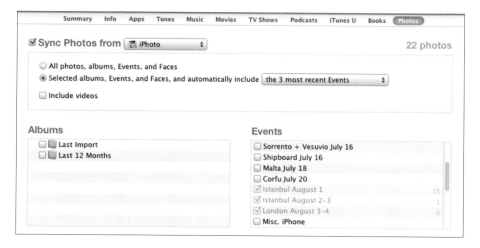

Figure 3-13: The Photos pane determines which photos will be synchronized with your iPad.

3. **To further refine what photos are synced, choose any of the following options:**

   • *Select albums, events, and more:* If you choose an application that supports photo albums, events, and/or facial recognition, as we have done in Figure 3-13, by choosing iPhoto, you can automatically include events by making a selection from the pop-up menu or select specific albums, events, and/or faces to sync by selecting them in the areas below.

   • *Search for photos to sync:* If you're using iPhoto, you can also type a word or phrase into the Search field (the oval with the magnifying glass) to search for a specific event(s).

   • *Select a folder of images:* If you choose a folder full of images, you can create subfolders inside it that appear as albums on your iPad.

   If you choose an application that doesn't support albums or events, or a single folder full of images with no subfolders, you have to transfer all or nothing.

Because iPhoto '09 and '11 — the two most recent releases — support events and faces in addition to albums, you also have the option of syncing events, albums, or faces — or all three.

4. **Click the Sync or Apply button in the lower-right corner of the window.**

Your photos are synced.

iCloud: Apple's Free-and-Easy Wireless Service

Apple's iCloud service is more than just a wireless hard drive in the sky. Rather, iCloud is a complete wireless storage and data synchronization solution. In a nutshell, iCloud stores and manages your digital stuff — your music, photos, contacts, events, and more — keeping everything updated on all your computers and i-devices automatically with no physical (wired) connection or action on your part. Like so many things Apple makes, iCloud just works.

iCloud "pushes" information such as e-mail, calendars, contacts, and bookmarks to and from your computer and to and from your iPad and other i-devices sporting iOS 5 or later, and then keeps those items updated on all devices wirelessly and without human intervention. It also includes non-synchronizing options, such as Photo Stream (see Chapter 9), e-mail (see Chapter 5), Find My iPad, Find My Friends, and 5GB of online storage.

Your free iCloud account includes 5GB of free storage, which is all many (if not most) users will need. If you find yourself needing more storage, 10, 20, and 50 gigabyte upgrades are available for $20, $40, and $100 a year, respectively.

A nice touch is that music, apps, books, periodicals, movies, and TV shows purchased from the iTunes Store, as well as photos in your Photo Stream, don't count against your 5GB of free storage. (If you don't know what your iPad's delicious Photo Stream and Shared Photo Streams are all about, find out more in Chapter 9.)

And, you'll find that the things that do count — such as mail, documents, account information, settings, and other app data — don't use much space. So, that free 5GB is all many users require.

If you want to have your e-mail, calendars, contacts, and bookmarks synchronized automatically and wirelessly (and — believe us — you do), here's how to enable iCloud syncing on your iPad:

1. **Tap Settings on your Home screen.**

2. **Tap iCloud in the list of settings on the left.**

3. **Provide your Apple ID and password.**

4. **Sign in.**

Now you can tap any of the individual On/Off switches to enable or disable iCloud sync for

- Mail
- Contacts
- Calendars
- Reminders
- Safari
- Notes
- Photo Stream
- Documents & Data
- Find My iPad

Note that even though iCloud lets you stream or download movies, TV shows, songs, podcasts, or other media files from the iTunes Store, if you don't have a speedy Internet connection, you may not be able to enjoy them because they will stutter or stall.

Part II
The Internet
iPad mini

The 5th Wave   By Rich Tennant

"He saw your iPad mini and wants to know if he can check his email."

*T*he first thing most people want to do with their iPad mini is surf the Internet with the delightfully large and colorful touchscreen. Safari, the iPad's web browser, is the place to start, and that's where this part begins as well — with an introduction to navigating the web with Safari.

Then we visit the Mail and Messages programs to see how easy it is to set up e-mail and iMessage accounts and to send and receive honest-to-goodness e-mail messages and attachments and iMessages.

Finally, in Chapter 6, we examine the new and improved Maps app. It can help you determine businesses and restaurants to visit, provide step-by-step driving directions and traffic info while you're en route, and take full advantage of the iPad's unerring ability to show you where you are on a map.

4

Going on a Mobile Safari

In This Chapter

▶ Surfing the 'Net with Safari

▶ Navigating the web

▶ Having fun with bookmarks and Reading Lists and History Lists

▶ Sharing websites

▶ Searching the World Wide Web

▶ Securing Safari

"**Y**ou feel like you're actually holding the web right in the palm of your hand."

Marketers use lines like that one because, well, that's what marketers do. Except that when an Apple marketer says such a thing to describe surfing the web on the iPad, a lot of truth is behind it, especially on the larger iPad's spectacular Retina display. But the 7.9-inch display on the iPad mini is no slouch. The screen, in combination with the snappy, dual-core, Apple-designed dual-core A5 chip inside the machine, makes browsing on the mini an absolute delight. In this chapter, you discover the pleasures — and the few roadblocks — in navigating cyberspace on your iPad mini.

TECHNICAL STUFF

Living on the EDGE

Wi-Fi is the chief way to prowl the virtual corridors of cyberspace (or send e-mail, access the App Store or iTunes Store, or check out YouTube) on the iPad. But for all the places you can find an Internet *hotspot* nowadays — airports, colleges, coffeehouses, offices, schools, and — yes — homes — Wi-Fi still isn't available everywhere.

If you bought an iPad mini Wi-Fi + Cellular model, you often have a viable alternative when Wi-Fi isn't available. In the United States, such models are available from AT&T, Verizon, and Sprint. In the United States, they work with geeky-sounding networks — CDMA EV-DO Rev. A and Rev. B, UMTS/HSPA+/DC-HSDPA, GSM/ EDGE, and LTE, depending on your carrier.

You can safely avoid the jargon. (These models also work with another wireless technology, *Bluetooth,* but it serves a different purpose and is addressed in Chapter 15.)

Cellular customers prepay for cellular access using credit cards. Monthly data is as follows: On AT&T, it's $14.99 for 250MB, $30 for 3GB, or $50 for 5GB; on Verizon, $20 for 1GB, up to $80 for 10GB; and on Sprint, it's $14.99 for 300MB, $34.99 for 3GB, $49.99 for 6GB, or $79.99 for 12GB. But plans vary, and are subject to change, and you might exhaust those limits quicker than you'd like and rack up higher charges.

Fortunately, no one- or two-year contract commitment is required, as is most likely the case with the cellphone in your pocket. That means if you're hiking in the Swiss Alps for a month or you're otherwise indisposed, you don't have to pay AT&T, Sprint, or Verizon for Internet access you'll never use.

You pay more money for an iPad mini with cellular upfront and whenever you need cellular service. But when a 4G network such as Long Term Evolution (LTE) is available — and the carriers are busily building their LTE networks, with Verizon available in more places than AT&T and Sprint as of this writing — you can surf at a blistering pace. See Chapter 2 for prepaid (but no contract) 4G data rates in the United States.

Cellular-ready iPads also work on GSM/UMTS network technologies that perform outside the United States, though you may have to pop in a SIM card to get it going abroad without Wi-Fi.

The iPad automatically hops onto the fastest available network, which is almost always Wi-Fi — the friendly moniker applied to the far-geekier 802.11 designation. And "eight-oh-two-dot-eleven" (as it's pronounced) is followed by a letter — typically (but not always) *b, g,* or *n.* You see it written as 802.11b, 802.11g, and so on. The letters relate to differing technical standards that have to do with the speed and range you can expect from the Wi-Fi configuration. But we certainly wouldn't have you lose any sleep over this issue if you haven't boned up on this geeky alphabet.

For the record, because the iPad adheres to dual-band 802.11a, b, g, and n standards, you're good to go pretty much anywhere you can find Wi-Fi. If you have to present a password to take advantage of a for-fee hotspot, you can enter it by using the iPad's virtual keyboard.

As we point out, the problem with Wi-Fi is that it's far from ubiquitous, which leads us right back to the cellular data network. Fortunately, 4G is appearing in more and more places.

When neither 3G nor 4G is available and you don't have Wi-Fi, the pokier EDGE on AT&T or its counterpart EV-DO, on Verizon, takes over — not the most pleasant experience.

If you're ever on a million-dollar game show and have to answer the question, *EDGE* is shorthand for Enhanced Datarate for GSM Evolution. It's based on the global GSM phone standard. You may also see an indicator for *GPRS,* shorthand for General Packet Radio Service, another poky data service.

4G, which stands for fourth generation, is your best bet among available cellular options for the iPad. The bottom line is this: Depending on where you live, work, or travel, you may feel like you're teetering on the EDGE in terms of acceptable Internet coverage, especially if Wi-Fi, 4G, or 3G is beyond your reach. We've used the iPad's cousin, the iPhone, in areas where web pages load extremely slowly, not-so-vaguely reminiscent of dialup telephone modems for your computer.

But the picture is brightening. 4G is in more places than ever. And the same can be said of Wi-Fi.

One last thing: At the risk of repeating ourselves, don't forget that streaming movies or downloading huge files will chew through your megabytes or gigabytes long before the end of your monthly plan, even in a matter of hours if you're not careful. Find some free Wi-Fi access if you want to watch movies or stream other large files.

To monitor your cellular network usage, tap Settings⇨General⇨Usage⇨Cellular Usage. We recommend tapping the Reset Statistics button at the bottom of the Usage pane (you may have to scroll down to see it) on the day you start your monthly data plan.

Surfin' Dude

One particular version of the Apple Safari web browser is a major reason that the 'Net on the iPad mini is very much like the 'Net you've come to expect on a more traditional computer, even with its smaller display. Safari for the Mac and for Windows is one of the best web browsers in the business. In our view, Safari on the iPhone has no rival as a cellphone browser. As you might imagine, Safari on the iPad mini is equally appealing.

Exploring the browser

We start our cyberexpedition with a quick tour of the Safari browser. Take a gander at Figure 4-1: Not all browser controls found on a Mac or PC are present. Still, Safari on the iPad has a familiar look and feel. We describe these controls and others throughout this chapter.

Before you plunge in, we recommend a little detour. Read the "Living on the EDGE" sidebar, earlier in this chapter, to find out more about the wireless networks that enable you to surf the web on the iPad in the first place.

Bookmarks, Reading List, and History

Next page

Previous page

Action

iCloud

Address field

Search field

Reload

Tab bar

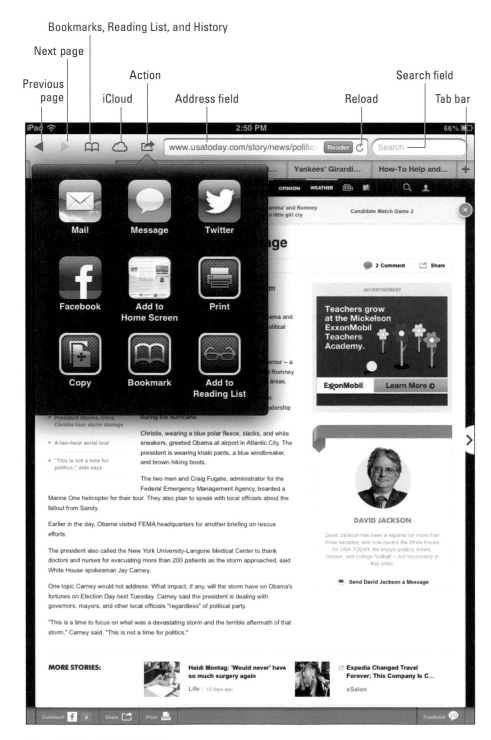

Figure 4-1: The iPad's Safari browser.

Blasting off into cyberspace

Surfing the web begins with a web address, of course. When you start by tapping the address field in iPad's Safari, the virtual keyboard appears.

Here are a few tips for using the keyboard in Safari (and see Chapter 2 for more help with using the virtual keyboard):

✔ Because so many web addresses end with the suffix `.com` (pronounced "dot com"), the virtual keyboard has a dedicated .com key. For other common web suffixes — `.edu`, `.net`, `.org`, `.us`, `.ro`, `.eu` — press and hold the .com key and choose the relevant domain type.

✔ Of equal importance, both the period (.) and the slash (/) are on the virtual keyboard because you frequently use them when you enter web addresses.

✔ The moment you tap a letter, you see a list of web addresses that match those letters. For example, if you tap the letter E (as we did in the example shown in Figure 4-2), you see web listings for ESPN, eBay, and others. Tapping U or H instead may display listings for *USA TODAY* or the *Houston Chronicle* (shameless plugs for the newspapers where we're columnists).

Figure 4-2: Web pages that match your search letter.

You don't see the Microphone icon on the virtual keyboard that appears in Safari. That rules out the use of dictation. But models with Siri can lend a hand, um, voice. If you call upon Siri and ask her to open the Safari app, she obliges. If you mention a specific website to Siri, such as "ESPN.com," Siri opens your designated search engine (Google, Bing, or Yahoo!) as discussed later in this chapter. And if Siri heard you right, the site you mentioned appears at the top of the search results.

The iPad has two ways to determine websites to suggest when you tap certain letters:

- ✔ **Bookmarks:** The websites you already bookmarked from the Safari or Internet Explorer browsers on your computer (and synchronized, as we describe in Chapter 3). More on bookmarks later in this chapter.

- ✔ **History:** Sites from the History List — those cyberdestinations where you recently hung your hat. Because history repeats itself, we also tackle that topic later in this chapter.

You might as well open your first web page now — and it's a full *HTML* page, to borrow from techie lingo:

1. **Tap the Safari icon docked at the bottom of the Home screen.**

   If you haven't moved the icon, it's a member of the Fantastic Four on the Dock (along with Mail, Videos, and Music). Chapter 1 introduces the Home screen.

2. **Tap the address field (refer to Figure 4-1).**

3. **Begin typing the web address, or *URL,* on the virtual keyboard that slides up from the bottom of the screen.**

4. **Do one of the following:**

   - *To accept one of the bookmarked (or other) sites that show up in the list, merely tap the name.*

     Safari automatically fills in the URL in the address field and takes you where you want to go.

   - *Keep tapping the proper keyboard characters until you enter the complete web address for the site you have in mind, and then tap the Go key on the right side of the keyboard.*

     You don't need to type **www** at the beginning of a URL. So, if you want to visit www.theonion.com (for example), typing **theonion.com** is sufficient to transport you to the humor site. For that matter, Safari can take you to this site even if you type **theonion** without the .com.

Because Safari on the iPad mini runs a variation of the iPhone mobile operating system, every so often you may run into a site that serves up the light, or mobile, version of a website, sometimes known as a WAP site. Graphics may be stripped down on these sites. Alas, the producers of these sites may be unwittingly discriminating against you for dropping in on them by using an iPad. In fact, you may be provided a choice of which site you want — the light or the full version. Bravo! If not, you have our permission to berate these site producers with letters, e-mails, and phone calls until they get with the program.

Zoom, zoom, zoom

If you know how to open a web page (if you don't, read the preceding section in this chapter), we can show you how radically simple it is to zoom in on pages so that you can read what you want to read and see what you want to see, without enlisting a magnifying glass.

Try these neat tricks for starters:

- ✔ **Double-tap the screen so that the area of the display that you make contact with fills the entire screen.** It takes just a second before the screen comes into focus. By way of example, check out Figure 4-3, which shows two views of the same *Sports Illustrated* web page. In the first view, you see what the page looks like when you first open it. In the second one, you see how the Top Stories box takes over much more of the screen after you double-tap it. The area of the screen you double-tapped is the area that swells up. To return to the first view, double-tap the screen again.

- ✔ **Pinch the page.** Sliding your thumb and index finger together and then spreading them apart (or as we like to say, *unpinching*) also zooms in and out of a page. Again, wait just a moment for the screen to come into focus.

Figure 4-3: Doing a double-tap dance zooms in and out.

✓ **Press down on a page and drag it in all directions, or flick through a page from top to bottom.** You're panning and scrolling, baby.

✓ **Rotate the iPad to its side.** This reorients from portrait mode to widescreen landscape mode. The keyboard is also wider in this mode, making it a little easier to enter a new URL.

However, this little bit of rotation magic doesn't happen if you've set and enabled the Screen Orientation Lock feature that we describe in Chapter 1.

Reader

Safari's superb Reader feature has been in the Mac and Windows versions of Safari for a while. You'll be glad that the feature is part of Safari for the iPad as well.

Think of Reader as a clutter remover. Just tap the Reader button in the Web Address field and you can read the article sans extraneous bits and pieces. A picture is, in this case, worth a thousand words, so feast your eyes on Figure 4-4 and compare it with Figure 4-1, which is the same page before invoking Reader.

Reader button

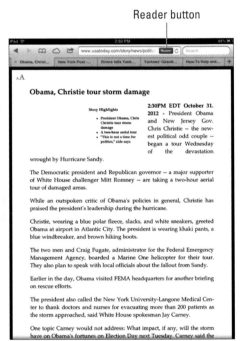

Figure 4-4: This is the same web page as Figure 4-1 but with Reader enabled.

Finding Your Way Around Cyberspace

In this section, we discuss ways to navigate the Internet on your iPad with links and tabs.

Looking at lovable links

Because Safari functions on the iPad mini the same way that browsers work on your Mac or PC, links on the device behave in much the same way.

Text links that transport you from one site to another are typically underlined or shown in blue, red, or bold type, or merely as items in a list. Tap the link to go directly to that site or page.

Tapping other links leads to different outcomes:

- ✔ **Open a map:** Tapping a map launches the Apple Maps application that is, um, addressed in Chapter 6.

- ✔ **Prepare an e-mail:** Tap an e-mail address, and the iPad opens the Mail program (see Chapter 5) and prepopulates the To field with that address. The virtual keyboard is also summoned so that you can add other e-mail addresses and compose a subject line and message. This shortcut doesn't always work when an e-mail address appears on a web page.

To see the URL for a link, press your finger on the link and hold it there until a list of options appears, as shown in Figure 4-5.

Use this method also to determine whether a picture has a link. Just hold your finger down on the picture and, if it's linked, you see the web address the link points to.

As for the other link options shown in Figure 4-5, here's what two of them do:

Figure 4-5: Press and hold on a link (Terms of Use), and a list of options appears.

- ✔ **Open:** Opens the page in this tab.

- ✔ **Copy:** Copies the link's URL to your iPad's clipboard so that you can paste it elsewhere.

You hear more about the other two options — Open in New Tab and Add to Reading List — a little later in this chapter.

Not every web link cooperates with the iPad. As this book goes to press, the iPad mini doesn't support some common web standards — most notably, Adobe Flash video. If you see an incompatible link, nothing may happen — or a message may appear, asking you to install a plug-in. For more about getting Flash to work on your iPad, see the nearby sidebar, "Support for the Flash-deprived."

Tabbed browsing

When we surf the web on a Mac or PC, we rarely go to a single web page and call it a day. In fact, we often have multiple web pages open at the same time. Sometimes, we choose to hop around the web without closing the pages we visit. Sometimes, a link automatically opens a new page without shuttering the old one. (If these additional pages are advertisements, this behavior isn't always welcome.)

Support for the Flash-deprived

The iPad's lack of support for Adobe Flash video is a void that, frankly, is unlikely to ever get addressed: Even Adobe is no longer embracing Flash for mobile devices. But because Flash has been the backbone of video and animations across cyberspace, you may still come across web destinations that rely on it. All is not lost, even with the absence of Flash. Apple does support an emerging standard for audio and video — HTML5, among others. And Adobe, too, is now backing HTML5.

In the meantime, you may be able to open Flash videos on the iPad through a couple of workarounds. Skyfire Labs sells a $4.99 iPad app that can support Flash on many sites. But Skyfire's alternative browser is limited to videos; it doesn't support Flash games or animations. Meanwhile, the free-to-try (free for ten minutes; the cost after the brief trial is $4.99) iSwifter app from YouWeb promises to address this shortcoming. So along with video, the iSwifter browser can deliver Flash games on Facebook and Google, though not on certain other sites.

Another workaround for some: Tap into your virtual private network (VPN) connection to control your desktop computer from the iPad. If such a connection is available, you can access the browser on that computer.

Safari on the iPad mini lets you open up to nine pages simultaneously, and through iOS gives you a brilliant rendition of tabbed browsing similar to the desktop version of browsers like Safari.

After you have one page open, here are two ways to open additional web pages in Safari so that they appear on the tab bar at the top of the screen (rather than replace the page you're viewing):

✔ **Tap the + button (see Figure 4-6) on the right side of the tab bar near the top of the screen.** A blank tab named Untitled appears, as shown in Figure 4-6. Now type a URL, tap a bookmark, or initiate a search and it will appear on this tab.

Figure 4-6: A new tab, ready to display any page you choose.

✔ **Hold your finger on a link until a list of options appears (refer to Figure 4-5), and then tap Open in New Tab.**

To switch tabs, simply tap the tab. To close a tab, tap the gray X that appears on the left edge of the active tab.

iCloud Tabs

Though the iPad is your likely traveling companion just about everywhere you go, we know that you also browse the web from your smartphone or personal computer. If that smartphone happens to be an iPhone and the computer is a Macintosh (or Windows PC with Safari and iCloud), you can take advantage of iCloud Tabs, a feature that lets you resume reading web pages that you started looking at on those other devices. It works with the iPod touch, too. To access iCloud Tabs, tap the icon that resembles a cloud near the upper-left corner of Safari (refer to Figure 4-1).

A window appears, revealing the tabs still open on your other devices. Tap the tab you want to return to on the list.

Revisiting Web Pages Time and Again

Surfing the web would be a real drag if you had to enter a URL every time you want to navigate from one page to another. That's why bookmarks, Web Clips, Reading Lists, and History Lists are useful — all so you can find those favorite websites in the future.

Book (mark) 'em, Dano

You already know how useful bookmarks are and how you can synchronize bookmarks from the browsers on your computer. It's equally simple to bookmark a web page directly on the iPad. Follow these steps:

1. **Make sure that the page you want to bookmark is open, and then tap the Action button at the top of the screen.**

   The Action button looks like an arrow trying to escape a rectangle.

2. **Tap Add Bookmark.**

   A new window opens with a default name for the bookmark, its web address, and its folder location.

3. **To accept the default bookmark name and default bookmark folder, tap Save.**

4. **To change the default bookmark name, tap the X in the circle next to the name, enter the new title (using the virtual keyboard), and then tap Save.**

5. **To change the location where the bookmark is saved, tap the > symbol in the Bookmarks field, tap the folder where you want the bookmark to be kept, tap the Add Bookmark button in the upper-left corner of the screen, and then tap Save.**

To open a bookmarked page after you set it up, tap the Bookmarks icon in the upper-left portion of the screen. (Refer to Figure 4-1.) If the bookmark you have in mind is buried inside a folder, tap the folder name first and then tap the bookmark you want. If you see History or Reading List (which you read more about in upcoming sections) instead of Bookmarks, tap the Bookmarks button at the top of the list, and then tap the appropriate bookmark.

If you tap Add to Home Screen rather than Add Bookmark in Step 1 of the preceding set of steps, your iPad adds an icon to your Home screen to let you quickly access the site, a topic we discuss in detail in the section "Clipping a web page," later in this chapter. If you tap Mail instead, the Mail program opens, with a link for the page in the message and the name of the site in the subject line. You find out more about using the Mail app in Chapter 5.

Altering bookmarks

If a bookmarked site is no longer meaningful, you can change it or get rid of it:

- **To remove a bookmark (or folder),** tap the Bookmarks icon and then tap Edit. Tap the red circle next to the bookmark you want to toss off the list, and then tap Delete.

  To remove a single bookmark or folder, swipe its name from left to right and then tap the red Delete button.

- **To change a bookmark name or location,** tap Edit and then tap the bookmark. The Edit Bookmark screen appears, showing the name, URL, and location of the bookmark already filled in. Tap the fields you want to change. In the Name field, tap the X in the gray circle and then use the keyboard to enter a new title. In the Location field, tap the > symbol and scroll up or down the list until you find a new home for your bookmark.

- **To create a new folder for your bookmarks,** tap Edit and then tap the New Folder button. Enter the name of the new folder and choose where to put it.

- **To move a bookmark up or down in a list,** tap Edit and then drag the three bars to the right of the bookmark's name to its new resting place.

If you take advantage of iCloud, the web pages you've bookmarked on your Mac and on your other iOS devices will be available on the iPad and vice versa.

Saving it for later with the Reading List

When you visit a web page you'd like to read, but not now, the Reading List feature is sure to come in handy. Here's how it works:

✔ **Save a page for later:** Tap the Action button and then tap Add to Reading List. Or, if you see a link to a page you'd like to read later, press on the link until a list of options appears (refer to Figure 4-5) and then tap Add to Reading List.

✔ **Read a page on your Reading List:** Tap the Bookmarks icon and tap the page in the Reading List, as shown in Figure 4-7.

✔ **Keep track of what you've read:** Any headlines you've already read appear in gray. The headlines that are still bold are unread.

✔ **Remove items from the Reading List:** Swipe the item from left to right or right to left, and then tap its red Delete button.

The Reading List feature doesn't require an active Internet connection. But for an alternative Reading List experience that lets you read web pages later *without* an Internet connection, check out Marco Arment's superb Instapaper app. It's only $4.99 in the App Store; you can read more about Instapaper in Chapter 19.

Finally, don't forget that you can share your Reading List (and Bookmarks) among your computers and iOS devices with iCloud, as described in Chapter 3.

Figure 4-7: Tap a page in the Reading List to read it.

Clipping a web page

You frequent lots of websites, but some way more than others. You're constantly online to consult your daily train schedule, for example. In their infinite wisdom, the folks at Apple let you bestow special privileges on frequently visited sites, not just by bookmarking pages but also by affording them their unique Home screen icons. Apple calls them *Web Clips,* and creating one is dead simple. Follow these steps:

1. **Open the web page in question and tap the Action button.**

2. **Tap Add to Home Screen.**

    Apple creates an icon out of the area of the page that was displayed when you saved the clip, unless the page has its own, custom icon.

3. **Type a new name for your Web Clip or leave the one that Apple suggests.**

4. **Tap Add.**

   The icon appears on your Home screen.

 As with any icon, you can remove a Web Clip by pressing and holding its icon until it starts to wiggle. Then tap the X in the corner of the icon and tap Delete. The operation is complete when you press the Home button. Of course, you can also move the Web Clip to a more preferred location on one of your Home screens.

Letting history repeat itself

Sometimes, you want to revisit a site that you failed to bookmark, but you can't remember the darn destination or what led you there in the first place. Good thing you can study the history books.

Safari records the pages you visit and keeps the logs on hand for several days. Here's how to access your history:

1. **Tap the Bookmarks icon and then tap the History icon.**

   The icon appears as a little clock at the bottom of the Bookmarks list.

2. **Tap the day you think you hung out at the site.**

3. **When you find the listing, tap it.**

   You're about to make your triumphant return.

 To clear your history so that nobody else can trace your steps (and just what is it you're hiding?), tap Clear History at the upper-right corner of the History List. Alternatively, starting on the Home screen, tap Settings⇨Safari⇨Clear History. In both instances, per usual, you have a chance to back out without wiping the slate clean.

Sharing Your Web Experiences

When you find a great website that you *must* share, Safari lets you tweet it, post it to Facebook, or — go old school — print it.

 To make Twitter and Facebook work, of course, the iPad must know your username and password, which you can fill in inside Settings (see Chapter 15).

Tweeting a web page

If you're one of the legions of people who tweets or merely a person who follows others on the enormously popular Twitter microblogging service, then you know that lots of folks share tidbits they come across on the web. Apple makes it a breeze to tweet web pages from the iPad. Tap the Action button and tap Tweet, and a window appears with the web page already attached. You're given room to add a comment of up to 120 characters of text. If you wish, you can tap Add Location to let everyone know from where it is you're tweeting. When you're ready, tap Send, or tap Cancel if you change your mind.

Sharing a page on Facebook

You probably noticed, while tapping the Action button, an icon for the world's most popular social network Facebook. If you tap that icon, you can share the page you're looking at with all your friends on Facebook. Once again, you have the option to add your location by— you guessed it — tapping Add Location.

Printing a web page

If you come to a web page that you want to print, tap the Action button. Tap Print from the menu that appears. You need a compatible AirPrint printer, as we explain in Chapter 2.

Saving web pictures

You can capture most pictures you come across on a website — but be mindful of any potential copyright violations, depending on what you plan to do with the images. To copy an image from a website, follow these steps:

1. **Press your finger against the image.**

2. **Tap the Save Image button that appears, as shown in Figure 4-8 (or tap Copy, depending on what you want to do with the image):**

   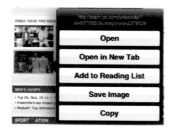

   Figure 4-8: Hold your finger against a picture in Safari to save it to the iPad.

   • Saved images end up in your Camera Roll, from which they can be synced back to a computer.

   • If you tap Copy instead, you can paste the image into an e-mail or as a link in a program, such as Notes.

In some cases — typically, advertisements — you also see an Open button or an Open in New Tab button, which takes you to the ad image. And sometimes, you see the Add to Reading List option as well.

Launching a Mobile Search Mission

Most people spend a lot of time using search engines on the Internet. And the search engines we summon most often are Google, Yahoo!, and Microsoft's Bing. So it goes on the iPad mini.

Although you can certainly use the virtual keyboard to type **google.com**, **yahoo.com**, or **bing.com** in the Safari address field, Apple doesn't require that tedious effort. Instead, you tap into Google, Yahoo!, or Bing by using the dedicated search box shown in Figure 4-9. The default search engine on the iPad is Google.

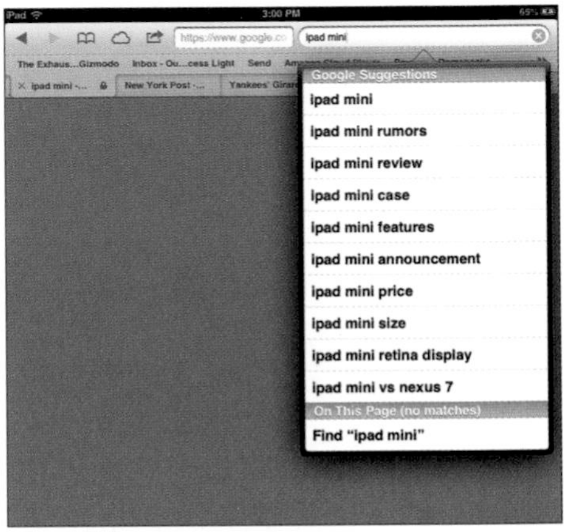

Figure 4-9: Conducting a Google search about iPads on the iPad.

To conduct a web search on the topic of the iPad, follow these steps:

1. **Tap the search field.**

   A funny thing happens. The search field expands (as if Google, Yahoo!, or Bing expected you to enter more text than could fit in the field initially). At the same time, the address bar gets smaller and your ever-obedient virtual keyboard slides up from the bottom. In Chapter 2, we explain how the keyboard adapts to what you're doing. The one that shows up now has a Search key.

2. **Enter your search term or phrase, and then tap the Search key to generate pages of results.**

3. **Tap any search result that looks promising.**

TIP

You can find a search word or phrase on the very web page you have open onscreen. Simply enter a search term in the search field as before. At the bottom of the search results list, tap On This Page. (Refer to Figure 4-9.) You may have to scroll down the list to see it. The first occurrence of your search term is highlighted. Tap the Next button at the lower-left corner of the screen to find the next match. Tap Next again for the match after that, and so on.

TIP

To switch the search box from Google to Yahoo! or Bing or whatever is your preference, check out the "Smart Safari Settings" section, later in this chapter.

Earlier in this chapter, we tell you that Siri can open Safari — all you have to do is ask. We also mention that she can (in some cases, anyway) take you to your favorite search engine, if you simply utter the name of a website.

Of course, much of what Suri can do is webcentric. So now is as good a time as any to recommend Chapter 14. You'll get an excellent sense of all that she can do.

Smart Safari Settings

Along with the riches galore found on the Internet are places in cyberspace where you're hassled. You might want to take action to protect your privacy and maintain your security.

To get started, tap the Settings icon on the Home screen and then tap Safari.

The following settings enable you to tell your iPad what you want to be private and how you want to set your security options:

- ✔ **Search Engine:** Tap the search engine you desire (as long as that search engine happens to be Google, Yahoo!, or Bing).

- ✔ **AutoFill:** Safari can automatically fill out web forms by using your personal contact information, usernames and passwords, or information from your other contacts. Tap AutoFill and then tap the On/Off switch to enable or disable AutoFill.

    Tap My Info to select yourself in your contacts so that Safari knows which address, phone numbers, e-mail addresses, and other information to use when it fills in a form.

    Tap the Names and Passwords On/Off switch to enable or disable Safari's capability to remember usernames and passwords for websites.

    Turning on AutoFill can compromise your security if someone gets hold of your iPad.

    Finally, tap Clear All to permanently delete all saved AutoFill names and passwords.

- ✔ **Open New Tabs in Background:** Enable this, and when you open new tabs in Safari, they load, even if you're reading a different page on another tab.

- ✔ **Always Show Bookmarks Bar:** Enable this option to always see Safari's Bookmarks bar between the Address field and Tab bar. (Refer to Figure 4-9.)

- ✔ **Private Browsing:** Enable this option, and Safari stops tracking the pages you visit, so your History won't reveal a trace of where you've been.

    The history of pages you've visited can be useful and a huge timesaver, so don't forget to disable the Private Browsing option again when you're done doing whatever it is that you don't want people to know you're doing.

✔ **Accept Cookies:** We're not talking about crumbs you may have accidentally dropped on the iPad. *Cookies* are tiny bits of information that a website places on the iPad when you visit so that the site recognizes you when you return. You need not assume the worst; most cookies are benign.

If this concept wigs you out, you can take action: Tap Accept Cookies and then tap Never. Theoretically, you will never again receive cookies on the iPad. A good middle ground is to accept cookies only from the sites you visit. To do so, tap From Visited. You can also tap Always to accept cookies from all sites.

If you set the iPad so that it doesn't accept cookies, certain web pages won't load properly, and other sites such as Amazon won't recognize you or make any of your preferred settings or recommendations available.

Tap Safari to return to the main Safari Settings page.

✔ **Clear History:** Tap this button to erase everything in Safari's History, leaving nary a trace of the pages you've visited.

✔ **Clear Cookies and Data:** Tap this button to clear all your stored cookies (for more details, see the earlier bullet about accepting cookies).

✔ **Fraud Warning:** Safari can warn you when you land on a site whose producers have sinister intentions. The protection is better than nothing, but don't let down your guard. The Fraud Warning feature isn't foolproof. The setting is on by default.

✔ **JavaScript:** Programmers use JavaScript to add various kinds of functionality to web pages, from displaying the date and time to changing images when you mouse over them. However, some security risks have also been associated with JavaScript. If you do turn it off, though, some things might not work as you expect.

✔ **Block Pop-Ups:** *Pop-ups* are those web pages that appear whether or not you want them to. Often, they're annoying advertisements. But on some sites, you welcome the appearance of pop-ups, so remember to turn off blocking under such circumstances.

✔ **Advanced:** Unless you happen to be a developer, you don't need to pay much attention to this setting. It lets you turn a debug console (showing errors, warnings, tips, logs, and similar details that developers find useful) on or off.

5

The E-Mail Must Get Through

*O*n any computing device, e-mails come and go with a variety of emotions. Messages may be amusing or sad, frivolous or serious. Electronic missives on the iPad mini are almost always touching.

The reason, of course, is that you're touching the display to compose and read messages. Okay, so we're having a little fun with the language. But the truth is, the built-in Mail application on the iPad is a modern program designed not only to send and receive text e-mail messages but also to handle rich HTML e-mail messages — formatted with font and type styles and embedded graphics. If someone sends you mail with a picture, it's quite likely that the picture is visible right in the body of the message. (That's the default behavior, but your results may vary, depending on the sender's e-mail capabilities and your iPad's mail settings.)

Furthermore, your iPad can read several types of file attachments, including (but not limited to) PDFs, JPG images, Microsoft Word documents, PowerPoint slides, and Excel spreadsheets, as well as stuff produced through Apple's own iWork software. Better still, all this sending and receiving of text, graphics, and documents can happen in the background so that you can surf the web or play a game while your iPad quietly and efficiently handles your e-mail behind the scenes.

With iOS 6, Apple even lets you grant VIP status to important senders so that there's almost no chance you'll miss mail from the people who matter most. Let's see, there's your spouse, your kids, your boss . . . are we missing anybody?

Prep Work: Setting Up Your Accounts

First things first. To use Mail, you need an e-mail address. If you have broadband Internet access (that is, a cable modem, FiOS, or DSL), you probably received one or more e-mail addresses when you signed up. If you're one of the handful of readers who doesn't already have an e-mail account, you can get one for free from Yahoo! (`http://mail.yahoo.com`), Google (`http://mail.google.com`), AOL (`www.aol.com`), or numerous other service providers.

Or you can get a free premium e-mail account (for example, *Your_Name@ me.com*) from Apple as part of iCloud. From your Home screen, just tap Settings⇨Mail, Contacts, Calendars⇨iCloud⇨Get a Free Apple ID.

Many free e-mail providers add a small bit of advertising at the end of your outgoing messages. If you'd rather not turn your email account into a billboard for your e-mail provider, either use the address(es) that came with your broadband Internet access (*yourname@comcast.net* or *yourname@ att.net*, for example) or pay a few dollars a month for a premium e-mail account that doesn't tack advertising (or anything else) onto your messages.

Finally, while the rest of the chapter focuses on the Mail app, you can also use Safari to access most e-mail systems, if that's your preference.

Setting up your account the easy way

Chapter 3 explains the option of automatically syncing the e-mail accounts on your Mac or Windows PC with your iPad. If you chose that option, your e-mail accounts should be configured on your iPad already. You may proceed directly to the later section "See Me, Read Me, File Me, Delete Me: Working with Messages."

If you haven't yet chosen that option but want to set up your account the easy way now, go to Chapter 3, read about syncing e-mail accounts, and then sync your iPad with your Mac or PC. Then you, too, can proceed directly to the section "See Me, Read Me, File Me, Delete Me: Working with Messages," later in this chapter.

Remember that syncing e-mail accounts doesn't have any effect on your e-mail messages; it merely synchronizes the *settings* for e-mail accounts so you don't have to set them up manually on your iPad.

Setting up your account the less-easy way

If you don't want to sync the e-mail accounts on your Mac or PC, you can set up an e-mail account on your iPad manually. It's not quite as easy as clicking a box and syncing your iPad, but it's not rocket science either. Here's how you get started:

- ✔ **If you have no e-mail accounts on your iPad,** the first time you launch Mail, you see the Welcome to Mail screen, shown in Figure 5-1. Your choices are iCloud, Microsoft Exchange (business e-mail), Gmail, Yahoo!, AOL, Microsoft Hotmail, and Other.

  Merely tap the account type you want to add to the iPad and follow the steps in the next section, the section after that ("Setting up an account with another provider"), or the section "Setting up corporate e-mail," later in this chapter.

- ✔ **If you have one or more e-mail accounts on your iPad already and want to add a new account manually,** tap Settings on the Home screen and then tap Mail, Contacts, Calendars⇨Add Account.

Figure 5-1: Tap a button to set up an account.

You see the Add Account screen with the same account options that are shown on the Welcome to Mail screen. Proceed to one of the next three sections, depending on the type of e-mail account you selected.

Setting up an e-mail account with iCloud, Gmail, Yahoo!, AOL, or Hotmail

If your account is with iCloud, Gmail (Google), Yahoo!, AOL, or Hotmail, follow these steps:

1. **Tap the appropriate button on the Welcome to Mail screen. (Refer to Figure 5-1.)**

2. **Enter your name, e-mail address, and password, and an optional description, as shown in Figure 5-2.**

   You can describe this account (such as Work or Personal), but the field tends to fill in automatically with the same contents in the Address field unless you tell it differently.

3. **Tap the Next button in the upper-right corner of the screen.**

   You're finished. That's all there is to setting up your account. You can now proceed to "See Me, Read Me, File Me, Delete Me: Working with Messages."

On June 30, 2012, Apple completed the transition from MobileMe to iCloud. Apple says that if you had an active MobileMe account when you signed up for iCloud, you can keep your me.com or mac.com e-mail address and any e-mail aliases you have created. You can move your MobileMe mail to iCloud, and for that matter, you can move your MobileMe contacts, calendars, and bookmarks.

Figure 5-2: Just fill 'em in and tap Next, and you're ready to rock.

Setting up an account with another provider

If your e-mail account is with a provider other than iCloud, Gmail (Google), Yahoo!, AOL, or Hotmail, you have a bit more work ahead of you. You need a bunch of information about your e-mail account that you may not know or have handy.

We suggest that you scan the following instructions, note the items you don't know, and go find the answers before you continue. To find the answers, look at the documentation you received when you signed up for your e-mail account or visit the account provider's website and search there.

Here's how you set up an account:

1. **Starting at the Home screen, tap Settings⇨Mail, Contacts, Calendars⇨Add Account⇨Other.**

2. **Under Mail, tap Add Mail Account.**

3. **Fill in the name, address, password, and description in the appropriate fields, and then tap Next.**

   With any luck, that's all you'll have to do. The iPad will look up and hopefully be able to retrieve your account credentials. If not, continue with Step 4.

4. **Tap the button at the top of the screen that denotes the type of e-mail server this account uses, IMAP or POP, as shown in Figure 5-3.**

5. **Fill in the Internet hostname for your incoming mail server, which looks something like `mail.providername.com`.**

6. **Fill in your username and password.**

7. **Enter the Internet hostname for your outgoing mail server, which looks something like `smtp.providername.com`.**

8. **Enter your username and password in the appropriate fields.**

9. **Tap the Next (sometimes Save) button in the upper-right corner to create the account.**

   You're now ready to begin using your account. See the later section "See Me, Read Me, File Me, Delete Me: Working with Messages."

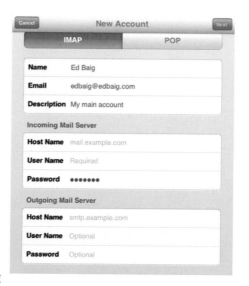

Figure 5-3: If you set up an IMAP or POP e-mail account, you may have a few more fields to fill in before you can rock.

Some outgoing mail servers don't need your username and password. The fields for these items on your iPad note that they're optional. Still, we suggest that you fill them in anyway. It saves you from having to add them later if your outgoing mail server does require an account name and password, which almost all do these days.

Setting up corporate e-mail

The iPad makes nice with the Microsoft Exchange servers that are a staple in large enterprises as well as in many smaller businesses.

What's more, if your company supports Microsoft Exchange ActiveSync, you can exploit push e-mail so that messages arrive pronto on the iPad, just as they do on your other computers. (To keep everything up to date, the iPad also supports push calendars and push contacts.) For push to work with an Exchange Server — at press time, anyway — your company must be simpatico with Microsoft Exchange ActiveSync 2003 (Service Pack 2), 2007 (Service Pack 1), or 2010. Ask your company's IT or tech department if you run into an issue.

Setting up Exchange e-mail isn't particularly taxing, and the iPad connects to Exchange right out of the box. You still might have to consult your employer's techie-types for certain settings.

Start setting up your corporate e-mail on your iPad by following these steps:

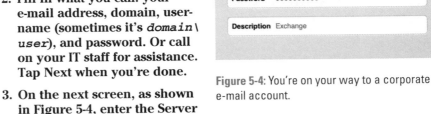

Figure 5-4: You're on your way to a corporate e-mail account.

1. **Tap the Microsoft Exchange icon on the Welcome to Mail or Add Account screen. (Refer to Figure 5-1.)**

2. **Fill in what you can: your e-mail address, domain, user-name (sometimes it's `domain\user`), and password. Or call on your IT staff for assistance. Tap Next when you're done.**

3. **On the next screen, as shown in Figure 5-4, enter the Server e-mail address, assuming that the Microsoft Autodiscover service didn't already find it. Tap Next when you're done.**

That server address may begin with `exchange.company.com`.

4. **Choose which infor-mation you want to synchronize through Exchange by tapping each item you want.**

   You can choose Mail, Contacts, and Calendars. After you choose an item, you see the blue On button next to it, as shown in Figure 5-5.

5. **Tap Save.**

The company you work for doesn't want just anybody having access to your e-mail — heaven forbid if your iPad is lost or stolen. So your bosses may insist that you change the passcode lock inside Settings on your iPad. (This is different from the password for your e-mail account.) Skip over to Chapter 15 to find instructions for adding or changing a passcode. (We'll

Figure 5-5: Keeping your mail, contacts, calendars, and reminders in sync.

wait for you.) And if your iPad ends up in the wrong hands, your company can remotely wipe the contents clean.

By default, the mini keeps e-mail synchronized for three days. To sync for a longer period, head to Settings; tap Mail, Contacts, Calendars; and then tap the e-mail account using ActiveSync. Tap Mail Days to Sync and tap No Limit or pick another time frame (1 day, 1 week, 2 weeks, or 1 month).

If you're moonlighting at a second job, you can configure more than one Exchange ActiveSync account on your iPad.

See Me, Read Me, File Me, Delete Me: Working with Messages

After your e-mail accounts are all set up, it's time to figure out how to receive and read the stuff. Fortunately, you've already done most of the heavy lifting when you set up your e-mail accounts. Getting and reading your mail are a piece of cake.

Your first clue that there's *unread* mail comes when you look at the Mail icon at the bottom of the Home screen. The cumulative number of unread messages appears in a little red oval in the upper-right area of the icon.

This "badge" is the default behavior. If you don't care for it, feel free to turn it off in the Settings app's Notification Center pane.

In the following sections, you find out how to read messages and attached files and send messages to the Trash or maybe a folder when you're done reading them. Or, if you can't find a message, check out the section on searching your e-mail messages. You can read your e-mail just like you can on a desktop or notebook computer; the way you do so just works a little differently on the iPad's touchscreen.

Reading messages

To read your mail, tap the Mail icon on the Home screen. Remember that what appears onscreen depends on whether you're holding the iPad in landscape or portrait mode, and on what was on the screen the last time you opened the Mail app:

- **Landscape:** Holding your iPad in landscape mode, you see All Inboxes at the top of the Inboxes section (see Figure 5-6), which, as its name suggests, is a repository for all messages across all your accounts. The number to the right of All Inboxes (604 in Figure 5-6) matches the number on the Mail icon on your Home page. Again, it's the cumulative tally of unread messages across all your accounts.

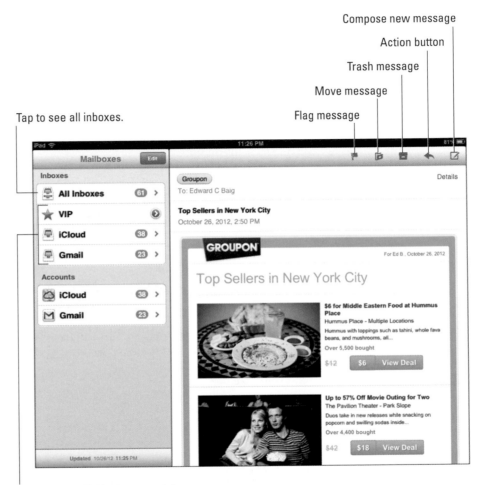

Compose new message

Action button

Trash message

Move message

Flag message

Tap to see all inboxes.

Tap to see individual account inboxes.

Figure 5-6: When you're holding the iPad sideways, Mail looks something like this.

Below the All Inboxes listing are the inboxes for your individual accounts. The number to the right of them, as you'd expect, is the number of unread messages in those accounts (601 in Gmail and 3 in Hotmail in Figure 5-6).

If you tap an account, you see the available subfolders for that account (Drafts, Sent Mail, Trash, and so on).

One of these accounts is the VIP Mailbox. The *VIP Mailbox* lists all the messages from senders you deem the most important. We tell you how to give someone VIP status in the later section "More things you can do with messages."

Depending on the last time the Mail app was open, you may alternatively see previews of the actual messages in your inbox in the left panel mentioned previously. Previews show the name of the sender, the time a message arrived, the subject header, and the first two lines of the message. (In Settings, you can change the number of lines shown in the preview from one line to five. Or you can show no preview lines.)

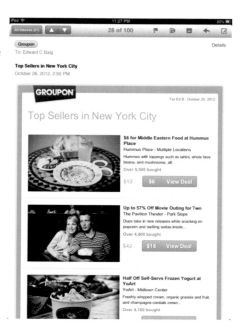

Figure 5-7: When you're holding the iPad in portrait mode, the message fills the screen.

✔ **Portrait:** When you hold the iPad in portrait mode, the last incoming message fills the entire screen. Figure 5-7 shows this view. You have to tap an Inbox button (in the upper-left corner of the screen) to summon a panel that shows other accounts or message previews. These overlay the message that otherwise fills the screen.

Messages display in *threads,* or conversations, making them easy to follow. Of course, you can still view accounts individually. Follow these steps to read your e-mail:

1. **If the e-mail mailbox you want to see isn't front and center, tap the Mailboxes button in the upper-left corner of the screen to summon the appropriate one.**

   Again, this button may say All Inboxes or another folder name, and it may say the name of the e-mail account that is currently open. Within an e-mail account, you can see the number of unread messages in each mailbox.

2. **(Optional) Swipe down and release the left panel listing your accounts to summon new messages.**

   You know the iPad is searching for new mail when you see a not-quite-closed circle with an arrow that is inside what appears to be a droplet. By the time you blink, the droplet icon morphs into a spinning gear.

3. **Swipe down one of the inboxes or accounts to refresh those specific mailboxes. To summon the unified inbox, tap All Inboxes instead.**

If a blue dot appears next to a message, the message hasn't been read. When you open a mailbox by tapping it, the iPad displays the number of "recent" messages that you specify in Settings — 50 by default, though you can display up to 1,000 recent messages. To see more than the number you specified, tap Load Additional Messages.

4. **Tap a message to read it.**

5. **Read additional messages.**

   When a message is onscreen, the buttons for managing incoming messages appear at the top, most of which you're already familiar with.

   - *In portrait mode:* Tap the up/down arrows that correspond to the next or previous message (refer to Figure 5-7).

   - *In landscape mode (and from within an account):* Tap a preview listing to the left of a message to read the next or previous message or any other visible message on the list. Scroll up or down to find other messages you may want to read.

A number next to one of the previews indicates the number of related messages in a thread or conversation.

Under a thread, only the first message of the conversation displays in the inbox. Tap that message to reveal all messages that are part of the thread. You can turn off message threading by choosing Settings➪Mail, Contacts, Calendars. Then tap Organize by Thread to toggle the setting on or off, depending on your preference.

Managing messages

Managing messages typically involves either moving the messages to a folder or deleting them. To herd your messages into folders, you have the following options:

- ✔ **To create a folder to organize messages you want to keep,** manage your mail account on your Mac or PC. You can't create a Mail folder on the iPad.

- ✔ **To file a message in another folder,** tap the File Message icon. When the list of folders appears, tap the folder where you want to file the message. It's kind of cool watching the entire message fly and land in the new folder that you've designated.

- ✔ **To read a message that you've filed away,** tap the folder where the message now resides and then tap the header or preview for the message in question.

- ✔ **To print a message,** tap the Action button (refer to Figure 5-6) and then tap Print.

✔ **To delete, move, or mark multiple messages,** tap Edit. In both portrait and landscape, *Edit* appears at the top of your inbox or another mailbox when those mail folders are selected. After tapping Edit, it becomes a Cancel button, and new Delete, Move, and Mark buttons appear at the bottom of the list, as shown in Figure 5-8. Tap each message you want to select so that a red check mark appears.

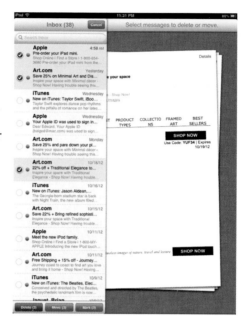

* *Tap Delete* to delete all selected messages.

* *Tap Move* to move all selected messages to another folder, and then tap the new folder in which you want those messages to hang out.

Figure 5-8: Wiping out, moving, or marking messages, *en masse.*

* *Tap Mark* to mark all selected messages as Read (and Unread) and Flagged (and Unflagged).

✔ **To delete a single message,** tap the Delete Message icon. You have a chance to cancel in case you tap the Delete Message icon by mistake.

✔ **To delete a single message without opening it,** swipe one finger across the message in the mailbox list and then tap the red Delete button that appears to the right of the message.

In certain Mail accounts, and Gmail is one, the Delete option may be replaced by an Archive option, depending on your preference. That means you're not so much getting rid of a message as stashing it aside, or to be precise, saving the deleted message in your All Mail folder. If the Archive message option does present itself, you can turn the feature on or off in Settings.

Searching e-mails

With Spotlight search, you can easily search a bunch of messages to find (fast) the one you want to read — such as that can't-miss stock tip from your broker. You can type **stock** or whichever search term seems relevant in the search box at the top of a mailbox preview pane. All matching e-mails that have already been downloaded appear. When you tap the search box in Mail, tabs appear that let you narrow the search to the From, To, or Subject field. It's too bad that (at press time, anyway) you can't run a search to find words within the body of an e-mail message from the Mail app. (But you can search using Spotlight; see Chapter 2.)

If you're using Exchange, iCloud, or certain IMAP-type e-mail accounts, you may even be able to search messages that are stored out on the server. When it's available, tap Continue Search on Server.

Don't grow too attached to attachments

Your iPad can even receive e-mail messages with attachments in a wide variety of popular file formats. (See the nearby sidebar "Keeping files in order" if you're not sure what file formats are.) Which file formats does the iPad support? Glad you asked:

- ✔ **Images:** `.jpg`, `.tiff`, `.gif`, `.png`
- ✔ **Microsoft Word:** `.doc`, `.docx`
- ✔ **Microsoft PowerPoint:** `.ppt`, `.pptx`
- ✔ **Microsoft Excel:** `.xls`, `.xlsx`
- ✔ **Web pages:** `.htm`, `.html`
- ✔ **Apple Keynote:** `.key`
- ✔ **Apple Numbers:** `.numbers`
- ✔ **Apple Pages:** `.pages`
- ✔ **Preview and Adobe Acrobat:** `.pdf`
- ✔ **Rich Text:** `.rtf`
- ✔ **Text:** `.txt`
- ✔ **Contact information:** `.vcf`

If the attachment is a file format that the iPad doesn't support (for example, a Photoshop `.psd` file), you see the name of the file but you can't open it on your iPad, at least without an assist from third-party apps that you may have installed.

Here's how to read a supported attachment:

1. **Open the mail message that contains the attachment.**

2. **Tap the attachment.**

   It appears at the bottom of the message, so you probably need to scroll down to see it.

   The attachment downloads to your iPad and opens automatically.

Keeping files in order

In very simple terms, computers of any type, including tablets like the iPad mini, and the software that runs on such machines have to have some way to recognize and appropriately act upon the files that run on the system. Long ago, the bright minds in technology cooked up standard ways to organize the layout of data so that files that serve a particular purpose adhere to a similar structure. You recognize such files by their extensions, the suffix that is separated by a dot or period after its name. Needless to say, many more file formats exist than most folks will ever need to become familiar with. But you, or more precisely, the hardware and software you're working with, will encounter some popular file types repeatedly, including such formats as .doc for Microsoft Word documents and .jpg for images. If you ever encounter files on any computer you are using that don't seem to open or respond, it's likely because you don't have the software on the machine to recognize such files. The good news is that the iPad supports most of the common file types it encounters, though not quite every file type.

3. **Read the attachment.**

4. **Tap the document you're reading (in the case of a document) and tap Done to return to the message text.**

   Or you can (again, for a document) open the Pages word processor if you have purchased that application for your iPad, or open the doc in certain other apps you may have added. Incidentally, the documents you create in the Pages app are automatically saved to your iPad. With the latest version of Pages, you can also save a document to iCloud where it can automatically be made available to the version of Pages for Mac computers.

You can open an attachment from a different app than may have otherwise been summoned to duty. Just touch and hold the attachment in the e-mail, and then tap the app from the options that present themselves. For example, you might open a Word document with Apple's Pages word processor if that optional app resides on your iPad.

More things you can do with messages

Wait! You can do even more with your incoming e-mail messages:

✔ **To see all recipients of a message,** tap Details (displayed in blue) to the right of the sender's name.

If all recipients are displayed, the word in blue is Hide rather than Details; tap it to hide all names except the sender's.

- **To add an e-mail recipient or sender to your contacts,** tap the name or e-mail address at the top of the message and then tap Create New Contact or Add to Existing Contact.

- **To make a sender a VIP,** tap the name or e-mail address at the top of the message and then tap Add to VIP. A star appears next to any incoming messages from a VIP. You can summon mail from all your VIPs by tapping the VIP folder in the list of Mailboxes. To demote a VIP to what we jokingly refer to as an NVIP (translation: not very important person), tap the name or e-mail at the top of the message and then tap Remove from VIP.

- **To mark a message as unread or to flag it,** tap the Flag icon at the top of a message. Two options appear:

  - *Mark as Unread:* Choose Mark as Unread for messages that you may want to revisit at some point but that don't necessarily have special significance. The message is again included in the unread-message count on the Mail icon on your Home screen, and its mailbox again has a blue dot next to it in the message list for that mailbox. You can tap Mark as Read if the message loses its significance.

  - *Flag:* Choose Flag for those messages that deserve special status or that you want to find again in a hurry.

- **To zoom in and out of a message,** use the pinch and unpinch gestures, at which we suspect you now excel. See Chapter 2 if you need help with your touchscreen moves.

- **To follow a link in a message,** tap the link. Links typically display in blue, but sometimes in other colors and sometimes underlined. If the link is a URL, Safari opens and displays the web page. If the link is a phone number, the iPad gives you the chance to add it to your contacts (or copy it). If the link is a map, Maps opens and displays the location. And last but not least, if the link is an e-mail address, a new, preaddressed, blank e-mail message is created.

If the link opens Safari, Contacts, or Maps and you want to return to your e-mail, press the Home button on the front of your iPad and then tap the Mail icon. Or double-press the Home button and select it from the gallery of running apps.

Darling, You Send Me (E-Mail)

Sending e-mail on your iPad is a breeze. You'll encounter several subspecies of messages: pure text, text with a photo, a partially finished message (a *draft*) that you want to save and complete later, or a reply to an incoming message.

You can also forward an incoming message to someone else — and in some instances print messages. The following sections examine these message types, one at a time.

Sending an all-text message

To compose a new e-mail message, tap Mail on the Home screen. Once again, what you see next depends on how you're holding your iPad. In landscape mode, your e-mail accounts or e-mail folders are listed in a panel along the left side of screen, with the actual message filling the larger window on the right.

Now, to create a new message, follow these steps:

1. **Tap the Compose New Message button. (Refer to Figure 5-6.)**

   The New Message screen like the one shown in Figure 5-9 appears (except your new message won't have text typed in the message body yet).

2. **Type the names or e-mail addresses of the recipients in the To field, or tap the + button to the right of the To field to choose a contact(s) from your iPad's contacts list.**

   If you start typing an e-mail address, e-mail addresses that match what you typed appear in a list below the To or Cc field. If the correct one is in the list, tap it to use it.

3. **(Optional) Tap the field labeled Cc/Bcc, From.**

   Doing so breaks the field into separate Cc, Bcc, and From fields (refer to Figure 5-9).

Figure 5-9: The New Message screen appears, ready for you to start typing the recipient's name.

The Cc/Bcc label stands for *carbon copy/blind carbon copy.* Carbon copy (a throwback term from another era) is kind of an FYI to a recipient. It's like saying, "We figure you'd appreciate knowing this, but you don't need to respond."

When using Bcc, you can include a recipient on the message but other recipients can't see that this recipient has been included. It's great for those secret agent e-mails! Tap the respective Cc or Bcc field to type names. Or tap the + symbol that appears in those fields to add a contact.

4. **(Optional) If you tap From, you can choose to send the message from any of your e-mail accounts on the fly, assuming, of course, that you have more than one account set up on the iPad.**

5. **Type a subject in the Subject field.**

The subject is optional, but it's considered poor form to send an e-mail message without one.

6. **Type your message in the message area.**

The message area is immediately below the Subject field. You have ample space to get your message across.

Apple includes a bunch of landscape-orientation keyboards in various applications, including Mail. When you rotate the iPad to its side, you can compose a new message using a wider-format virtual keyboard.

7. **Tap the Send button in the upper-right corner of the screen.**

Your message wings its way to its recipients almost immediately. If you aren't in range of a Wi-Fi network or a cellular network when you tap Send, the message is sent the next time you're in range of one of these networks.

Sending a photo with an e-mail message

Sometimes a picture is worth a thousand words. When that's the case, here's one way to send an e-mail message with a photo attached:

1. **Tap the Photos icon on the Home screen.**

2. **Find the photo you want to send.**

3. **Tap the Action button (the little rectangle with the curved arrow springing out of it) in the upper-right corner of the screen.**

4. **Tap the Mail button.**

An e-mail message appears onscreen with the photo already attached. In fact, the image may appear to be embedded in the body of the message, but the recipient receives it as a regular e-mail attachment.

On the Cc/Bcc line of your outgoing message, you see the size of the attached image. If you tap on the size of the image shown, a new line appears, giving you the option to choose an alternative size among Small, Medium, Large, or Actual Size (in other words, keeping what you have). Your choice affects both the visible dimensions and file size of the photo (with the actual sizes of the file as measured in kilobytes or megabytes shown for each possible choice).

5. **Choose a size for sending your photo.**

6. **Address the message and type whatever text you like, as you did for an all-text message in the preceding section, and then tap the Send button.**

If you've read the introduction to this section closely, you've probably already surmised that there's an alternative way to send photos in an e-mail. And it's quite easy: Press and hold your finger against the body of the message where you normally enter text. You see the Insert Photo or Video tab. Tap the tab, and you can select an image (or a video) from any of your photo albums.

Saving an e-mail to send later

Sometimes you start an e-mail message but don't have time to finish it. When that happens, you can save it as a draft and finish it another time. Here's how:

1. **Start an e-mail message, as described in one of the two previous sections.**

2. **When you're ready to save the message as a draft, tap the Cancel button in the upper-left corner of the screen.**

3. **Tap the Save Draft button if you want to save this message as a draft and complete it another time.**

If you tap the Delete Draft button, the message disappears immediately without a second chance. Don't tap Delete Draft unless you mean it.

To work on the message again, tap the Drafts mailbox. A list of all messages you saved as drafts appears. Tap the draft you want to work on, and it reappears on the screen. When you're finished, you can tap Send to send it or tap Cancel to save it as a draft again.

The number of drafts appears to the right of the Drafts folder, the same way that the number of unread messages appears to the right of other mail folders, such as your inbox.

Replying to, forwarding, or printing an e-mail message

When you receive a message and want to reply to it, open the message and then tap the Action button (the curved arrow at the upper-right corner of the screen, as shown in Figure 5-10). Then tap the Reply, Reply All, Forward, or Print button, described as follows:

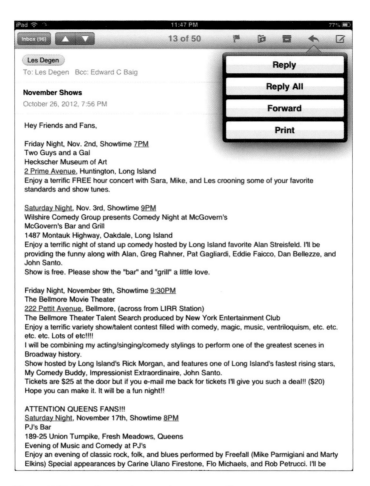

Figure 5-10: Reading and managing an e-mail message.

- ✓ **Reply and Reply All:** The Reply button creates an e-mail message addressed to the sender of the original message, with the content of that original message embedded in your reply. The Reply All button creates an e-mail message addressed to the sender and all other recipients of the original message, plus Ccs. (The Reply All option appears only if more than one recipient was on the original e-mail.) In both cases, the subject is retained with the *Re:* prefix added. So if the original subject were *iPad Tips,* the reply's subject would be *Re: iPad Tips.*

- ✓ **Forward:** Tapping the Forward button creates an unaddressed e-mail message that contains the text of the original message. Add the e-mail address(es) of the person or people you want to forward the message to, and then tap Send. In this case, rather than the *Re* prefix, the subject is preceded by *Fwd.* So this time, the subject would be *Fwd: iPad Tips.*

✔ **Print:** Of course, you tap Print if you want to print using an AirPrint-capable printer.

If you want to add a level of indentation when you forward or reply to a message, tap Settings⟹Mail, Contacts, Calendars⟹Increase Quote Level. Tap to turn the switch to On (if it's not on already).

You can edit the subject line of a reply or a forwarded message or edit the body text of a forwarded message the same way you'd edit any other text. It's usually considered good form to leave the subject lines alone (with the *Re:* or *Fwd:* prefix intact), but you may want to change them sometimes. Now you know that you can.

To send your reply or forwarded message, tap the Send button as usual.

Settings for sending e-mail

You can customize the mail you send and receive in lots of ways. In this section, we explore settings for sending e-mail. Later in this chapter, we show you settings that impact the way you receive and read messages. In each instance, start by tapping Settings on the Home screen.

You can customize your mail in the following ways:

✔ **To hear an alert when you successfully send a message:** From the main Settings screen, tap Sounds. Make sure that the Sent Mail setting is turned on. You'll know because you'll see a sound type listed — "Swoosh," by default. If you tap Sent Mail in settings, you can select another sound besides Swoosh or choose None if going silent is your preference.

If you want to change other settings, tap the Sounds button at the top of the screen, which is shaped like a left-pointing arrow. If you're finished setting the settings, tap the Home button on the front of your iPad.

No matter what setting you've just accessed, if you want to continue using Settings, tap whichever left-pointing button appears at the top of the screen — sometimes it's General, sometimes Mail, sometimes Contacts, or sometimes something else. After you return to the previous screen, you can change other settings. Similarly, you can tap the Home button on the front of your iPad when you're finished setting any setting. That action always saves the change you just made and returns you to the Home screen.

✔ **To add a signature line, phrase, or block of text to every e-mail message you send:** Tap Settings⟹Mail, Contacts, Calendars⟹Signature on the right. The default signature is *Sent from my iPad.* You can add text before or after it or delete it and type something else. Your signature is affixed to the end of all your outgoing e-mail.

✔ **To have your iPad send you a copy of every message you send:** Tap Settings⇨Mail, Contacts, Calendars, and then turn on the Always Bcc Myself setting.

✔ **To set the default e-mail account for sending e-mail from outside the Mail application:** Tap the Settings icon on the Home screen, and then tap Mail, Contacts, Calendars⇨Default Account. Tap the account you want to use as the default. For example, when you want to e-mail a picture directly from the Photos application, this designated e-mail account is the one that's used. Note that this setting applies only if you have more than one e-mail account on your iPad.

Setting Your Message and Account Settings

This final discussion of Mail involves more settings that deal with your various e-mail accounts. (If you're looking for settings that let you apply a signature and other settings related to sending e-mail, read the preceding section.)

Checking and viewing e-mail settings

Several settings affect the way you can check and view e-mail. You might want to modify one or more, so we describe what they do and where to find them:

✔ **To specify how often the iPad checks for new messages:** Tap the Settings icon on the Home screen; tap Mail, Contacts, Calendars⇨Fetch New Data. You're entering the world of *fetching* or *pushing.* Check out Figure 5-11 to glance at your options. If your e-mail program (or more precisely, the e-mail server behind it) supports push and the Push setting is enabled on your iPad (the On button displays), fresh messages are sent to your iPad automatically as soon as they hit the server. If

Figure 5-11: Fetch or push? It's your call.

you turned off push or your e-mail program doesn't support it in the first place (Off displays), the iPad fetches data instead. Choices for fetching are Every 15 Minutes, Every 30 Minutes, Hourly, and Manually. Tap the one you prefer.

Tap Advanced to determine the push and fetch settings for each individual account. Tap the account in question. Push is shown as an option only if the e-mail account you tapped supports the feature. It's worth pointing out that with push e-mail, messages can show up on the lock screen and in Notification Center.

✔ **To hear an alert sound when you receive a new message:** Tap Sounds on the main Settings screen, and then tap the New Mail setting. The Ding sound is there by default. Do nothing if you're satisfied with the ding you hear each time a new message arrives. If you aren't satisfied, tap New Mail and select an alternative sound from the list, or tap None if you don't want to hear any such alert.

✔ **To set the number of recent messages that appear in your inbox:** From the main Settings screen, tap Mail, Contacts, Calendars➪Show. Your choices are 50, 100, 200, 500, and 1,000 recent messages. Tap the number you prefer.

You can always see more messages in your inbox regardless of this setting by scrolling all the way to the bottom and tapping Load Additional Messages.

✔ **To set the number of lines of each message to be displayed in the message list:** From the main Settings screen, tap Mail, Contacts, Calendars➪Preview; then choose a number. Your choices are None, 1, 2, 3, 4, and 5 lines of text. The more lines of text you display in the list, the fewer messages you can see at a time without scrolling. Think before you choose 4 or 5.

✔ **To specify whether the iPad shows the To and Cc labels in message lists:** From the main Settings screen, tap Mail, Contacts, Calendars and turn the Show To/Cc Label setting on or off.

✔ **To turn the Ask before Deleting warning on or off:** From the main Settings screen, tap Mail, Contacts, Calendars; then turn the Ask before Deleting setting on or off. If this setting is turned on, you need to tap the Trash icon at the bottom of the screen and then tap the red Delete button to confirm the deletion. When the setting is turned off, tapping the Trash icon deletes the message, and you never see a red Delete button.

✔ **To specify whether the iPad will automatically load remote images:** Tap Load Remote Images so that the On button displays. If it's off, you can still manually load remote images. Certain security risks have been associated with loading remote images.

✔ **To organize your mail by thread:** Tap Organize by Threads so that the setting is toggled on.

Altering account settings

The last group of settings we explore in this chapter deal with your e-mail accounts. You most likely will never need most of these settings, but we'd be remiss if we didn't at least mention them briefly. So here they are, whether you need 'em or not:

- ✔ **To stop using an e-mail account:** Tap the Settings icon on the Home screen; tap Mail, Contacts, Calendars⇨*Account Name* and flip the switch so that Off rather than On is showing.

  This setting doesn't delete the account; it only hides it from view and stops it from sending or checking e-mail until you turn it on again. (You can repeat this step to turn off Calendars, Contacts, Reminders, and Notes within a given account.)

- ✔ **To delete an e-mail account:** Tap the Settings icon on the Home screen; tap Mail, Contacts, Calendars⇨*Account Name*⇨Delete Account⇨Delete. Tap Cancel if you change your mind and don't want your account blown away.

You can find still more advanced Mail settings, reached the same way: Tap the Settings icon on the Home screen; tap Mail, Contacts, Calendars; and then tap the name of the account you want to work with.

The settings you see under Advanced and how they appear vary by account. This list describes some of the settings you might see:

- ✔ **To specify how long until deleted messages are removed permanently from your iPad:** Tap Advanced⇨Remove. Your choices are Never, After One Day, After One Week, and After One Month. Tap the choice you prefer.

- ✔ **To choose whether drafts, sent messages, and deleted messages are stored on your iPad or on your mail server:** Tap Advanced and then choose the setting under Mailbox Behaviors stored On My iPad or stored On the Server. You can decide for Drafts, Sent Messages, and Trash. If you choose to store any or all of them on the server, you can't see them unless you have an Internet connection (Wi-Fi or cellular). If you choose to store them on your iPad, they're always available, even if you don't have Internet access.

  We strongly recommend that you don't change these next two items unless you know exactly what you're doing and why. If you're having problems with sending or receiving mail, start by contacting your ISP (Internet service provider), e-mail provider, or corporate IT person or tech department. Then change these settings only if they tell you to. Again, these settings, and exactly where and how they appear, vary by account.

✔ **To reconfigure mail server settings:** Tap Host Name, User Name, or Password in the Incoming Mail Server or Outgoing Mail Server section of the account settings screen and make your changes.

✔ **To adjust Use SSL, Authentication, IMAP Path Settings, or Server Port:** Tap Advanced and then tap the appropriate item and make the necessary changes.

And that, as they say in baseball, retires the side. You're now fully qualified to set up e-mail accounts and send and receive e-mail on your iPad. But, as the late Apple cofounder Steve Jobs was wont to say, there is one more thing. . . .

Getting the iMessage

The Messages app lets you exchange iMessages, pictures, contacts, videos, audio recordings, and locations with anyone using an Apple i-device with iOS 5 or higher or with a Mac running OS X Mountain Lion.

In the following sections, find out how each of the iMessages features works.

Sending iMessages

Tap the Messages icon on the Home screen to launch the Messages app, and then tap the Compose New Message button, the little pencil-and-paper icon in the upper-left corner of the screen (on the Messages list) to start a new text message.

At this point, with the To field active and awaiting your input, you can do three things:

✔ **If the recipient *is* in your contacts list, type the first few letters of the name.** A list of matching contacts appears. Scroll through it if necessary and tap the name of the contact.

The more letters you type, the shorter the list becomes. And, after you've tapped the name of a contact, you can begin typing another name so that you can send this message to multiple recipients at once.

✔ **Tap the blue + icon on the right side of the To field to select a name from your contacts list.**

✔ **If the recipient *isn't* in your contacts list, type his or her cellphone number or e-mail address.**

You have a fourth option if you want to compose the message first and address it later. Tap inside the text-entry field (the oval-shaped area just above the keyboard and to the left of the Send button) to activate it, and then type your message. When you've finished typing, tap the To field and use one of the preceding techniques to address your message.

You are not limited to sending an iMessage to a single person. To initiate a group message, type the names or phones numbers of everyone you want to include in the To field.

When you've finished addressing and composing, tap the Send button to send your message on its merry way. And that's all there is to it.

Being a golden receiver: Receiving iMessages

First things first: Decide whether you want to hear an alert when you receive a message:

- ✓ **If you want to hear an alert sound when you receive a message,** tap the Settings icon on your Home screen, tap Sounds⇨Text Tone, and then tap one of the available sounds. You can audition the sounds by tapping them. (Ed, as a film buff, prefers the Noir sound.) If you have a Mac, you can create your own text tones in GarageBand.

  You hear the sounds when you audition them in the Settings app, even if you have the ring/silent switch set to Silent. After you exit the Settings app, however, you *won't* hear a sound when a message arrives if the ring/silent switch is set to Silent.

- ✓ **If you *don't* want to hear an alert when a message arrives,** instead of tapping one of the listed sounds, tap the first item in the list: None.

- ✓ **If you don't want any messages, you can turn iMessages off.** The Do Not Disturb that arrived with iOS 6 lives up to its name. Flip the switch in Settings so that the setting is turned On and you see the Moon icon on the status bar. And you won't be inundated with messages. For more about this feature and other settings, head to Chapter 15.

The following pointers explain what you can do with iMessages that you receive:

- ✓ **Receiving a message when your iPad is asleep:** All or part of the text and the name of the sender appear on the Unlock screen, as shown in Figure 5-12. Slide any of the green message icons to the right to reply to a specific message, as we're doing to the first message in Figure 5-12.

- ✓ **Receiving a message when your iPad is awake and unlocked:** All or part of the message and the name of the sender appear at the top of the screen in front of whatever's already there. If what's already there is your Home screen, as shown in Figure 5-13, you'll notice that the Messages icon displays the number of unread messages.

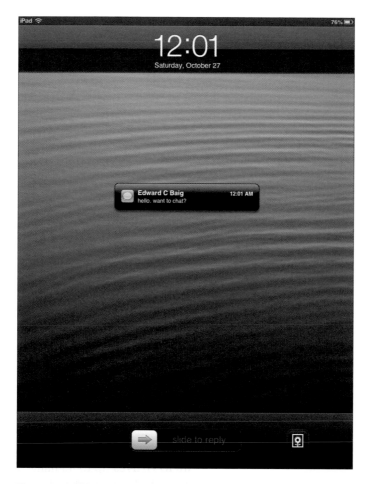

Figure 5-12: This is what message notifications look like when your iPad is slumbering.

All these notifications are on by default; turn them off in the Settings app's Notification Center pane if you don't care for them.

Figure 5-13: This is what a notification looks like when your iPad is awake.

- **To read or reply to a message:** Tap the Messages icon on your Home screen, swipe downward with four fingers to display the Notification Center, or tap the notification if you can be quick about it (it fades away in a few seconds).

- **Following the conversation:** Each conversation you have is saved as a series of text bubbles. Your messages appear on the right side of the screen in blue bubbles; the other person's messages appear on the left in gray ones, as shown in Figure 5-14.

- **Forwarding a conversation:** If you want to forward all or part of a conversation to another iMessage user, first tap the Action button (the little rectangle with the arrow coming out of it) and then tap the text bubbles you want to forward so that the red check mark appears in the circles to their left. Then tap the blue Forward button at the lower-right corner of the screen. The contents of the text bubbles with check marks are copied to a new text message; specify a recipient and then tap Send.

- **Deleting part of a single conversation thread:** Tap the Action button in the upper-right corner of the conversation, and a circle appears to the left of each text bubble. Tap a text bubble, and a red check mark appears in the circle. When you've added a red check mark to all the text bubbles you want to delete, tap the red Delete button at the lower left of the screen. Or, to delete the entire conversation in one fell swoop, tap the Clear All button in the upper-left corner of the screen.

- **To delete an entire conversation thread:** Tap the Edit button at the upper left of the Messages list, tap the red – (minus) icon that appears to the left of the person's name, and then tap the Delete button that appears to the right of the name.

Sending pix and vids in a message

To send a picture or video in a message, follow the instructions for sending a text message and then tap the Camera icon to the left of the text-entry field at the bottom of the screen. You then have the option of using an existing picture or video or taking a new one. You can also add text to photos or videos. When you're finished, tap the Send button.

If you *receive* a picture or video in a message, it appears in a bubble just like text (refer to Figure 5-14). Tap it to see it full-screen.

Tap the Action button in the upper-right corner for additional options, such as sharing the image on Facebook or assigning it to a contact. If you don't see the icon, tap the picture or video once and the icon will magically appear.

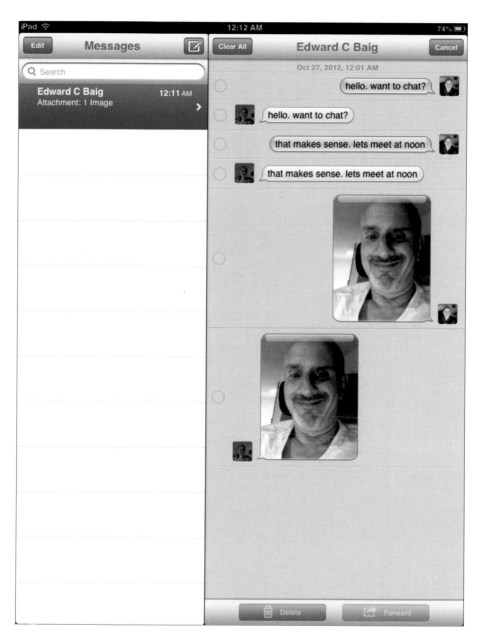

Figure 5-14: This is what an iMessage conversation looks like.

Smart messaging tricks

Here are some more things you can do with messages:

- ✔ **Search your messages for a word or phrase.** Type the word or phrase in the Search field at the top of the Messages screen.

- ✔ **Send Read Receipts to allow others to be notified when you have read their missives.** Tap Settings⇨Messages, and slide the switch so that Send Read Receipts is on.

  You can see within iMessages when your own message has been delivered and read, and when the other person is readying a response.

- ✔ **Use a Bluetooth keyboard for typing instead of the onscreen keyboard.** Follow the instructions in Chapter 15 to pair your Bluetooth keyboard with your iPad.

  The Apple Wireless Keyboard ($69) works with the iPad and iPhones. Find out more in Chapter 17. Or search for a full-size Bluetooth keyboard that also includes a numeric keypad.

- ✔ **Dictate a message.** Tap the Microphone key on your keyboard and start talking. Tap the Microphone key again when you're done.

- ✔ **Open a URL included in an iMessage.** Tap it to open that web page in Safari.

- ✔ **Send an e-mail to an address included in an iMessage.** Tap it to open a preaddressed e-mail message in Mail.

- ✔ **See an included street message in an iMessage.** Tap it to see it on a map in Maps.

And that's all there is to it. You're now an official iMessage maven.

6

Maps Are Where It Is

In This Chapter

▶ Finding out where you are

▶ Searching

▶ Navigating by viewing, zooming, and panning

▶ Bookmarking

▶ Reaching your destination quickly: routes and real-time traffic

*I*n another book we wrote, *iPhone For Dummies* (John Wiley & Sons, Inc.), we say that the Maps feature was one of the sleeper hits of our iPhone experience and an application we both use more than we expected, because it's so darn handy. Since we first discovered the Maps app via our iPhones, the app has become better and more capable. With Maps on the iPad or iPhone, you can quickly and easily discover exactly where you are, find nearby restaurants and businesses, get turn-by-turn driving instructions from any address to any other address, and see real-time traffic information and a photographic street view of many locations as well.

Apple is touting the iPad mini as "beautifully designed from the ground up (and the sky down)." We have to agree — it's more beautiful than ever. But beyond its good looks, zooming in and out is noticeably faster, it now offers spoken, turn-by-turn navigation with real-time traffic updates, and it has a cool, new 3D view.

To be fair, turn-by-turn driving instructions and traffic updates are all but useless on a Wi-Fi-only iPad.

You can't use the Maps app unless you're connected to the Internet via Wi-Fi, 3G, or 4G (LTE). See Chapter 1 to find out how to connect.

Directions

3rd of 3 Suggested Routes
15 minutes - 4.4 miles - Howard St

4939 Greenwood St, Skokie, IL 60077, United States

0.2 miles
At the end of the road, turn right onto Skokie Blvd

1.7 miles
Turn left onto Howard St

2.5 miles
The destination is on your right: Howard St

?727 Howard St, Chicago, IL ?45-1303, United States

Finding Your Current Location with Maps

We start with something supremely simple yet extremely useful — determining your current location. At the risk of sounding like self-help gurus, here's how to find yourself:

1. **Make sure Location Services is enabled by tapping Settings⇨Privacy⇨Location Services.**

   Tap the Location Services and Maps switches, if necessary, to turn them on.

2. **Tap the Home button to return to the Home screen.**

3. **Tap the Maps icon on your Home screen.**

4. **Tap the little Arrow icon in the lower-left corner of the screen.**

   The Arrow icon turns a soothing purple to let you know that Location Services is doing its thing and that you'll soon see a blue circle (see Figure 6-1), which indicates your approximate location. And if you move around, your iPad can update your location and adjust the map so that the location indicator stays in the middle of the screen.

Just so you know, if you tap the screen, drag the map, or zoom in or out, your iPad continues to update your location, though it doesn't continue to center the marker. That's a good thing, but it also means that the location indicator can move off the screen.

Tap to find your location

Your location

Figure 6-1: A blue marker shows your GPS location.

Searching

The Maps app wouldn't be useful if you couldn't use it to find things. In the following sections, we show you how to search for places you want to go and people you want to see — including people you have stored as contacts.

Finding a person, place, or thing

To find a person, place, or thing with Maps, follow these steps:

1. **Tap the Search field in the upper-right corner of the screen to make the keyboard appear, and then type what you're looking for.**

   You can search for addresses, zip codes, intersections, towns, landmarks, and businesses by category and by name, or combinations, such as *New York, NY 10022; pizza 60645* or *Auditorium Shores Austin, TX.*

2. **(Optional) If the letters you type match names in your contacts list, the matching contacts appear in a list below the Search field; tap a name to see a map of that contact's location.**

   Maps is smart about it, too; it displays only the names of contacts that have a street address. See the section "Connecting maps and contacts," later in this chapter, for more details.

3. **When you finish typing, tap Search.**

   After a few seconds, a map appears. If you searched for a single location, it's marked with a pushpin. If you searched for a category (*pizza 60645,* for example), you see multiple pushpins, one for each matching location, as shown in Figure 6-2.

Figure 6-2: If you search for *pizza 60645,* you see pushpins for all nearby pizza joints.

You can tap the little circle with three horizontal lines on the right in the Search field, and a drop-down list of matching locations appears (refer to Figure 6-2).

Connecting maps and contacts

Maps and contacts go together like peanut butter and jelly. For example, here are two helpful tasks that illustrate maps and contacts at work.

To see a map of a contact's street address, follow these steps:

1. **Tap the little Bookmarks icon to the left of the Search field.**

2. **Tap the Contacts button at the bottom of the overlay.**

3. **Tap the contact's name whose address you want to see on the map.**

   Alternatively, simply type the first few letters of a contact's name in the Search field, and then tap the name in the Suggestions list that appears below the Search field whenever the characters you type match one or more contact names.

If you find a location by typing an address into the Search field, you can add that location to one of your contacts or create a new contact with a location you've found. To do either one, follow these steps:

1. **Tap the location's pushpin on the map.**

2. **Tap the little *i* in a blue circle to the right of the location's name or description (as shown next to Gullivers — refer to Figure 6-2).**

   That contact's Info screen opens. (See Figure 6-3.)

Figure 6-3: The Info screen for Gullivers appears as an overlay.

How does Maps do that?

Maps uses iPad's Location Services to determine your approximate location using available information from your wireless data network. Wi-Fi–only models use local Wi-Fi networks; iPad Wi-Fi + 3G and 4G models use assisted GPS plus cellular data. If you're not using Location Services, turning it off conserves your battery. (To turn it off, tap Settings➪General➪Location Services.) Don't worry if Location Services is turned off when you tap the Arrow icon — you're prompted to turn it on. Finally, Location Services may not be available in all areas at all times.

3. **Tap the Add to Contacts button to create a new entry for the location in your contacts list.**

4. **Tap Create New Contact or Add to Existing Contact, whichever is applicable.**

5. **Fill in the new contact information and tap Done. Or select an existing contact from the list that appears.**

You work with your contacts by tapping the Contacts icon on your Home screen. Go to Chapter 12 to find out more about the Contacts app.

Don't forget that you can swipe across your iPad screen with four or five fingers to switch apps. So if you're in Contacts, a four- or five-finger swipe from right to left should bring you back to the Maps app.

And don't forget you can also use a four-finger swipe upward to reveal the multitasking bar at the bottom of the screen.

If nothing happens when you swipe with four or five fingers, tap Settings➪ General, scroll down to the Multitasking Gestures On/Off switch, and make sure it's set to On.

You can also get driving, walking, and public transit directions from most locations, including a contact's address — to any other location, including another contact's address. You see how to do that in the "Smart Map Tricks" section, later in this chapter.

Viewing, Zooming, and Panning

The preceding section talks about how to find just about anything with Maps. Now here's a look at some ways that you can use what you find. First, find out how to work with what you see on the screen. Three views are available at any time: Standard, Hybrid, and Satellite. (Figures 6-1 and 6-2 show the Standard view). Select one view by tapping the curling page in the lower-right corner of the screen. The map then curls back and reveals the view buttons, as shown in Figure 6-4.

In Standard, Hybrid, or Satellite view, you can zoom to see either more or less of the map — or scroll *(pan)* to see what's above or below, or to the left or right of, what's on the screen:

Figure 6-4: The map "curls" to reveal these buttons.

 ✔ **Zoom out:** Pinch the map or tap using *two* fingers. To zoom out even more, pinch or tap using two fingers again.

  To tap with two fingers, merely tap with two fingers touching the screen simultaneously instead of with the usual one finger. (This concept may be new to you.)

 ✔ **Zoom in:** Unpinch (some people say *spread*) the map, or double-tap (in the usual way — with only one finger) the spot you want to zoom in on. Unpinch or double-tap with one finger again to zoom in even more.

The *unpinch* action is the opposite of pinch. Start with your thumb and a finger together and then spread them apart.

You can also unpinch with two fingers or two thumbs, one from each hand, but you'll probably find the single-handed pinch and unpinch handier.

 ✔ **Scroll:** Flick or drag up, down, left, or right.

Tap the 3D button in the lower-left corner to see the map from a three-dimensional, bird's-eye view.

Chapter 6: Maps Are Where It Is

Saving Time with Bookmarks, Recents, and Contacts

In Maps, three tools can save you from typing the same locations repeatedly. You see these options on the overlay that's displayed when you tap the little Bookmarks icon to the left of the Search field.

At the bottom of this overlay, you see three buttons: Bookmarks, Recents, and Contacts. The following sections give you the lowdown on these buttons.

Bookmarks

Bookmarks in the Maps application work like bookmarks in Safari. When you have a location you want to save as a bookmark so that you can reuse it later without typing a single character, follow these steps:

1. **Tap the little _i_ in a blue circle to the right of the location's name or description.**

   The Info screen for that location appears (refer to Figure 6-3).

2. **Tap the Add to Bookmarks button.**

   You may have to scroll down the Info screen to see the Add to Bookmarks button.

After you add a bookmark, you can recall it at any time. To do so, tap the Bookmarks icon, tap the Bookmarks button at the bottom of the overlay, and then tap the bookmark name to see it on a map.

The first things you should bookmark are your home and work addresses and your zip codes. These are things you use all the time with Maps, so you might as well bookmark them now to avoid typing them over and over.

Use zip code bookmarks to find nearby businesses. Choose the zip code bookmark, and then type what you're looking for, such as _78729 pizza, 60645 gas station,_ or _90201 Starbucks._

To manage your bookmarks, tap the Edit button in the upper-left corner of the Bookmarks overlay. Then:

> ✔ **To move a bookmark up or down in the Bookmarks list:** Locate the little icon with three gray bars on it that appears to the right of the bookmark. Drag the icon upward to move the bookmark higher in the list or downward to move the bookmark lower in the list.

✔ **To delete a bookmark from the Bookmarks list:** Tap the minus-sign-in-a-red-circle to the left of the bookmark's name, and then tap the red Delete button.

When you're finished using bookmarks, tap anywhere outside the overlay to return to the map.

You can also drop a pin anywhere on the map. A *pin* is similar to a bookmark but is often handier than a bookmark because you can drop it by hand. Why? If you don't know the exact address or zip code for a location but you can point it out on a map, you can drop a pin (but you can't create a bookmark).

To drop a pin:

1. **Tap the curling page in the lower-right corner.**

2. **Tap the Drop Pin button (refer to Figure 6-4).**

   A pin drops onscreen, and you see a purple "dropped pin" with an *i* in a blue circle on its right.

3. **Press the purple dot on the head of the pin, and drag it as close as possible to your destination.**

4. **Tap the little *i*.**

   The Dropped Pin overlay appears. You can fill in details about the pin and take similar actions to those that appear on the Info screen (refer to Figure 6-3).

Recents

The Maps app automatically remembers the locations you've searched for and directions you've viewed in its Recents list. To see this list, tap the Bookmarks icon and then tap the Recents button at the bottom of the overlay. To see a recent item on the map, tap the item's name.

To clear the Recents list, tap the Clear button in the upper-left corner of the overlay, and then tap the big red Clear All Recents button at the bottom of the overlay. Or tap Cancel if you change your mind.

When you finish using the Recents list, tap anywhere outside the overlay to return to the map.

Contacts

To see a list of your contacts, tap the Bookmarks icon and then tap the Contacts button at the bottom of the overlay. To see a map of a contact's location, tap the contact's name in the list.

To limit the contacts list to specific groups (assuming that you have groups in your contacts list), tap the Groups button in the upper-left corner of the overlay, and then tap the name of the group. Now only contacts in this group display in the list.

When you're finished using the contacts list, tap the Done button in the upper-right corner of the overlay to return to the map.

Smart Map Tricks

The Maps application has more tricks up its sleeve. Here are a few nifty features you may find useful.

Getting route maps and driving directions

You can get route maps and driving directions to any location from any other location (within reason — our tech editor tried unsuccessfully to get driving directions from 1600 Pennsylvania Avenue in Washington, D.C., to 10 Downing Street in London). Follow these steps:

1. **Tell your iPad to get directions for you.**

   You can do so in a few ways:

   - *When you're looking at a map screen:* Tap the Directions button in the upper-left corner of the screen. The Search field transforms into Start and End fields.

   - *If a pin is already on the screen:* Tap the pin and then tap the little *i* in a blue circle to the right of the name or description. This action displays the item's Info screen. Tap either the Directions to Here or Directions from Here button to get directions to or from that location, respectively.

   - *Ask Siri for directions:* Press and hold the Home button and ask, "How do I get to [my destination]."

2. **Tap in the Start and End fields to designate the starting and ending points of your trip.**

   You can either type them or choose them from a list of your bookmarks, recent maps, or contacts.

3. **(Optional) If you need to swap the starting and ending locations, tap the little swirly Arrow button between the Start and End fields.**

4. **(Optional) Tap the car or pedestrian above the Start and End fields to choose driving or walking directions.**

If you tap the Bus icon in the current version of iOS, you see a list of available public transportation apps with links to them in the App Store. What you don't see is anything resembling directions. So tap it, if you like, but be prepared to download (and possibly pay for) a separate app.

5. **When the starting and ending locations are correct, tap the Route button in the upper-right corner of the Directions overlay.**

   Suggested routes appear on the map, as shown in Figure 6-5.

   If multiple possible routes exist, Maps shows you as many as three (refer to Figure 6-5). To switch routes, tap the route you want to switch to. Notice that the text at the top of the screen updates to tell you the approximate time and distance of the selected route (15 minutes, 4.4 miles, and the third of three suggested routes in Figure 6-5).

Route 1   Start button

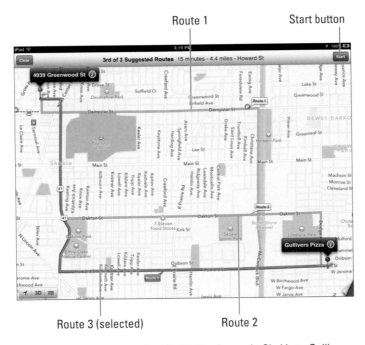

Route 3 (selected)   Route 2

Figure 6-5: The route map from Bob's first house in Skokie to Gullivers in Chicago.

6. **Tap the Start button in the upper-right corner of the screen to begin receiving directions.**

   When you tap the Start button, a series of big green "road signs" appear across the top of the map, one for each step in the directions, as shown in Figure 6-6.

Highlighted step   Overview button

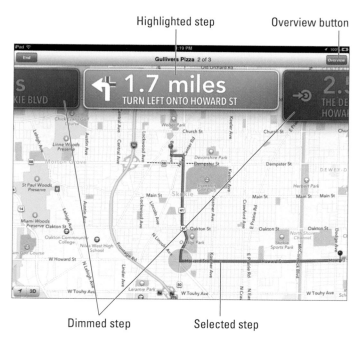

Dimmed step   Selected step

Figure 6-6: The green signs show you each step of your route.

7. Navigate your directions by using one of these methods:

- *Swipe a road sign:* Swipe right or left on a road sign to see the next or previous step in your route. The current step is high-lighted, and a blue circle appears on the map to indicate the location of that step. The other (next or previous) steps are dimmed slightly (refer to Figure 6-6).

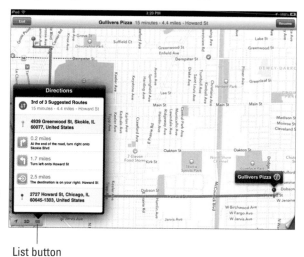

List button

Figure 6-7: Step-by-step driving directions, displayed as a list.

- *Choose from a list:* If you prefer to see all steps in your driving directions displayed at one time in a list, tap the List button near the bottom-left corner of the screen. The steps appear in an overlay, as shown in Figure 6-7.

If you've already tapped the Start button, tap the Overview button in the upper-right corner of the screen to make the List button reappear.

Tap any step in the list to see that leg of the trip displayed on the map.

If you want to return to the step-by-step road sign directions and map again, tap the Start button in the upper-left corner of the screen or tap any step in the list overlay.

The list disappears, and the road signs and map reappear.

Getting traffic info in real time

You can find out the traffic conditions for the map you're viewing by tapping the curling page in the lower-right corner of the screen and then tapping the Traffic switch so that it says On. When you do this, major roadways are color-coded to inform you of the current traffic speed, as shown in Figure 6-8. Here's the key:

- **Orange dots:** Traffic slowdowns

- **Red dashes:** Stop-and-go traffic

- **Incident marker:** A marker you can tap for more info

Figure 6-8: Downtown Chicago in the middle of a Saturday afternoon has more traffic than many other cities during rush hour.

Traffic info doesn't work in every location, but the only way to find out is to give it a try. If no color codes appear, assume that it doesn't work for that particular location.

Getting more info about a location

If a location has a little *i* in a blue circle to the right of its name or description (refer to Figure 6-2), you can tap the letter to see additional information about that location.

As we explain earlier in this chapter, you can get directions to or from that location, add the location to your bookmarks or contacts, or create a new contact from it. You can do two more things with some locations from their Info screens:

- Tap its e-mail address to launch the Mail application and send an e-mail to it.
- Tap its URL to launch Safari and view its website.

Not all locations have these options, but we thought you should know anyway.

Part III
The Multimedia iPad mini

The 5th Wave — By Rich Tennant

©RICHTENNANT

"I build bookshelves and Bernice buys an iPad mini."

Your iPad is arguably the best iPod ever invented. So in this part we look at the multimedia side of your tablet — audio, video, pictures, and books. Never before has a tablet been this much fun to use; in this part, we show you how to wring the most out of every multimedia bit of it.

First we explore how to enjoy listening to music, podcasts, and audiobooks on your iPad mini. Then we look at some video, both literally and figuratively. You find out how to use the video camera, how to find good video for your iPad, and instructions for watching video on your iPad.

In Chapter 9, you find everything you always wanted to know about taking, managing, and displaying photos: how to take still photos with your iPad, how to find photos on your iPad, how to use the iPad's unique Picture Frame feature, how to create and display slide shows, and how to do other interesting things with them.

Finally, in Chapter 10, you visit the iBookstore, Apple's nifty digital bookstore. You'll be amazed at how many books you can carry without breaking your back.

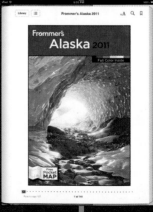

Get in Tune(s): Audio on Your iPad mini

In This Chapter

▶ Checking out your iPad's inner iPod

▶ Browsing your library

▶ Taking control of your tunes

▶ Customizing your audio experience

▶ Shopping with the iTunes app

Your iPad is perhaps the best iPod ever — especially for working with audio and video. In this chapter, we show you how to use your iPad mini for audio; in Chapter 8, we cover video.

We start with a quick tour of the iPad's Music application. Then we look at how to use your iPad as an audio player. After you're nice and comfy with using it this way, we show you how to customize the listening experience so that it's just the way you like it. Then we offer a few tips to help you get the most out of using your iPad as an audio player. Finally, we show you how to use the iTunes application to buy music, audiobooks, videos, and free content such as podcasts and iTunes U courses.

We assume that your iPad already contains audio content — songs, podcasts, or audiobooks. If you don't have any audio on your iPad yet, we humbly suggest that you get some before you read the rest of this chapter — or Chapter 8, for that matter. You can get audio by syncing (flip to Chapter 3 and follow the instructions) or buying it from the iTunes Store (see the last section in this chapter) on your iPad.

Okay, now that you have some audio content on your iPad to play with, are you ready to rock?

Introducing the iPod inside Your iPad mini

To use your iPad as an iPod, tap the Music icon on the right side of the Dock at the bottom of the screen (unless you've moved the app elsewhere).

Figure 7-1 provides a quick overview of the Music app for your enjoyment and edification.

At the top of the screen are the music controls and buttons; at the bottom are five tabs: Playlists, Songs, Artists, Albums, and More. Because the Songs tab is selected in Figure 7-1, the middle of the screen displays the songs available on our iPad.

If you don't see every song in your library, chances are you've typed something into the Search field or you're looking at a shared Music library instead of the songs on your iPad.

Along the right side of the screen, you see the letters of the alphabet, from A to Z. Tap one to jump to that letter instantly when you're browsing playlists, songs, artists, or albums.

If you don't see the alphabet on the right side of the screen, you may not have enough items on that tab to warrant it, or you may be looking at a category such as Genres (described in the "Browsing among the tabs" section, later in the chapter), which doesn't have an alphabetical index. Don't worry.

You can find a particular song, artist, album, genre, composer, podcast, audiobook, or iTunes U course by either using the Search field or browsing the tabs. The following sections show you how.

Rewind/Previous Track
Play/Pause
Volume control
Fast Forward/Next track
Scrubber bar
Genius
Repeat
Shuffle
AirPlay

Store
Tabs
Search field
Alphabet

Figure 7-1: These components are what you find on the Music app's main screen.

iTunes Match: All your music, all the time, on all your devices

If you own more music than your iPad can hold, or if you'd prefer to devote your gigabytes to something other than music — such as photos or videos — you'll like the Apple iTunes Match service. For a mere $24.99 a year, Apple stores your music library — as many as 25,000 songs — on iCloud (see Chapter 3) and lets you stream or download any of them any time you like on up to ten devices.

It all happens in iTunes, and it works beautifully. When you enable iTunes Match, the first thing it does is compare your iTunes Library with tracks available in the iTunes Store (20 million tracks and growing). If it finds a match, the song is already available from iCloud, and you can listen to it or download it to your device at any time (as long as you have an Internet connection, of course).

After it matches all the songs it can, iTunes uploads all songs it couldn't match (to a maximum of 25,000). In a few hours (or days), those songs are also available from iCloud on all your devices on demand.

Here are three more cool things you should know about iTunes Match:

- Songs purchased from the iTunes Store don't count against your total of 25,000 songs.

- Your iTunes Match content doesn't count against your free 5GB of iCloud storage.

- All the songs that iTunes matches (with its 20 million-plus tracks) are 256 Kbps AAC DRM-free files, even if your original was of lower quality. The songs you stream or download from iCloud are therefore likely to sound better than the originals in your iTunes Library.

For only $25 a year, you can ignore the whole syncing thing between your Mac or PC and your iPad (Chapter 3 covers syncing), at least for music. As long as Internet access is available, your entire music library is available on your iPad (and up to nine other devices).

Finding music with the Search field

With the Music app open, the easiest way to find music is to type a song, an artist, an album, or a composer name into the Search field in the lower-right corner of the screen.

You can also find songs (or artists, for that matter) without opening the Music app by typing their names in a Spotlight search, as we mention in Chapter 2.

Browsing among the tabs

To browse your music library, tap the appropriate tab at the bottom of the screen — Playlists, Songs, Artists, or Albums — and all items of that type appear. Or tap the More button to browse genres or composers or to connect to a shared library, as described later in this chapter.

Now you can find a song, an artist, an album, a genre, or a composer by

- **Flicking upward or downward** to scroll up and down the list until you find what you're looking for

  or

- **Tapping one of the little letters on the right side of the screen** to jump to that letter in the list (all categories except Genres)

Then, when you find what you're looking for, here's what happens, based on which tab is selected:

- **Playlists:** A grid of available playlists on this iPad appears. Tap a playlist, and the songs it contains appear in a list (refer to Figure 7-1). Tap a song to play it.

- **Songs:** The song plays.

  If you're not sure which song you want to listen to, try this: Tap the Shuffle button at the top of the screen (shown earlier, in Figure 7-1). Your iPad then plays songs from your music collection at random.

- **Artists:** A list of artists' names appears. Tap an artist, and all the albums and songs by that artist appear; tap a song, and it plays.

  To see the list of artists, you can either tap the Artists button near the upper-left corner of the screen or tap the Artists tab at the bottom of the screen.

  Figure 7-2 is what you see after you tap an artist's name. (In this case, the artist is Dirk Etienne, one of Bob's favorite singers.)

- **Albums:** The Albums option works much the same way as Artists, except that you see a grid of album covers instead of a list of artists. Tap an album, and its contents appear.

Figure 7-2: Bob tapped Dirk Etienne in the list of artists, and this appeared.

To play one of the songs on the album, tap the song. To return to the grid of album covers, tap anywhere outside the overlay.

✔ **More:** Tap More to see one of these elements:

- *Genres:* When you tap Genres, a grid of genres — Comedy, Rock, Pop, Hip Hop/Rap, and so on — appears. Tap a genre, and a list of the songs in that genre appears.

  If the list of songs in an overlay is long enough, you may have to flick upward to see the rest of the songs.

- *Composers:* A list of composers appears. Tap a composer, and all the albums and songs by that composer appear. Tap a song, and it plays; tap an album cover, and all the songs from that album play; or tap the Play All Songs button, just below the Search field, to play all songs from all albums by that composer. Tap the Composers button near the top of the screen and just to the right of the word *Library,* or tap the Composers tab at the bottom of the screen to return to the list of composers.

- *Shared:* You see this item only when a computer with Home Sharing enabled in iTunes is sharing the Wi-Fi network with your iPad mini.

If you're looking for other iTunes content — such as movies, TV shows, iTunes U courses, or podcasts — you find them in their own, separate apps (Video, iTunes U, and Podcasts), which we cover in Chapter 8.

What's the difference between artists and composers?

If you're wondering about the difference between an artist and a composer, imagine this, if you will: You have a recording in your iTunes Library of a track entitled *Symphony No. 5 in C Minor.* The composer will always be Ludwig van Beethoven, but the artist can be the London Symphony Orchestra, the Los Angeles Philharmonic, the Austin Klezmer Ensemble, or many other performers. Here's another example: The ballad "Yesterday" was composed by John Lennon and Paul McCartney but has been performed by artists that include The Beatles, Ray Charles, Boyz II Men, Dave Grusin, Marianne Faithful, and many others.

Now you may be wondering where your iPad gets this kind of info, because you know you didn't supply it. Check this out: Click a track in iTunes on your computer, choose File➪Get Info, and then click the Info tab at the top of the window.

That's only some of the information that can be embedded in an audio track. These bits of embedded information, sometimes referred to as the track's *tags,* is what your iPad uses to distinguish between artists and composers. If a track doesn't have a composer tag, you won't find it on the Composers tab on your iPad.

Taking Control of Your Tunes

If you're reading along in this chapter, you have the iPad mini's musical basics down and can find and play songs. Here we take a look at some of the things you can do with your iPad when it's in Music mode.

Playing with the audio controls

First things first: In this section, we look at the controls you use after you tap the title of a song to play it. Take a peek at Figure 7-1, earlier in this chapter, to see exactly where all these controls are located on the screen:

- **Volume control:** Drag the little dot to the left or right to reduce or increase the volume level.

- **Previous Track/Rewind button:** When a track is playing, tap once to go to the beginning of the track, or tap twice to go to the start of the preceding track in the list. Touch and hold this button to rewind the track at double speed.

- **Play/Pause button:** Tap to play or pause the track.

- **Next Track/Fast Forward button:** Tap to skip to the next track in the list. Touch and hold this button to fast-forward at double speed.

Figure 7-3: These controls appear — even if you're using another app — when you double-tap the Home button and swipe the multitasking bar from left to right while a track plays.

You can display playback controls anytime a track is playing. Better still, this trick works even when you're using another app or your Home screen(s): Double-tap the Home button and swipe the multitasking bar from left to right, and the controls appear at the bottom of the screen, as shown in Figure 7-3.

The playback controls *don't* appear if you're using an app that has its own audio, such as many games, any app that records audio, or VoIP (Voice over Internet Protocol) apps such as Skype.

A similar set of controls appears at the *top* of the screen when you double-tap the Home button while your iPad is locked.

- **Scrubber bar and Playhead:** Drag the little dot (the *Playhead*) along the Scrubber bar to skip to any point within the track.

You can adjust the scrub rate by sliding your finger downward on the screen as you drag the Playhead along the Scrubber bar. Check out the section on the hidden iTunes scrub-speed tip in Chapter 20 for additional details. By the way, this slick trick also works in many other apps that use a Scrubber bar — most notably, the Videos app.

✔ **Repeat:** Tap once to repeat all songs in the current *list* (that is, playlist, album, artist, composer, or genre) and play them all over and over. Tap again to repeat the current *song* again and again. Tap again to turn off Repeat.

The button appears in blue after one tap, in blue with a little numeral 1 inside after two taps, and in black-and-white when Repeat is turned off.

✔ **Shuffle:** Tap this button to play songs at random; tap again to play songs in the order they appear onscreen.

✔ **Genius:** This feature is so cool that we devote an entire section to it. See the section "It doesn't take a Genius," later in this chapter.

But wait — there's more. If you tap the album art for the song that's playing (between the Fast Forward/Next Track button and the Repeat button at the top of the screen), the album art fills the screen. Tap anywhere to see the controls and tabs at the top and bottom of the screen.

Notice that when album art is onscreen, the Store button and Search field at the bottom of the screen disappear and the Back and Track List buttons take their places, as shown in Figure 7-4.

Figure 7-4: You see these additional buttons after you tap the album art.

Earlier in this section, we explain how to use the volume control, Rewind/Previous Track button, Play/Pause button, Fast Forward/Next Track button, and Scrubber bar/Playhead. These elements may look slightly different on this screen, but they work in exactly the same way.

These new buttons are at the bottom of the screen:

✔ **Back:** Tap this button to return to the preceding screen.

✔ **Track List:** Tap this button to see all the tracks on the album that's playing, as shown in Figure 7-5.

Tap any song in this list to play it. Or swipe your finger across the dots just beneath the Scrubber bar to rate the song from one to five stars.

Figure 7-5: We've given this tune a rating of four (out of five) stars.

In Figure 7-5, we've rated the song that's playing — "Across the Universe" — four stars.

Why would you want to assign star ratings to songs? One reason is that you can use star ratings to filter songs in iTunes on your Mac or PC. Another is that you can use them when you create Smart Playlists (described later in this chapter) in iTunes. And last but not least, they look cool.

It doesn't take a Genius

Genius selects songs from your music library that go great together. To use it, tap the Genius button, and your iPad generates a Genius playlist of 25 songs that it picked because it thinks they go well with the song that's playing.

If you tap the Genius button on the main screen (refer to Figure 7-1) and no song is playing, an alphabetical list of songs appears. You need to select a song before the Genius playlist can be generated.

When you create a Genius playlist, you find an item called Genius in your library list; tap it and you see the 25 songs that Genius selected. You see three buttons in the upper-right corner of the list:

- **New:** Select a different song to use as the basis for a Genius playlist.
- **Refresh:** See a list of 25 songs that "go great with" the song you're listening to (or the song you selected).
- **Save:** Save this Genius playlist so that you can listen to it whenever you like.

When you save a Genius playlist, it inherits the name of the song it's based on and appears in your library with the Genius icon, which looks like the Genius button. And the next time you sync your iPad, the Genius playlist magically appears in iTunes.

The less popular the song, artist, or genre, the more likely Genius will "choke" on it. When it chokes, you see an alert that asks you to try again because this song doesn't have enough related songs to create a Genius playlist.

If you like the Genius feature, you can also create a new Genius playlist in iTunes and then sync it with your iPad.

A brief AirPlay interlude

You may or may not see one icon in your iPad's Music app, and it's the AirPlay icon, which looks like the image on the left in the figure. *AirPlay* is a wicked-cool technology baked into every copy of iOS. AirPlay lets you wirelessly stream music, photos, and video to AirPlay-enabled devices, such as Apple's AirPort Extreme, AirPort Express Wi-Fi base stations, and Apple TV, as well as third-party AirPlay-enabled devices, including (but not limited to) speakers and (someday, we hope) HDTVs.

AirPlay Selector appears only if it detects an AirPlay-enabled device on the same Wi-Fi network. Bob has an Apple TV in his den, so he sees the options in the figure on the right when he taps the AirPlay Selector icon. Tapping Family Room Apple TV sends whatever is playing on the Music app to the Apple TV in his den. The Apple TV is, in turn, connected to his home theater audio system and to HDTV via HDMI and/or optical audio cables.

If you use an Apple TV as your AirPlay-enabled device, you can also stream music, video, and photos from your iPad to your HDTV.

Finally, the iPad mini offers a cool video-mirroring option when used with a second- or

third-generation Apple TV. To use this new feature, double-tap the Home button and swipe the multitasking bar from left to right to reveal the music controls. Now tap the AirPlay Selector and then Apple TV. Switch on the Mirroring option, and whatever appears on the iPad's screen also appears on the HDTV screen.

If you have an HDMI-equipped TV and/or a decent sound system and you have decent Wi-Fi bandwidth, you'll love Apple TV and AirPlay.

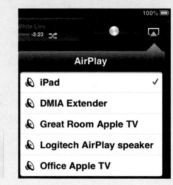

Creating playlists

A *playlist* lets you organize songs around a particular theme or mood: operatic arias, romantic ballads, British invasion — whatever. Younger folks sometimes call it a *mix*.

Although it may be easier to create playlists in iTunes on your computer, your iPad makes it relatively easy to create (and listen to) playlists:

✔ **To create a playlist on your iPad,** tap the Playlists tab at the bottom of the screen, and then tap the New button in the upper-right corner of the screen. You're asked to name your playlist. Do so and then tap Save. After you do this, you see a list of the songs on your iPad in alphabetical order. Tap the ones you want to have in this playlist, or tap the Add All Songs button to add them all. Songs you add turn gray, as shown in Figure 7-6.

After you've tapped every song you want in the list, tap the Done button in the upper-right corner.

Figure 7-6: Creating a playlist on your iPad.

You can select tracks for your playlist from the Artists, Albums, Genres, or More (Composers, Audiobooks, or Podcasts) tab by tapping the appropriate tab at the bottom of the screen.

✔ **To listen to a playlist,** tap its name in your library, and you see a list of the songs it contains. If the list is longer than one screen, flick upward to scroll down. Tap a song in the list, and the song plays. When that song is over or you tap the Next Song button, the next song in the playlist plays. This continues until the last song in the playlist has played, at which point your iPad stops playing music.

Of course, songs don't play in order if you've enabled the Shuffle or Repeat functions (both discussed in "Playing with the audio controls," earlier in this chapter).

Although you can't create Smart Playlists on your iPad, they totally rock. What is a Smart Playlist? Glad you asked. A *Smart Playlist* is a special playlist that selects tracks based on criteria you specify, such as artist name, date added, rating, genre, year, and many others. Fire up iTunes on your computer and choose File⇨New Smart Playlist to get started.

That's all there is to selecting, creating, and playing songs in a playlist.

Customizing Volume and Equalizer Settings

You can tweak volume and equalizer settings to customize your iPad-as-an-iPod experience. If you've noticed, and been bothered, that the volume of some songs is higher than others, check out the iTunes Sound Check feature. If you want to adjust certain frequencies, the equalizer enables you to do so. And if you want to set a maximum volume limit, tell your iPad to make it so. The following sections explain how.

Play all songs at the same volume level

The iTunes Sound Check option automatically adjusts the level of songs so that they play at the same volume relative to each other. That way, one song never blasts out your ears even if the recording level is much louder than that of the song before or after it. To tell the iPad to use these volume settings, you first have to turn on the feature in iTunes on your computer. Here's how to do that:

1. **Choose iTunes⇨Preferences (Mac) or Edit⇨Preferences (PC).**
2. **Click the Playback tab.**
3. **Select the Sound Check check box to enable it.**

Now you need to tell the iPad to use the Sound Check settings from iTunes. Here's how to do *that:*

1. **Tap the Settings icon on the iPad's Home screen.**
2. **Tap Music in the list of settings.**
3. **Tap the Sound Check On/Off switch so that it says On.**

Choose an equalizer setting

An *equalizer* increases or decreases the relative levels of specific frequencies to enhance the sound you hear. Some equalizer settings emphasize the bass (low-end) notes in a song; other equalizer settings make the higher frequencies more apparent. The iPad has more than a dozen equalizer presets, with names such as Acoustic, Bass Booster, Bass Reducer, Dance, Electronic, Pop, and Rock. Each one is ostensibly tailored to a specific type of music.

The way to find out whether you prefer using equalization is to listen to music while trying different settings. To do that, first start listening to a song you like. Then, while the song is playing, follow these steps:

1. **Tap the Home button on the front of your iPad.**
2. **Tap the Settings icon on the Home screen.**

3. Tap Music in the list of settings.

4. Tap EQ in the list of Music settings.

5. Tap different EQ presets (Pop, Rock, R&B, or Dance, for example), and listen carefully to the way they change how the song sounds.

6. When you find an equalizer preset that you think sounds good, tap the Home button and you're finished.

If you don't like any of the presets, tap Off at the top of the EQ list to turn off the equalizer.

At the risk of giving away one of the tips in Chapter 20, we feel obliged to mention that you may improve the battery life if you turn off EQ.

Set a volume limit for music (and videos)

You can instruct your iPad to limit the loudest listening level for audio or video. To do so, here's the drill:

1. Tap the Settings icon on the Home screen.

2. Tap Music in the list of settings.

3. Tap Volume Limit in the list of Music settings.

4. Drag the slider to adjust the maximum volume level to your liking.

5. (Optional) Tap Lock Volume Limit to assign a four-digit passcode to this setting so that others can't easily change it.

The Volume Limit setting limits the volume of only music and videos; it doesn't apply to podcasts or audiobooks. And although the setting works with any headset, headphones, or speakers plugged into the headset jack on your iPad, it doesn't affect the sound played on your iPad's internal speaker.

By the way, speaking of that lone internal iPad speaker, it's not in stereo — although it sounds pretty good just the same. Of course, when you plug in headphones, you hear rich stereo output.

Shopping with the iTunes App

Last but certainly not least, the iTunes app lets you use your iPad to download, buy, or rent just about any song, album, movie, or TV show. And if you're fortunate enough to have an iTunes gift card or gift certificate in hand, you can redeem it directly from your iPad.

If you want to do any of that, however, you must first sign in to your iTunes Store account. Follow these steps:

1. **Tap the Settings icon on the Home screen.**
2. **Tap Store in the list of settings.**
3. **Tap Sign In.**
4. **Type your username and password.**

Or, in the unlikely event that you don't have an iTunes Store account already, follow these steps:

1. **Tap the Settings icon on the Home screen.**
2. **Tap Store in the list of settings.**
3. **Tap Create New Account.**
4. **Follow the onscreen instructions.**

After the iTunes Store knows who you are (and, more importantly, knows your credit card number), tap the iTunes icon on your Home screen (or the Store button in the Music app) and shop until you drop. It works almost exactly the same as the iTunes App Store, which you can read about in Chapter 11.

If you had an iPad before buying your iPad mini, you should know that in iOS 6, you no longer download and manage podcasts and iTunes U courses with the iTunes app. For that, download the free Podcasts and iTunes U apps from the App Store, as described in Chapter 11.

8

iPad mini Video: Seeing Is Believing

In This Chapter

▶ Finding and playing videos

▶ Restricting movies

▶ Capturing, editing, and deleting video on your iPad

▶ Facing up to FaceTime

*P*icture this scene: The smell of popcorn permeates the room as you and your family congregate to watch the latest Hollywood blockbuster. A motion picture soundtrack swells up. The images on the screen are stunning. And all eyes are fixed on the iPad.

Okay, here comes the reality check. The iPad mini won't replace a wall-size, high-definition television as the centerpiece of your home theater (though, as you discover, you can watch material that originates on the iPad on the bigger screen). But the 7.9-inch screen on your mini is very good, if not quite up to high-definition standards or the beautiful Retina display on the most recent full-size iPads. (In technical terms, it has 1024-by-768-pixel resolution at 163 pixels per inch.)

The bottom line: Watching movies and other videos on Apple's new mini tablet is a cinematic treat. What's more, your mini is equipped with front and rear cameras that can help turn you, under certain circumstances, into a filmmaker — directly from the device.

And video on the iPad ventures into another area: video chat. You can keep in touch with friends and loved ones by gazing into each other's pupils. It's all done through a version of *FaceTime,* a clever video chat program that comes with your iPad mini. In the interest of equal time, we'd like to point out that you can also do video chats on your iPad by downloading a popular third-party app, such as Skype.

We get to FaceTime later in this chapter. For now, and with no further ado, we get on with the show!

Finding Stuff to Watch

You have a few main ways to find and watch videos on your iPad mini. You can fetch all sorts of fare from the iTunes Store, whose virtual doors you can open directly from the iPad.

Or you can sync content that already resides on your Mac or PC. (If you haven't done so yet, now is as good a time as any to read Chapter 3 for all the details on syncing.)

The videos you can watch on the iPad generally fall into one of the following categories:

- **Movies, TV shows, and music videos from the iTunes Store:** You can watch these by tapping the Videos icon on the Home screen.

    The iTunes Store features dedicated sections for purchasing or renting episodes of TV shows, as shown in Figure 8-1, and for buying or renting movies, as shown in Figure 8-2.

Figure 8-1: Buying and watching TV on the iPad is gleeful.

Figure 8-2: You can spend hours watching movies on the iPad.

Pricing varies, but it's not atypical as of this writing to fork over $1.99 to pick up an episode of a popular TV show in standard definition or $2.99 for high-def versions. You can rent certain shows commercial-free for 99 cents. And a few shows are free. You can also purchase a complete season of a favorite show. The final season of a classic show, such as *Lost,* for example, costs $24.99 in standard-def and $34.99 in high-def.

A new release feature film typically costs $19.99 in high definition or $14.99 in standard def. But you can find HD movies for as little as $9.99 and sometimes even cheaper than that.

You can also rent many movies, typically for $2.99, $3.99, or $4.99. We're not wild about current rental restrictions — you have 30 days to begin watching a rented flick and a day to finish watching after you've started, though you can watch as often as you want during the 24-hour period.

But that's showbiz for you. Such films appear in their own Rented Movies section in the video list, which you get to by tapping Videos. The number of days before your rental expires displays.

As shown in Figure 8-3, by tapping a movie listing in iTunes, you can generally preview a trailer before buying (or renting) and check out additional tidbits: the plot summary, credits, reviews, and customer ratings, as well as other movies that appealed to the buyer of this one. And you can search films by genre or top charts (the ones other people are buying or renting) or rely on the Apple Genius feature for recommendations based on stuff you've already watched. (Genius works for movies and TV much the way it works for music, as we explain in Chapter 7.)

- ✓ **The boatload of video podcasts, just about all free, featured in the iTunes Store on your computer:** Podcasts started out as another form of Internet radio, although, rather than listen to live streams, you download files onto your computer or iPod to take in at your leisure. You can still find lots of audio podcasts, but the focus here is on video. You can watch free episodes that cover *Sesame Street* videos, sports programming, investing strategies, political shows (across the ideological spectrum), and so much more. You can access these on your iPad via Apple's free Podcasts app.

- ✓ **Videos that play via entertainment apps:** For example, Netflix offers an app that enables you to use your Netflix subscription, if you have one, to stream video on your iPad. We like it so much, it made our list of favorites in Chapter 18. In summer 2012, Amazon added its appealing Amazon Instant Video streaming app for members of its service. Similarly, the ABC television network offers an appealing app so that you can catch up on its shows on your iPad. The Hulu Plus subscription app also lets you catch up on favorite TV. And if you're an HBO subscriber, go for the HBO Go app.

- ✓ **Seminars at Harvard, Stanford, or numerous other prestigious institutions:** iTunes U boasts more than 500,000 free lectures from around the world, many of them videos, in what Apple calls the world's largest catalog of educational content. In early 2012, Apple created a free iTunes U app, shown in Figure 8-4, so you no longer go directly through the iTunes Store to "enroll" in such lectures. Better yet, you get no grades, and you don't have to apply for admission, write an essay, or do homework. But you can take notes while watching. Some interactive textbook e-books (see Chapter 10) can also be accessed via iTunes U. Bring on our sheepskins.

- ✓ **The movies you've created in iMovie software or other software on the Mac or, for that matter, other programs on the PC:** Plus, you can view all the other videos you may have downloaded from the Internet, though sometimes you must convert these to a format the iPad recognizes.

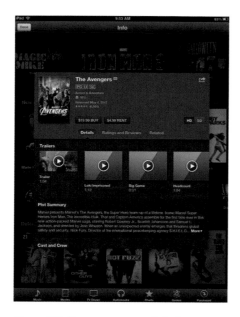

Figure 8-3: Bone up on a movie before buying or renting it.

Figure 8-4: Get smart. iTunes U offers a slew of lectures on diverse topics.

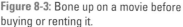 **Videos you've given birth to using the rear- or front-facing camera on the iPad mini:** Oh, and now a version of iMovie is made especially for iPads with cameras. The optional app costs $4.99. Check out the "Shooting Your Own Videos" section, later in this chapter, for direction on creating movies with the iPad.

You may have to prepare some videos so that they'll play on your iPad. To do so, highlight the video in question after it resides in your iTunes library. In iTunes, choose Advanced⇨Create iPad or Apple TV Version. Alas, creating an iPad version of a video doesn't work for all the video content you download off the Internet, including video files in the AVI, DivX, MKV, Flash, WMV, and Xvid formats.

For a somewhat technical workaround without potential conversion hassles, try the $2.99 Air Video app from InMethod s.r.o. The utility app can deliver AVI, DivX, MKV, and other videos that wouldn't ordinarily play on your iPad. You can also check out a limited free version. You have to download the free Air Video Server software to your Mac or PC to stream content to your iPad. Or try the excellent (and free) HandBrake application (from www.handbrake.fr) to convert most video formats to iPad-compatible versions.

For more on compatibility, check out the nearby "Are we compatible?" sidebar (but read it at your own risk).

TECHNICAL STUFF

Are we compatible?

The iPad works with a whole bunch of video, although not everything you'll want to watch will make it through. Several Internet video standards — notably, Adobe Flash — are not supported.

The absence of Flash is a bugaboo because Flash has been the technology behind much of the video on the web, though the landscape is changing. Even Adobe is pulling support for mobile versions of Flash.

Fortunately, Apple backs other increasingly popular standards — HTML5, CSS 3, and JavaScript. But the company was apparently sensitive enough to the issue that in the early days of the iPad, Apple made mention of several sites where video *would* play on the iPad. The list included CNN, *The New York Times,* Vimeo,

Time, ESPN, Major League Baseball, NPR, The White House, *Sports Illustrated,* TED, Nike, CBS, Spin, and *National Geographic.* What's more, entertainment apps from Netflix and ABC help fill the TV/movie void, as do many others.

With the appropriate utility software, you might also be able to convert some nonworking video to an iPad-friendly format on your computer. But if something doesn't play now, it may in the future because Apple has the capability to upgrade the iPad through software.

In the meantime, you can find a description of the video formats that iPad supports on Apple's website; point your browser to

`www.apple.com/ipad/specs`

Playing Video

After you know what you want to watch, here's how to watch it:

1. **On the Home screen, tap the Videos icon.**

   Videos stored on your iPad are segregated by category — Movies, Rented Movies, TV Shows, Music Videos, and Shared. For each category, you see the program's poster art, as shown in Figure 8-5. Categories such as Rented Movies and Shared appear only if you have that type of content loaded on the machine.

Figure 8-5: Choosing the movie, TV show, or music video to watch from Ed's Shared library.

You can view podcasts and iTunes U content through their dedicated apps.

2. **At the top of the screen, select the tab that corresponds to the type of video you want to watch.**

3. **Tap the poster that represents the movie, TV show, or other video you want to watch.**

   You sometimes see a full description of the movie you want to watch, along with a listing of cast and filmmakers, and sometimes only the cast, as shown in Figure 8-6. Tap the Chapters tab to browse the chapters. You see thumbnail images and the length of the chapter. Tap the Info tab to return to a description.

4. **To start playing a movie (or resume playing from where you left off), tap the Play button.**

   Alternatively, from Chapters view (see Figure 8-7), tap any chapter to start playing from that point.

   If you go to Settings from the Home screen and tap Videos, you can change the setting to start playing from where you left off rather than to start playing from the beginning, or vice versa.

5. **(Optional) Rotate your iPad to landscape mode to maximize a movie's display.**

   If you hold the iPad in portrait mode, you can see black bars on top of and below the screen where the movie is playing. Those bars remain when you rotate the device to its side, but the iPad plays the film in a wider-screen mode (depending on the video).

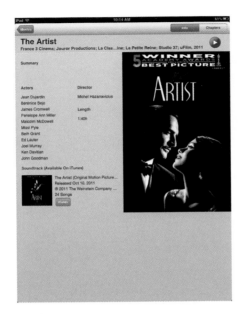

Figure 8-6: Who's who in the movie you're about to watch?

Figure 8-7: Start playing from any chapter.

For movies, this is a great thing. You can watch flicks as the filmmaker intended, in a cinematic *aspect ratio.* But we should point out that you might experience pillarboxing (see the following section) on flicks that aren't optimized to the iPad's aspect ratio proportions.

Finding and Working the Video Controls

While a video is playing, tap the screen to display the controls shown in Figure 8-8. Then you can tap a control to activate it. Here's how to work the controls:

- **To play or pause the video,** tap the Play/Pause button.

- **To adjust the volume,** drag the volume slider to the right to raise the volume and to the left to lower it. The volume adjusts relative to how the physical Volume buttons are controlling audio levels.

- **To restart or go back,** tap the Restart/Rewind button to restart the video, or tap and hold the same button to rewind.

- **To skip forward,** tap and hold Fast Forward to advance the video. Or skip ahead by dragging the Playhead along the Scrubber bar.

- **To set how the video fills the screen,** tap the Scale button, which toggles between filling the entire screen with video or fitting the video to the screen. Alternatively, you can double-tap the video to go back and forth between fitting and filling the screen.

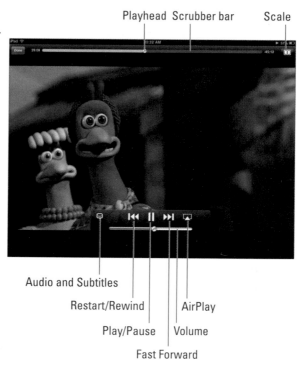

Fitting the video to the screen displays the film in its theatrical aspect ratio. Again, you may see black bars above and below the video (or to its sides), which some people don't like. The bars on the top and bottom are an example of *letterboxing;* on the sides, it's *pillarboxing. Filling* the entire screen with the video may crop or trim the sides or top of the picture, so you don't see the complete scene that the director shot.

Playhead Scrubber bar Scale

Audio and Subtitles

Restart/Rewind AirPlay

Play/Pause Volume

Fast Forward

Figure 8-8: Controlling the video.

✔ **To select language and subtitle settings,** tap the Audios and Subtitles button. You see options to select a different language, turn on or hide subtitles, and turn on or hide closed captioning. The control appears only if the movie supports any of these features or if you've turned on closed captioning by choosing Settings⟳Video.

✔ **To make the controls go away,** tap the screen again (or simply wait for them to go away on their own).

✔ **To tell your iPad you're done watching a video,** tap Done. You return to the last Videos screen that was visible before you started watching the movie.

Watching Video on a Big TV

We love watching movies on the iPad, but we also recognize the limitations of a smaller screen. Friends won't crowd around to watch with you, so Apple offers two ways to display video from your iPad to a TV:

✔ **AirPlay:** Through the AirPlay feature, you can wirelessly stream movies — commercial flicks or videos you shot — as well as photos and music from the iPad to an Apple TV box that's connected to an HDTV. Start watching the movie on the iPad and tap the AirPlay button that appears in the video controls. (Refer to Figure 8-8.) You can watch only one screen at a time. Tap Apple TV to stream to the TV through the Apple TV box. Tap iPad to watch on the iPad.

You can multitask while streaming a video. Therefore, while the kids are watching a flick on the TV, you can surf the web or catch up on e-mail.

Although you can stream from an iPad to an Apple TV and switch screens between the two, you can't stream to the iPad a rented movie that you start watching on Apple TV.

✔ **AV Adapter cables:** Apple sells a pair of $49 cable adapters — one for the digital AV (HDMI)) and one for a VGA connection. These cables let you connect to large, widescreen televisions, projectors, or other devices that have either of these inputs.

If you have a more recent iPad, however, the Digital AV (HDMI) adapter also lets you *mirror* the iPad screen on the connected TV or projector. So not only can you watch a movie or video, but you can also view anything else that's on the iPad's screen: your Home screens, web pages, games, other apps — you name it.

The Digital AV adapter doesn't include an HDMI cable, so you have to supply one yourself. For more on accessories, check out Chapter 17.

Restricting Video Usage

If you've given an iPad mini to your kid or to someone who works for you, you may not want that person spending time watching movies or television. You might want him to do something more productive, such as homework or the quarterly budget. That's where parental restrictions come in. Please note that the use of this iron-fist tool can make you really unpopular.

Tap Settings⇨General⇨Restrictions⇨Enable Restrictions. You're asked to establish or enter a previously established passcode. Twice. Having done so, you can set restrictions based on movie ratings (PG, R, and so on) and TV shows. You can also restrict FaceTime usage or use of the camera (which when turned off also turns off FaceTime). For more on restrictions, flip to Chapter 15, where we explain the settings for controlling (and loosening) access to iPad features.

Deleting Video from Your iPad

Video takes up space — lots of space. After the closing credits roll and you no longer want to keep a video on your iPad, here's what you need to know about deleting video:

✔ To delete a video manually, tap and hold its movie poster until the small, circled *x* shows up on the poster. To confirm your intention, tap the larger Delete button that appears or tap Cancel if you change your mind.

✔ Deleting a movie from the iPad only removes it from the iPad. It remains in the iTunes library on your Mac or PC (assuming that you synced it to your computer) and iCloud. That means if you want to watch it on your iPad again in the future, you can do so, as long as you either sync it again or download the movie from iCloud. You can also download purchased videos again from the iTunes Store at no charge.

✔ If you delete a rented movie before watching it on your iPad, it's gone. You have to spend (more) loot if you hope to watch it in the future on the iPad.

Shooting Your Own Videos

Apple equipped the iPad mini with two splendid cameras. The 5-megapixel iSight camera takes terrific stills (see Chapter 9) and lets you capture 1080p video, or the highest of the high-definition specifications. Another bonus is that it has built-in video stabilization, which helps compensate for a slightly jittery videographer.

The front FaceTime camera on the mini does high-def too, but up to the 720p video standard. It lets you capture 1.2-megapixel stills as well. Given its name, of course, you also know that it serves a vital role in FaceTime video chats.

Now that we've dispensed with that little piece of business, here's how to shoot video on the iPad:

1. **Tap the Camera icon on the Home screen.**

2. **Drag the little onscreen button at the lower-right corner of the display from the camera position to the video camera position.**

The button is labeled in Figure 8-9. The camera button is for stills, a subject we cover in Chapter 9.

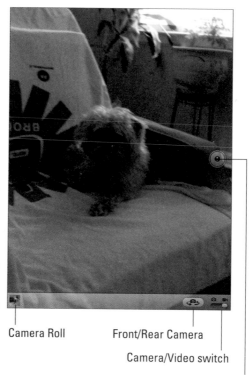

Camera Roll   Front/Rear Camera

Camera/Video switch

Record button

Figure 8-9: Lights, camera, action.

You can't switch from the front to the rear camera or vice versa while you're capturing a scene. So before shooting anything, think about which camera you want to use and then tap the front/rear camera button at the bottom-right corner of the screen when you've made your choice.

3. **To begin shooting a scene, tap the Record button (a large, silver button with a red dot in the center) on the center-right side of the screen.**

4. **Tap the Record button again to stop recording.**

   Your video is automatically saved to the Camera Roll, alongside any other saved videos and digital stills.

Editing what you shot

We assume that you've captured some great-looking footage, but you probably shot some stuff that belongs on the cutting-room floor as well. No big whoop because you can perform simple edits right on your mini. Remember to tap the Camera Roll at the lower-left corner of the Camera app to find your recordings. Then:

1. **Tap a video recording to display the onscreen controls, as shown in Figure 8-10.**

2. **Drag the start and end points along the frame viewer at the top of the screen to select only the video you want to keep.**

   Hold your finger over the section to expand the frame viewer to make it easier to apply your edits. Tap the Play button to preview your surgery.

3. **Choose what to do with your trimmed clip:**

   • Tap *Trim Original* to permanently remove scenes from the original clip.

   • Tap *Save as New Clip* to create a newly trimmed video clip; the original video remains intact, and the new clip is stored in the Camera Roll.

   • Tap *Cancel* to start over.

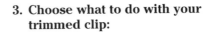

Figure 8-10: Getting a trim.

We should point out that this method lets you edit footage captured only on an iOS device, not video from a digital camcorder or camera, even if you sync it to the iPad mini.

For more ambitious editing on the iPad, consider iMovie for iPad, a $4.99 app that resembles a lighter version of iMovie for Mac computers. Through iMovie, you can export your finished video to YouTube, Vimeo, and Facebook. And iMovie for iPad lets you produce Hollywood-style movie trailers, just like on a Mac.

Any video edited with the iOS version of iMovie has to have originated on an iOS device. You can't mix in footage shot with a digital camera or obtained elsewhere.

Sharing video

You can play back what you've just shot in portrait mode or landscape mode. And if the video is any good, you likely want to share it with a wider audience. To do so, display the playback controls by tapping the screen and then tap the Action button, the icon that resembles an arrow trying to escape a rectangle. From there, you can e-mail the video (if the video file isn't too large), or send it as an iMessage (see Chapter 5). If you download the YouTube app, you can send it there too.

Seeing Is Believing with FaceTime

We'd bet you can come up with a lengthy list of people you'd love to be able to eyeball in real time from afar. Maybe it's your old college roommate. Maybe it's your old college sweetheart. And maybe it's your grandparents, who've long since retired to warm climates somewhere.

That's the beauty of *FaceTime,* the video chat app on the iPad mini. FaceTime exploits the two cameras built into the devices, each serving a different purpose. The front camera lets you talk face to face. The back camera shows the person you're talking to what you're seeing.

To take advantage of FaceTime, here's what you need:

✔ **Access to Wi-Fi or cellular:** And the people you're talking to need Internet access, too. On an iOS device, you used to need Wi-Fi. With iOS 6, Apple made FaceTime available to cellular connections. A third-generation or more recent iPad is required. On a Mac, you need an upstream or downstream Internet connection of at least 128 Kbps. You also need at least a 1 Mbps upstream and downstream connection for HD-quality video calls.

Using FaceTime over a cellular connection can quickly run through your monthly data allotment and prove hazardous to your budget.

✔ **FaceTime:** On your conversation partner's own iPad or Intel-based Mac computer (OS X 10.6.6 or later), on a recent-model iPod touch, or on an iPhone 4, 4S or 5. (FaceTime first appeared on Apple's prized smartphone.)

The iPad's inviting screen would seem to be made for FaceTime, but it helps to have halfway decent lighting and a robust Internet connection.

Getting started with FaceTime

When you use FaceTime for the first time, after you tap the app's icon from the Home screen, you're required to sign in to FaceTime using your Apple ID, which can be your iTunes Store account, iCloud ID, or another Apple account. (You may have previously supplied this info during setup of your iPad.) If you don't have an account, tap Create New Account to set one up within FaceTime. You also must supply an e-mail address or phone number that callers use to call you from their own FaceTime-capable iPads, Macs, iPhones, or iPod touches.

If this is the first time you've used a particular e-mail address for FaceTime, Apple sends an e-mail to that address to verify the account. Tap (or click) Verify Now and enter your Apple ID and password to complete the FaceTime setup. If the e-mail address resides in Mail on the iPad, you're already good to go.

If you have multiple e-mail addresses, callers can use any of them for FaceTime. To add an e-mail address after the initial setup, tap Settings⇨ FaceTime⇨Add Another Email. And phone numbers work too with iOS 6.

In fact, it's often a good idea to allocate separate e-mail addresses for FaceTime, assuming you have more than one Apple product that can take advantage of it. That way, a call to you when you're on your Mac, for example, won't ring on the iPad instead.

You can turn FaceTime on or off within Settings, but if you don't turn it off, you don't have to sign back in when you launch the app.

Making a FaceTime call

Now the real fun begins — making a call.

Follow these steps:

1. **Start the FaceTime app from the Home screen or by asking Siri to open the app on your behalf.**

   You can check out what you look like in a window before making a FaceTime call. So powder your nose and put on a happy face.

2. **Choose someone to call. Pick among the following:**

   • *Your contacts:* Tap a name or number, and then tap the e-mail address or phone number that contact has associated with FaceTime. To add a contact, tap Contacts and tap +.

   • *Your recent calls:* Tap Recents and then tap the appropriate number or name.

   • *Your favorites:* You can add frequent callers to a favorites list. Once again, merely tap a name to call.

3. **Check or change what you display on the screen, if needed.**

   When a call is under way, you can still see what you look like to the other person through a small picture-in-picture window that you can drag to any corner of the video call window. It's a great way to know whether your mug has dropped out of sight.

4. **(Optional) To toggle between the front and rear cameras, tap the Camera button that is also labeled in Figure 8-11.**

5. **Tap End when you're ready to hang up.**

While you're on a FaceTime call, the following tips are handy to know:

✔ **Rotate the iPad to its side to change the orientation.**

✔ **Silence or mute a call by tapping the Microphone icon (labeled in Figure 8-11).**

Call window shows who you're talking to

How you look to the other person

Mute Voice   Switch Cameras

Hang up

Figure 8-11: Bob can see Ed, and Ed can see Bob in FaceTime.

Be aware that you can still be seen even if not heard (and you can still see and hear the other person).

🎯 TIP

✔ Momentarily check out another iPad app by pressing the Home button and then tapping the icon for the app you have in mind, or by double-tapping the Home button to select the app from the multitasking bar. At this juncture, you can still talk over FaceTime, but you can no longer see the person. Tap the green bar at the top of the iPad screen to bring the person and the FaceTime app back in front of you.

Receiving a FaceTime call

Of course, you can get FaceTime calls as well as make them. FaceTime doesn't have to be open for you to receive a video call. Here's how incoming calls work:

✔ **You hear the call:** When a call comes in, the caller's name prominently displays on the iPad's screen, as shown in Figure 8-12. You simultaneously hear the phone ring.

✔ **You accept or decline the call:** Tap Accept to answer the call or tap Decline if you'd rather not. If your iPad is locked when a FaceTime call comes in, slide the green arrow button to the right to answer. To decline it, do nothing and wait for the caller to give up.

✔ **You silence the ring:** You can press the Sleep/Wake button at the top of the iPad to silence the incoming ring. If you know you don't want to be disturbed by FaceTime calls before the phone even rings, flip the side switch on the iPad to Mute. Make sure that you're using the side switch as a mute control rather than as a rotation lock. Otherwise, head to Settings (see Chapter 15) to change the function of this switch back to mute.

Figure 8-12: Tap Accept to answer the call.

And with that, we hereby silence this chapter. But you can do more with the cameras on your iPad. And we do that in Chapter 9.

You Oughtta Be in Pictures

In This Chapter

▶ Shooting pictures

▶ Importing your pictures

▶ Viewing and admiring pictures

▶ Creating a slide show

▶ Working with pictures even more

▶ Deleting your photos

▶ Hamming it up in Photo Booth

We often sing the praises of the grown-up iPads' vibrant multitouch display. You'd be hard-pressed to find a more appealing portable screen for watching movies or playing games — and, yes, for appreciating photos. Though the screen on the iPad mini is smaller (and of lower resolution) than the iPads with Retina displays that preceded it, the mini tablet you have recently purchased (or are lusting after) is also a first-rate photo viewer. Images are crisp and vivid, at least those that you shot properly. (C'mon, we know Ansel Adams is a distant cousin.)

What's more, you can shoot some of those pictures directly with your prized tablet. The reasons, of course, are the front and rear cameras that are built into the device. If you've already read Chapter 8, you already know you can put those cameras to work capturing video. In this chapter, you get to see the big picture on shooting still images.

Okay, we need to get a couple of things out of the way. The iPad mini will never substitute for a point-and-shoot digital camera, much less a pricey digital SLR. As critics, we can quibble about the lack of a flash or about the grainy images you may produce after shooting in low light. And shooting can be awkward.

But we're here, friends, to focus on the positive. And having cameras on your iPad may prove to be a godsend when no better option is available, and they represent decent solutions for close-up "macro shots." In Chapter 8, we tell you about the capability to capture full, high-definition video, up to the 1080p standard, as techies refer to it.

In this chapter, we point out other optical enhancements in the iPad mini. The 5-megapixel iSight camera has backside illumination and boasts what's known as an f/2.4 aperture and a five-element lens. It also has a hybrid infra-red filter (like the one on an SLR) that helps lead to more uniform colors. Oh, and face detection ensures that the balance and focus are just right for as many as ten faces on the screen.

All these features are simply photographer-speak for "potentially snapping darn sweet pictures."

And we can think of certain circumstances — selling real estate, say, or shopping for a new home — where tablet cameras are quite convenient.

Meanwhile, you're in for a real treat if you're new to *Photo Booth*, a yuk-it-up Mac program that's on the iPad mini as well. It may be the best, or at least the most fun, use of the cameras yet.

We get to Photo Booth at the end of this chapter. But over the next few pages, you discover the best ways to make the digital photos on the iPad come alive, no matter how they managed to arrive on your machine.

Shooting Pictures

To start shooting pictures on iPads with cameras, tap the Camera icon on the Home screen. The screen resembles a closed camera shutter. When that shutter opens an instant later, you're peering through, in effect, a 7.9-inch viewfinder. Here's what to do next:

1. **In this example, make sure that the Camera/Video switch at the lower-right corner of the screen (and shown in Figure 9-1) is turned to Camera mode. If it isn't, slide the switch from right to left.**

2. **Use the viewfinder to frame the image.**

3. **Tap the portion of the screen in which you see the face or object you want as the image's focal point.**

   A small rectangle surrounds your selection, and the iPad automatically adjusts the exposure and focus of that part of the image.

4. **(Optional) To zoom in or out, tap the screen with two fingers and spread (unpinch) to zoom in or pinch to zoom out.**

The iPad has a 5X digital zoom, which basically crops and resizes an image. Such zooms are nowhere near as effective, quality-wise, as optical zooms on many digital cameras. Be aware that zooming works only with the rear camera still in Camera mode; it doesn't work with the front camera or when you shoot video.

5. **(Optional) To see grid lines to help compose your picture, tap the Options button and then tap the Grid switch (so that it says On).**

To toggle between the front and rear cameras, tap the Front/Rear Camera button (refer to Figure 9-1) in the lower-right corner of the screen.

We should point out that the front camera is of lower quality than its rear cousin, but it's perfectly adequate for the kinds of demands you put on it, including using FaceTime and Photo Booth.

Options button   Front/Rear camera

Camera Roll   Camera/Video switch

Shutter release button

Figure 9-1: Using the iPad as a camera.

6. **When you're satisfied and ready to snap an image, tap the shutter release button in the right-center of the screen.**

We've also found, when we use the onscreen shutter button, that we often get better results when we hold a finger against the button while composing a shot and then release it only when the moment is right. This way, you're less prone to shake the iPad — and blur your pictures — than when you're tapping the screen.

As an alternative to the shutter release, use the Volume Up/Down control on the side of the iPad, which some people, under certain circumstances, will find more comfortable. Don't cover the lens with your fingers!

You hear a shutter sound unless you've turned the Mute switch to Silent, as we explain in Chapter 1.

The image you shoot lands in the Camera Roll in the lower-left corner of the screen. We explain what you can do with the images on the iPad later in this chapter.

Importing Pictures

Of course, you don't need to shoot pictures on the iPad mini to place images on your tablet. You can add them in several ways, in fact. Alas, at least one of the methods involves buying an accessory. We zoom in on this topic in the following sections.

Syncing pix via computer

We devote an entire chapter (see Chapter 3) to synchronizing data with the iPad, so we don't dwell on it here. But because syncing pictures is still the most common way to import images to the iPad, we'd be remiss not to mention it in this chapter. (The assumption in this section is that you already know how to put pictures on your computer.)

When the iPad is connected to your computer, click the Photos tab on the iPad Device page in iTunes on the Mac or PC. Then select a source from the Sync Photos From pop-up menu.

On a Mac, you can sync photos (and videos) via iPhoto software version 6.06 or later or Aperture 3.02 or later. On a PC, you can sync using Adobe Photoshop Elements 8.0 or later. Alternatively, with both computers, you can sync with any folder that contains pictures.

After you make a selection from the Sync Photos From menu, you may see one or more check boxes or radio buttons enabling you to sync different combinations of albums, events, faces, or folders. The boxes or buttons you see are based on your selection on the Sync Photos From menu.

So what are events and faces, anyway? Here's a quick look at these staple features in iPhoto and Aperture on the Mac:

- **Events:** In their infinite wisdom, the folks at Apple figured that most pictures shot on a given day are tied to a specific occasion, such as Junior's birthday party or a wedding. So the iPhoto program on a Mac automatically groups them accordingly, by placing all pictures taken on the same day into a single collection. Don't worry: You can split a day's worth of pictures into more than one event if, say, the birthday party was in the morning and the wedding was at night. Apple automatically names an event by its date; you can change it to something more descriptive (such as Timmy's Softball Game or Geri's Graduation).

- **Faces:** As its name implies, Faces is a collection of pictures on a single common thread: whose mug is in them. In our experience with Faces, the technology, although pretty darn impressive, isn't perfect.

Photo Stream: Sync photos among your devices effortlessly

The Photo Stream feature, when enabled, uploads and stores up to 1,000 photos from the last 30 days on iCloud and automatically downloads them to all your devices that have Photo Stream enabled when connected to Wi-Fi.

You need to enable two settings if you want to use your Photo Stream. First, instruct your iPad's camera to send photos *to* your Photo Stream by following these steps:

1. **Tap Settings on your Home screen.**
2. **Tap iCloud on the left side of the screen.**
3. **Tap Photo Stream.**
4. **Tap the switch to turn on Photo Stream (it should say On).**

Second, if you want to see your Photo Stream in the Photos app, do this:

1. **Tap Settings on your Home screen.**
2. **Tap Photos & Camera on the left side of the screen.**
3. **Tap the switch to turn on Photo Stream (it should say On).**

That's it. Turn it on, and you'll always have access to your last 30 days of pictures.

If you're a Mac user, iPhoto '11 (versions 9.2 and higher) supports Photo Stream. To enable it, launch iPhoto on your Mac and do this:

1. **Choose iPhoto⇨Preferences.**
2. **Click the Photo Stream tab at the top of the Preferences window.**
3. **Select the Enable Photo Stream check box.**

A bit later in this chapter, we tell you about a cool variation that lets you share Photo Streams with friends and family.

Connecting a digital camera or memory card

Almost all the digital cameras we're aware of come with USB cables that you can use to transfer images to a computer. Of course, the iPad isn't a regular computer, and it isn't equipped with a USB port.

Instead, Apple sells optional $29 Lightning–to–SD–Card Camera Readers and Lightning–to–USB Camera Adapters, $29 apiece; here's how the latter product works:

1. **Connect the Lightning end of the connector to the iPad mini.**

2. **Connect the other end of the connector to the USB cable that is, in turn, connected to your digital camera.**

   Kindly use the USB cable that comes with your camera, or another that fits, because no such cable comes with the Apple adapter.

3. **Make sure that the iPad is unlocked.**

4. **If you haven't already done so, turn on the camera and ensure that it's set to transfer pictures.**

   Consult the manual that came with the camera if you're unsure of which setting to use.

   The Photos app on the iPad opens and displays the pictures that you can import from the camera.

5. **Tap Import All to select the entire bunch, or tap the individual pictures you want to include if you'd rather cherry-pick.**

   A check mark appears next to each image you select. And that's pretty much it: The iPad organizes the pictures into albums and such, as we describe later in this chapter.

At this point, you're free to erase the pictures from your camera.

The Lightning–to–SD–Card Reader connector accommodates the SD memory cards that are common to many digital camera models. The procedure works almost identically to the USB connector, except that you're inserting the SD gizmo into the Lightning connector port rather than into the USB connector we mentioned. Insert the SD gently to prevent damage.

The two connectors support many common photo formats, including JPEG and Raw. The latter format is favored by photo enthusiasts. They also support common standard and high-definition video formats.

You might be able to connect certain USB computer keyboards, MIDI keyboards, media readers, and microphones to your iPad mini with the Lightning–to–USB–Camera Adapter and then watch those peripherals come alive. We're making no guarantees, of course, but, hey — it never hurts to try.

Saving images from e-mails and the web

You can easily save pictures that arrive in e-mails or pictures that you come across on the web: Just press and hold your finger against the image, and then tap Save Image when the button pops up a second later. Pictures are stored in the Camera Roll, as noted in the next section.

Where Have All My Pictures Gone?

So where exactly do your pictures hang out on the iPad? Well, we explain in the preceding section what happens to images saved from e-mails and the Internet: They reside in the Camera Roll. (We wanted to see whether you're paying attention.)

Other imported images are grouped into the same albums as they were on the computer, or lumped together as Events or Faces or — when the embedded *metadata* inside an image identifies where a picture was shot — under the very cool Places feature. We have more to say about Places later in this chapter.

So now that you know where the pictures are, you're ready to discover how best to display them and share them with others — and how to dispose of the duds that don't measure up to your lofty photographic standards.

Get ready to literally get your fingers on the pics (without worrying about smudging them). The following steps walk you through the basics of navigating among your pictures with the Photos app:

1. **Tap the Photos app on the Home screen.**

   The app opens with a grid of thumbnail images on top of a black background, as shown in Figure 9-2. The Photos tab at the top of the screen is highlighted because you're in Photos view. If the thumbnail you have in mind doesn't appear on this screen, flick your finger up or down to scroll through the pictures rapidly, or use a slower

Figure 9-2: The landing spot for photos.

dragging motion to pore through the images more deliberately. So, if you have more photos than can possibly show up on the screen at any one time, which is highly probable, your flicking and dragging skills will improve quickly.

2. **Tap or pinch the photo you want to display.**

   These actions lead to slightly different outcomes. When you *tap* an image, the picture rapidly gets bigger, practically jumping off the screen. If you *pinch* or *unpinch* instead, by putting your thumb and forefinger together and then spreading them apart, you have more control over how the image shrinks or grows. You can also keep your finger pressed against the image to drag it around.

3. **To navigate collections of images, tap Albums, Events, Faces, or Places at the top of your iPad screen. Or pinch them.**

   You see stacks or collections of pictures. Tap an Album, Event, or Faces pile, and all the underlying pictures scatter into a mass of individual images. It's an orderly escape because the individual pictures once again appear in a grid. Most likely, you'll have to scroll up or down again to see all the pictures in the collection. As before, tap any of the individual pictures you want to focus on.

   But what if you unpinch a collection instead of tapping? The answer depends on how you pinch. If you pinch just a little bit, the pictures spread out slowly enough that you can preview some of the images in the pile. Let go, and the collection opens (unless, that is, you hadn't pinched far enough and the images retreat into a stack). If you do a *wider pinch* by spreading your fingers even more, the entire collection opens. As before, tap a picture to see a large view of it.

4. **With an individual photo on the screen, tap the picture to open the picture controls at the top and bottom of the screen.**

   The controls are shown in Figure 9-3. Later in this chapter, we discuss what they do, but we want you to know how to summon them, because we're certain that you'll be calling on them.

5. **To make the controls disappear, tap the screen again. Or just wait a few seconds and they go away on their own.**

6. **Press the Home button when you're finished with the Photos app.**

Tap to see slideshow.

Tap to edit this photo.

Tap to send as an e-mail or iMessage, assign to contact, use as wallpaper, tweet, print or copy.

Tap to return to main screen.

Number of photos in this album/event

Slide finger to skim through album.

Figure 9-3: Picture controls.

Improving Pictures

iOS includes a welcome quartet of photo editing tools: Rotate, Enhance, Red-Eye, and Crop — to use any of them, tap the Edit button in the upper-right portion of the screen, and a toolbar with four buttons appears at the bottom of the screen:

- **Rotate:** Tap to turn the image a quarter-turn counterclockwise.
- **Enhance:** Tap to improve the lighting, contrast, and color balance of the image. Tap Enhance again to remove the effect.
- **Red-Eye:** Tap to enable, and then tap on the red eye in the image. Tap again to undo.

  If the tool doesn't recognize a red eye, it politely informs you that it didn't find a red eye to correct.

- **Crop:** Tap to crop or straighten the image. Tap the corners of the overlay to set the cropping area; tap the Constrain button to make the cropped image conform to popular proportions, such as 5 x 7, 8 x 10, 4 x 6, and so on.

If you've applied more than one of the tools to your image, you can use the Undo button in the upper-left corner to step backward through time, undoing one step for each tap. Or tap the Revert to Original button to remove all the improvements at one time.

Admiring Pictures

Photographs are meant to be seen, of course, not buried in the digital equivalent of a shoebox. And the iPad affords you some neat ways to manipulate, view, and share your best photos.

You've no doubt already figured out (from the preceding section) how to find a photo, view it full-screen, and display picture controls. But you can do a lot of maneuvering of your pictures without summoning those controls. Here are some options:

- **Skip ahead or view the previous picture:** Flick your finger left or right.
- **Landscape or portrait:** The iPad's wizardry (or, more specifically, the device's accelerometer sensor) is at work. When you turn the iPad sideways, the picture automatically reorients itself from portrait to landscape mode, as the images in Figure 9-4 show. Pictures shot in landscape mode fill the screen when you rotate the iPad. Rotate the device back to portrait mode, and the picture readjusts accordingly.

  The Screen Orientation Lock to the left of the iPad controls on the multitasking bar must be switched off. See Chapter 2 for the gory details.

Figure 9-4: The same picture in portrait (left) and landscape (right) modes.

Show a picture to a friend by flipping the iPad over. The iPad always knows which side is up.

✔ **Zoom:** Double-tap to zoom in on part of an image. Double-tap again to zoom out. Alternatively, spread and pinch with your thumb and index finger to zoom in and zoom out. The downside to zooming is that you can't see the entire image.

✔ **Pan and scroll:** This cool little feature is practically guaranteed to make you the life of the party. After you zoom in on a picture, drag it around the screen with your finger. Besides impressing your friends, you can bring front and center the part of the image you care most about. That lets you zoom in on Fido's adorable face, as opposed to, say, the unflattering picture of the person holding the dog in his lap.

✔ **Skim:** A bar appears at the bottom of the screen when you summon picture controls. Drag your finger across the bar in either direction to quickly view all the pictures in an open album.

✔ **Map it:** If you tap the Places tab instead of an album, or an Event or Faces collection, a map like the one shown in Figure 9-5 appears. Notice the red pins on the map. These indicate that pictures were taken in the location shown on the map. Now tap a pin, and a stack representing all the images on the iPad that were shot in that location appears, as shown in the middle of Figure 9-5. As before, you can tap or pinch the collection to open it.

The iPad is pretty smart when it comes to geography. So as long as Location Services is turned on in Settings and the specific location settings (also under Location Services in Settings) for the camera are turned on, pictures you take with the iPad cameras are *geotagged,* or identified by where they were shot.

Be aware that Apple placed the various options for Location Services under a Privacy setting. For more on Settings, see Chapter 15.

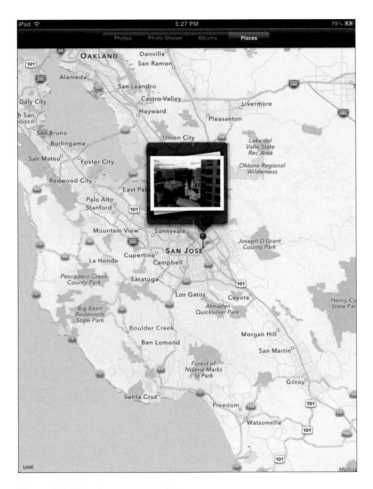

Figure 9-5: Mapping out your pictures.

Spread your fingers on a map to enlarge it and narrow the pictures taken to a particular area, town, or even neighborhood. For more on Maps, flip to Chapter 6.

Launching Slide Shows

Those who store a lot of photographs on computers are familiar with running slide shows of those images. You can easily replicate the experience on the iPad, and through AirPlay, stream the slide show wirelessly to an Apple TV or, lacking that device, via an optional cable that connects to a TV, projector, or even (you still have one of these?) a VCR. Follow these steps:

1. **Open an album by tapping it or display all your photos in Photos view.**

2. **Tap the Slideshow button in the upper-right corner of the screen.**

   The Slideshow Options window, as shown in Figure 9-6, appears. We explore these and other options in the next section. But if you just want to start the slide show from here, continue to Step 3.

3. **Tap Start Slideshow.**

   Your only obligation is to enjoy the show.

Figure 9-6: Tap the Slideshow button to see slide show options.

Adding special slide show effects

Both the Settings options and the Slideshow button enable you to add special effects to your slide shows. Under Settings, you can alter the length of time each slide is shown, change the transition effects between pictures, and display images in random order. With Slideshow Options, you can add transitions and music.

From the Home screen, tap Settings⇨Photos & Camera. Then tap any of the following options to make changes:

- **Play Each Slide For:** You have five choices: 2 seconds, 3 seconds, 5 seconds, 10 seconds, and 20 seconds. When you're finished, tap the Photos button to return to the main Settings screen for Photos.

- **Repeat:** If this option is turned on, the slide show continues to loop until you stop it. The Repeat control may be counterintuitive. If Off displays, tap it to turn on the Repeat function. If On displays, tap it to turn off the Repeat function.

- **Shuffle:** Turning on this feature plays slides in random order. As with the Repeat feature, if it says Off, tap to switch it to On. Conversely, if it says On, tap to switch it to Off.

Tap the Home button to leave Settings and return to the Home screen.

To select transitions and music for your slide shows, tap the Slideshow button within the Photos app to select options (refer to Figure 9-6):

- ✔ **Transitions:** You can change the effect you see when you move from one slide to the next. Again, you have five cool choices: Cube, Dissolve, Ripple, Wipe, or, a personal favorite of ours, Origami, in which the images fold out in ways similar to the Japanese folk art of paper folding. Why not try them all to see what you like?

- ✔ **Music:** Adding music to a slide show couldn't be easier. From the Slideshow Options window, tap the Play Music option so that it's turned on. Then tap Music in the Slideshow Options overlay (refer to Figure 9-6) to choose your soundtrack from the songs stored on the device. Ed loves backing up slide shows with Sinatra, Sarah Vaughan, or Gershwin, among numerous other artists. Bob loves using songs by The Beatles or stately classical music.

Tap anywhere onscreen during a slide show to display additional information and controls; tap the Photos button in the upper-left corner to exit the slide show.

Admiring pictures on the TV

The AirPlay feature lets you stream music and videos wirelessly from the iPad to an Apple TV (see Chapter 8), and it works with photos, too. For wired connections to a TV, let us direct you to Chapter 17 on accessories.

To watch the slide show or view individual pictures on a big-screen TV via Apple TV, tap the AirPlay button shown in the upper-right corner of Figure 9-3, and then tap Apple TV from the list. If the AirPlay button isn't visible, make sure that the iPad and Apple TV share the same Wi-Fi network. Tap the iPad button to view the slide show again on the iPad. We can tell you the experience is very cool.

Turning the iPad into a picture frame

Even when the iPad is locked, it can do something special — turn into a handsome, animated, digital picture frame — a variation on the slide show feature. To turn on this feature, tap the Picture Frame icon in the lower-right corner of the Lock screen. (It can also be used as a camera when locked, so you don't have to fumble when the perfect shot unexpectedly presents itself.)

Inside Picture Frame Settings, and reachable like all other settings when you tap the Settings icon on the Home screen, you can choose one of two transitions (Dissolve or Origami), turn a "zoom in on faces" feature on or off, and arrange to play slides in random mode or shuffle mode. And, of course, you can pick the albums or photos to include in your slide show.

You can pause or stop a slide show by tapping the Picture Frame icon or sliding the slider to unlock the iPad. To disable the feature altogether, tap General under Settings, tap Passcode Lock so that it's on (you have to enter your passcode at this point, if you have one), and tap Picture Frame so that the setting is off.

Sharing Photo Streams

The Photo Streams feature we discuss earlier in the chapter is generally a terrific and hassle-free way for you to make sure the pictures you've shot end up on your devices without fretting about how they land there. But Apple, in its infinite wisdom, recognizes that you also might want to share your best images with friends and family and have those pictures automatically show up on those people's devices. The impressive, aptly named solution Shared Photo Streams arrived on the iPad — and, of course, on the iPad mini and the iPhone and iPod touch — with iOS 6 (and a bit earlier on Macs running OS X Mountain Lion). The feature lets you share pictures with other folks and lets you subscribe in kind to the shared photo streams that they make available to you. Here's how:

1. **Tap Settings on your Home Screen.**

2. **Tap Photos & Camera on the left side of the screen.**

3. **Tap the Shared Photo Streams option so that On is showing.**

4. **Open the Photos app and choose the photos you want to share in a Shared Photo Stream.**

5. **Tap the Share button and tap the Photo Stream option in the Share dialog that appears.**

   Take note of some of your other options here: sharing via Mail, Twitter, and Facebook, as discussed in the next section.

6. **Choose whether you want to create a new Photo Stream or add to an existing one.**

   If you're adding your photos to an existing Photo Stream, tap the appropriate Photo Stream that appears on your list of Photo Streams. To create a new Photo Stream, tap New Photo Stream.

7. **In the Share dialog that appears (see Figure 9-7), type the e-mail addresses**

Figure 9-7: Preparing to stream your pictures to friends.

for each person you want to receive your Photo Stream or tap the + button to add names from your contacts.

8. **Enter a name for your Photo Stream and tap Next.**

Share your Photo Stream with everyone through a public gallery on iCloud.com. To do that, flip the Public Website switch to On.

9. **Enter a comment (optional) and then tap Post.**

More (Not So) Stupid Picture Tricks

You can take advantage of the photos on the iPad in a few more ways. In most cases, you tap the picture and make sure that the picture controls are displayed. Then tap the Share (or Action) button in the upper-right corner. (It looks like an arrow trying to escape from a rectangle.)

Here's what each choice does:

- **Email Photo:** Some photos are so precious that you just have to share them with family members and friends. When you tap Mail, the picture is automatically embedded in the body of an outgoing e-mail message. Use the virtual keyboard to enter the e-mail addresses and subject line and any comments you want to add — you know, something profound, like "Isn't this a great-looking photo?" (Check out Chapter 5 for more info on using e-mail.)

- **Message:** When e-mail just won't do, this option lets you send the photo in an iMessage. The caveat, of course, is that the recipient has to have an i-device with iOS 5 or higher or Mac with Mountain Lion. To send a picture this way, tap the Messages icon on the Home screen, and tap the Camera icon adjacent to the field where you type text to a recipient. That gives you the Take Photo or Video option (self-explanatory, don't you think?) or Choose Existing option (still evident). Select a picture you already have on hand, and it's embedded in the message.

- **Assign to Contact:** You can assign a picture to someone in your contacts list. To make it happen, tap Assign to Contact from the Share options window. (Yep, we're back to starting out in the Photos app.) Your list of contacts appears on the screen. Scroll up or down the list to find the person who matches the picture of the moment. You can drag and resize the picture to get it just right. Then tap Use.

  You can also assign a photo to a contact by starting out in Contacts, as we explain in Chapter 12. Here's a sneak peek at that chapter: From Contacts, choose the person, tap Edit, and then tap Add Photo. At that point, you can select an existing portrait from one of your on-board picture albums or take a new picture.

To change the picture you assigned to a person, tap her name in the contacts list, tap Edit, and then tap the person's thumbnail picture, which also carries the Edit label. From there, you can select another photo from one of your albums, edit the photo you're already using (by resizing and dragging it to a new position), or delete the photo you no longer want.

- **Use As Wallpaper:** When you unlock the iPad mini, the default background image shows what appears to be calm waves on a hazy day. You also see this same image (unless you change it) on the Lock screen.

  But you probably have what you consider to be an even better photograph to use as the iPad's wallpaper — perhaps a picture of your spouse, your kids, or your pet.

  When you tap the Use As Wallpaper button, you see what the present image looks like as the iPad background picture. You can move and resize the picture through the now-familiar action of dragging or pinching across the screen with your fingers. When you're satisfied with the wallpaper preview, tap the Set Home Screen button to make it your new Home background, or tap Set Lock Screen to have the image appear when the iPad is locked. Or you can tap Set Both to set that image as your Home and Locked wallpaper screens. Per usual, you also have the option to tap Cancel. (You can find out more about wallpaper in Chapter 15.)

- **Twitter:** Tap this button to tweet this picture to your Twitter followers. (Try saying that three times, fast.) For it to work, you have to add or create a Twitter account in Settings. Once it's set up, you can add your location to the tweet by tapping Add Location in the Tweet dialog that appears.

- **Facebook:** If you've configured a Facebook account in Settings, you can share the photo (and, if you wish, your location) on the world's most popular social network.

- **Print:** In the 21st century, people are accustomed to viewing pictures on computer screens, digital frames, smartphones, and tablets. In the last century, most viewed prints. But something is still special about printing pictures to give away, carry around, or place in an old-fashioned photo frame or album. Through AirPrint, you can print photos from an iPad onto a compatible printer. Tap Print from the menu. The iPad tries to find the printer. You can select the number of copies. If your printer has a tray for photo paper in addition to plain paper, the printer may automatically switch to that tray when you try to print a picture.

- **Copy Photo:** Tap this button when you want to copy a photo and paste it elsewhere.

  Alternatively, you can also press and hold your finger against a photo until the Copy button appears. Tap that button, and you can paste the image into an e-mail, for example, by preparing a message, holding your finger against the screen until a Paste button appears, and then pressing the button to paste it into the body of the message.

In addition to describing the photo tricks that come ready to use on your iPad, we encourage you to check out the App Store, which we explore in greater depth in Chapter 11. As of this writing, hundreds of photography-related applications, some free, are available. These come from a variety of sources and range from Photobucket for iPad, which is free, to Adobe Photoshop Touch, a $9.99 app that brings layers, filters, and other photographic tools to the tablet. Apple even produces iPhoto for iPad, a custom $4.99 version of the popular photography program on Macs.

Deleting Pictures

We told a tiny fib by intimating that photographs are meant to be seen. We should have amended our statement by saying that *some* pictures are meant to be seen. Others, well . . . you can't get rid of them fast enough. Fortunately, the iPad makes it a cinch to bury the evidence:

- ✔ **Deleting photos in the Camera Roll albums or Photo Stream:** Some pictures — namely, those you saved from an e-mail or web page and that now reside in the Camera Roll album or Photo Stream — are easy to dispose of. Just tap the soon-to-be-whacked picture to open it, and then tap the Trash icon that appears in the upper-right corner when you summon picture controls. To finish the job, tap the big red Delete Photo button. Or tap anywhere else on the screen if you have second thoughts and decide to keep the picture on your iPad.

  If you dispose of images in Photo Stream, the images are removed from the Photo Stream on all your devices.

- ✔ **Deleting multiple photos in Camera Roll or Photo Stream:** When the Saved Photos or Camera Roll or Photo Stream albums are open, tap the Edit button in the upper-right corner, and a red Delete button appears in the upper-left corner of the screen, though it's somewhat dim. Now tap each photo that you want to get rid of; a check mark appears on each one and the red Delete button brightens. When you've identified the doomed bunch, tap Delete Selected Photos, or tap Cancel to save them.

- ✔ **Removing synced photos:** The Trash icon appears only in the Saved Photos or Camera Roll album. That's because the other pictures on your iPad — those you synced through your Mac or PC — must first be deleted from the photo album on your computer. Then when you resync those albums, the photos are no longer on your iPad.

Entering the Photo Booth

Remember the old-fashioned photo booths at the local 5 and Dime? Remember the 5 and Dime? Okay, if you don't remember such variety stores, your parents probably do, and if they don't, their parents no doubt do. The point is that photo booths (which still exist) are fun places to ham it up solo or with a friend as the machine captures and spits out wallet-size pictures.

In the Photo Booth app included on the iPad mini, Apple has cooked up a modern alternative to the real-life photo booth. The app is a close cousin to a similar application on the Mac. Here's how Photo Booth works:

1. **Tap the Photo Booth icon.**

   A red curtain opens, revealing the tic-tac-toe-style grid, as shown in Figure 9-8.

2. **Point the front-facing camera at your face.**

   You see your mug through a prism of eight rather wacky special effects: Thermal Camera, Mirror, X-Ray, Kaleidoscope, Light Tunnel, Squeeze, Twirl, and Stretch. The center square (what is this, *Hollywood Squares?*) is the only one in which you come off looking normal — or, as we like to kid, like you're supposed to look.

   You can also use the rear camera in Photo Booth to subject your friends to this form of, um, visual abuse.

Figure 9-8: Photo booths of yesteryear weren't like this.

3. **Choose one of the special effects (or stick with Normal) by tapping one of the thumbnails.**

   Ed chose Mirror for the example shown in Figure 9-9, because, after all, two Eds are better than one. (Sorry — couldn't resist.)

4. **If you're not satisfied with the effect you've chosen, tap the icon at the lower-left corner of the app to return to the Photo Booth grid and select another.**

5. **(Optional) After choosing an effect, doctor things up even further by pinching or unpinching with your fingers.**

6. **When you have your bizarre look just right, tap the shutter release on the screen to snap the picture.**

   Your pic lands (as do other pictures taken with the iPad cameras) in the Camera Roll album.

   From the Camera Roll album, pictures can be shared or — you might want to seriously consider this, given the distortions you've just applied to your face — deleted.

Nah, we're only kidding. Keep the image and take a lot more. Photo Booth may be a blast from the past. But it's also a blast.

Figure 9-9: When one co-author just isn't enough.

10

Curling Up with a Good iBook

In This Chapter

▶ Getting the skinny on e-books

▶ Opening up to iBooks

▶ Reading books

▶ Shopping for iBooks

▶ Reading electronic periodicals

Don't be surprised if you have to answer this question from an inquisitive child someday: "Is it true, Grandpa, that people once read books on paper?"

That time may still be a ways off, but it somehow doesn't seem as far-fetched any more, especially now that Apple has signed on as a major proponent of the burgeoning electronic books revolution.

Don't get us wrong; we love physical books as much as anyone and are in no way urging their imminent demise. But we also recognize the real-world benefits behind Apple's digital publishing efforts, and those by companies like Amazon, which manufactures what is, for now, the market-leading Kindle electronic reader. As you discover in this chapter, the Kindle plays a role on the iPad mini as well.

For its part, the iPad mini makes a terrific electronic reader, with color and dazzling special effects, including pages that like they're in a paper book. You can even make the case that the iPad mini is a superior electronic reader than larger iPads because it's closer in size to a paperback and is more easily carried in one hand or slipped into a jacket pocket.

We open the page on this chapter to see how to find and purchase books for your iPad, and how to read them after they land on your virtual bookshelf. But first we look at why you might want to read books and periodicals on your iPad.

Why E-Books?

We've run into plenty of skeptics who ask, "What's so wrong with the paper books that folks have only been reading for centuries that we now have to go digital?" The short answer is that nothing is wrong with physical books — except maybe that paper, over the long term, is fragile, and they tend to be bulky, a potential impediment for travelers.

On the other hand, when asked why he prefers paper books, Bob likes to drop one from shoulder height and ask, "Can your iPad (or Kindle) do that?"

Having said that, though, now consider the electronic advantages:

- **No more weight or bulk constraints:** You can cart a whole bunch of e-books around when you travel, without breaking your back. The same goes for students on campus. To the avid bookworm, this potentially changes the whole dynamic in the way you read. Because you can carry so many books wherever you go, you can read whatever type of book strikes your fancy at the moment, kind of like listening to a song that fits your current mood. You have no obligation to read a book from start to finish before opening a new bestseller, just because that happens to be the one book, maybe two, that you have in your bag. In other words, weight constraints are out the window.

- **Feel like reading a trashy novel?** Go for it. Rather immerse yourself in classic literature? Go for that. You might read a textbook, cookbook, or biography. Or gaze in wonder at an illustrated beauty. What's more, you can switch among the various titles and styles of books at will, before finishing any single title.

- **Flexible fonts and type sizes:** With e-books, or what Apple prefers to call *iBooks,* you can change the text size and fonts on the fly — quite useful for people with less than 20/20 vision.

- **Get the meaning of a word:** No more searching for a physical dictionary. You can look up an unfamiliar word on the spot.

- **Search with ease:** Need to do research on a particular subject? Enter a search term to find each and every mention of the subject in the book you're reading.

- **Read in the dark:** The iPad has a high-resolution backlit display so that you can read without a lamp nearby, which is useful in bed when your partner is trying to sleep.

- **See all the artwork in color:** Indeed, you're making no real visual sacrifices anymore. For example, the latest iBooks software from Apple lets you experience (within certain limits) the kind of stunning art book once reserved for a coffee table. Or you can display a colorful children's picture book.

Truth is, there are two sides to this backlit story. The grayscale electronic ink displays found on Amazon's Kindle and several other e-readers may be easier on the eyes and reduce fatigue, especially if you read for hours on end. And although you may indeed have to supply your own lighting source to read in low-light situations, those screens are easier to see than the iPad screen when you're out and about in bright sunshine. And some newer E Ink-type readers from Amazon, Barnes & Noble, and others include displays that do light up.

You can *buy* an iBook using iTunes on your Mac or PC, but as we write this, you can't *read* that iBook using iTunes (or any other app we know of) on your Mac or PC. You can *read* iBooks from Apple's iBookstore only on an iPhone, iPad, or iPod touch.

Beginning the iBook Story

To start reading iBooks on your iPad, you have to fetch the iBooks app in the App Store. (For more on the App Store, consult Chapter 11.)

As you might imagine, the app is free, and it comes with access to Apple's iBookstore, about which we have more to say later in this chapter. For now, just know that iBookstore is an inviting place to browse and shop for books 24 hours a day. All the other books you end up purchasing for your iPad library turn up on the handsome wooden bookshelf, as shown in Figure 10-1.

Follow these guidelines to navigate the iBooks main screen:

- **Change the view:** If you prefer to view a list of your books rather than use this Bookshelf view, tap the button toward the upper-right corner of the screen (labeled in Figure 10-1). In this view, you can sort the list by title, author, or category (as shown in Figure 10-2), or you can rearrange where books appear on the bookshelf.

- **Rearrange books in Bookshelf view:** Hold your finger on the book you want to move. Wait a second or two and it will increase in size slightly to let you know it's now moveable. Without lifting your finger, drag the book to its new location and then release.

- **Rearrange books in List view:** Tap Edit (in the upper-right corner) and then press on the three horizontal lines to the right of the book you want to move. Now drag the book up or down the list.

- **Remove a book from the bookshelf:** In either view, tap Edit and then tap the book(s) you want to remove. Each book you tap displays a check mark; tap the book again to remove the check mark and thus deselect the book. When all the books you want to delete have check marks, tap the red Delete button at top left.

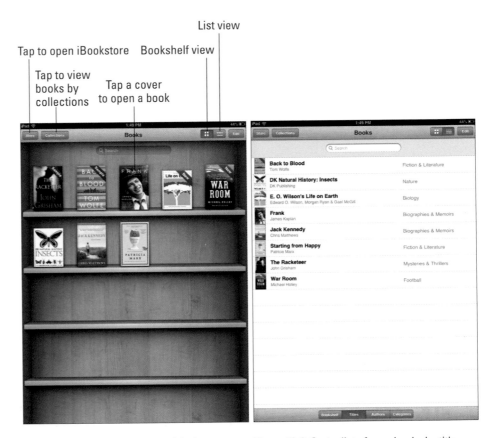

List view

Tap to open iBookstore   Bookshelf view

Tap to view
books by
collections   Tap a cover
to open a book

Figure 10-1: You can read a book by its cover.   Figure 10-2: Sort a list of your books by title,
author, category, or bookshelf.

As with other content you purchase from Apple, you can restore
(download) any book you've purchased from the Purchased tab of the
iBookstore.

✔ **Organize books by collections:** If you have a vast library of e-books, you
might want to organize titles by genre or subject by creating collections
of like-minded works. You might have collections of mysteries, classics,
biographies, children's books, how-to's, textbooks — even all the *For
Dummies* books you (hopefully) own. Apple has already created two collections on your behalf: books for all titles and PDFs for the Adobe PDF
files you may have on your iPad. (Apple doesn't let you edit or remove
the premade Books or PDFs collections.) To create, rename, or remove
a collection of your own, tap the Collections button (also labeled earlier,
in Figure 10-1) to show off your current list of collections and choose
from the following options:

- Tap New to add a new collection.

- Tap Edit and the red circle with the white dash to delete a collection. Tap Delete to finish the job.

  If the collection has books in it, you're asked if you want to remove the contents of this collection from your iPad. If you choose not to remove them, they're returned to their original collections (Books, PDFs, or any other collection).

- If you want to change the name of a collection, tap its name.

- If you want to move a book or PDF to a collection, go to the bookshelf, tap each work you want to move, and then tap Move. Select the new collection for these titles.

A book can reside in only one collection at a time.

Of course, here we are telling you how to move or get rid of a book before you've even had a chance to read it. How gauche. The next section helps you start reading.

Reading a Book

To start reading a book, tap it. The book leaps off the shelf, and at the same time, it opens to either the beginning of the book or the place where you left off. (And you may have left off on an iPhone, iPod touch, or another iPad because, via your Apple ID, your virtual place in a book is transported from device to device as long as both devices have an Internet connection.)

Even from the title page, you can appreciate the color and beauty of Apple's app as well as the navigation tools, as shown in Figure 10-3.

If you rotate the iPad to the side, the one-page book view becomes a two-page view, though all the navigational controls remain the same. On the newer multitouch books, you may have a scrolling view of a book (when you hold the iPad in portrait mode) rather than the typical one-page view. And you have the option of a scrolling display for any title by changing the Book theme to the Scroll theme. Tap the Fonts button, labeled in Figure 10-3, to do that.

While you're lounging around reading, and especially if you're lying down, we recommend that you use the Screen Rotation Lock (shown in Chapter 1) to stop the iPad from inadvertently rotating the display.

You can take advantage of the iPad's VoiceOver feature to have the iPad read aloud to you. It may not be quite like having Mom or Dad read you to sleep, but it can be a potential godsend for people with impaired vision. For more on the VoiceOver feature, consult Chapter 15.

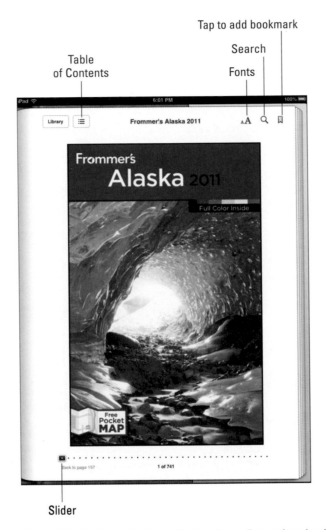

Table of Contents

Tap to add bookmark

Search

Fonts

Slider

Figure 10-3: Books on the iPad offer handy reading and navigation tools.

The VoiceOver feature is useful under certain circumstances. But we're not at the point where the iPad's loquacious virtual assistant Siri can read a book aloud. Maybe someday. For now, Siri can open the iBooks app, though. Read Chapter 14 for more on Siri.

Turning pages

You've been turning pages in books your entire life, so you don't want this simple feat to become a complicated ordeal just because you're now reading electronically. Fear not, it's not. You have no buttons to press.

Instead, to turn to the *next* page of a book, do any of the following:

- ✔ **Tap or flick your finger near the right margin of the page.** If you tap or flick, the page turns in a blink.

- ✔ **Drag your finger near the margin,** and the page folds down as it turns, as if you were turning pages in a real book.

- ✔ **Drag down from the upper-right corner of the book,** and the page curls from that spot. The effect is so authentic that you can make out the faint type bleeding from the previous page on the next folded-down page.

- ✔ **Drag up from the lower-right corner,** and the page curls up from that spot.

- ✔ **Drag from the middle-right margin,** and the entire page curls.

To turn to the *previous* page in a book, tap, flick, or drag your finger in a similar fashion, except now do so closer to the left margin. You'll witness the same cool page-turning effects.

That's what happens by default anyway. If you go into the main iPad Settings and tap iBooks under Apps on the left side of the screen, you have the option to go to the next page instead of to the previous page when you tap near the left margin.

The iPad is smart, remembering where you left off. So if you close a book by tapping the Library button in the upper-left corner or by pressing the main Home button, you automatically return to this page when you reopen the book. It isn't necessary to bookmark the page (though you can, as we describe later in this chapter). The lone proviso: You need an Internet connection when you "close" the book, because, otherwise, the server at Apple doesn't get the new bookmark info to pass on when you open the book on another device. And similarly, you need an Internet connection when you reopen it to retrieve the information that was passed on.

Jumping to a specific page

When you're reading a book, you often want to go to a specific page. Here's how:

1. **Tap anywhere near the center of the page you're reading to summon page navigator controls, if they're not already visible.**

   The controls are labeled earlier, in Figure 10-3.

2. **Drag your finger along the slider at the bottom of the screen until the chapter and page number you want appear.**

3. **Release your finger and — *voilà* — that's where you are in the book.**

Going to the table of contents

Most books you read on your iPad have tables of contents, just like many other books. Here's how you use a table of contents on your iPad:

1. **With a book open on your iPad, tap the Table of Contents button near the top of the screen.**

   The Table of Contents screen, as shown in Figure 10-4, appears.

2. **Tap the chapter, title page, or another entry to jump to that page.**

   Alternatively, tap the Resume button that appears at the upper-left corner of the screen to return to the previous location in the book.

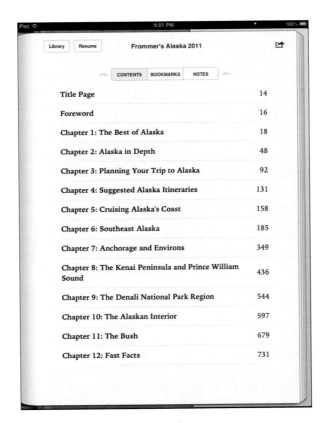

Figure 10-4: The table of contents for *Frommer's Alaska 2011*.

Adding bookmarks

Moving around to a particular location on the iPad is almost as simple as moving in a real book, and as we explain in the earlier section "Turning pages," Apple kindly returns you to the last page you were reading when you closed a book.

Still, occasionally, you want to bookmark a specific page so that you can easily return to it. To insert a bookmark somewhere, merely tap the Bookmark icon near the upper-right reaches of the screen. A red ribbon slides down over the top of the Bookmark icon, signifying that a bookmark is in place. Tap the ribbon if you want to remove the bookmark. Simple as that.

After you set a bookmark, here's how to find it later:

1. **Tap the Table of Contents/Bookmark button.**

2. **Tap Bookmarks (if it's not already selected).**

   Your bookmark is listed along with the chapter and page citations, the date you bookmarked the page, and a phrase or two of surrounding text, as the example in Figure 10-5 shows.

3. **Tap a bookmark to return to that page in the book.**

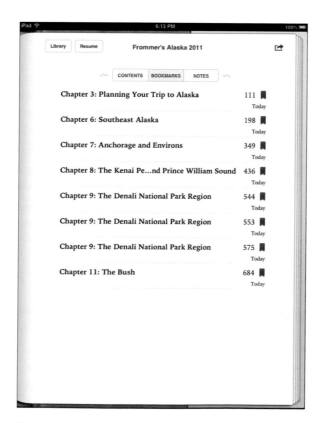

Figure 10-5: Finding the pages you bookmarked.

You can also remove a bookmark from the Bookmarks list by swiping your finger in either direction along a bookmark and then tapping the red Delete button that appears.

Adding highlights and notes

Bookmarks are great for jumping to pages you want to read again and again. Of course, you may instead want to highlight specific words or passages within a page. And sometimes you want to add your own annotations or comments, which is handy for school assignments. Pardon the pun, but Apple is on the same page. Here's how to do both:

1. **Press and hold your finger against any text on a page. Then lift your finger to summon the Highlight and Note buttons.**

   These two buttons appear side by side, sandwiched along with the Define and Search buttons that we address in a moment.

   You see grab points along the highlighted word.

2. **(Optional) Refine the highlighted section by expanding the grab points.**

3. **Choose a button to add a highlight or note:**

   - *When you tap the Highlight button,* the word or passage you selected is highlighted in yellow. You can later read the highlight by returning to the Table of Contents page in the same way that you find a bookmark. (See the preceding section, and refer to Figure 10-5.)

   - *Tap Note,* and a Post-it–like note appears on the screen. Using the virtual keyboard, type your note.

After you add a highlight or note, the following tips are handy to know:

- ✔ **To remove a highlight or note:** Tap the highlighted text or note and, from the toolbar that appears, tap the circle icon with a red line running diagonally inside. Alternatively, from the Highlights & Notes section under the Bookmarks list, swipe your finger in either direction along an entry and tap the red Delete button that appears.

- ✔ **To change the highlighted color of a highlight or note:** You can change the color from the default yellow to green, blue, pink, or purple. And you can underline. Touch the highlighted selection for a moment and lift your finger. From the toolbar, tap the icon with the color that you prefer.

- ✔ **To e-mail or print notes:** From the Table of Contents page, in the upper-right corner of the screen, tap the Action button (it looks like an arrow trying to escape a rectangle). Tap Email to e-mail your notes, or tap Print to print them (provided you have a compatible printer). See Chapter 2 for details about printing. Meanwhile, to see other possibilities for notes and iBooks generally, read the nearby sidebar, "The iPad goes to school."

The iPad goes to school

Apple has been pushing the use of the iPad in K–12 and higher education. As part of its vision for the iPad and with the iBooks 3 app, the company is throwing its considerable weight behind digital textbooks, works that include interactive captions, quizzes, 3D objects, and video. Apple even unveiled free software for the Mac, iBooks Author, to encourage teachers and others to produce their own interactive books for learning.

In the meantime, among the early high school textbooks produced for the iPad are titles that cover algebra, environmental sciences, physics, and other subjects.

E. O. Wilson's *Life on Earth* is an especially rich, interactive, digital biology textbook like none you've seen, from 3D models of DNA to animated maps of global photosynthesis. The introduction to the book was made available for free, after which you can purchase additional chapters as they're released — $1.99 as this book was being published. (In general, publishers will have to work out pricing on most of the emerging textbooks.)

Meanwhile, if a book supports it, you can turn your notes into study cards — a great way for students to learn vocabulary or prepare for exams. (If the option is available, you see an icon that looks like a notepad just to the right of the Table of Contents button.) You can swipe the cards to move from one to another, or tap a card to see one side with glossary terms or

material you've highlighted, on the other any notes you've supplied. At the time we wrote this book, there weren't a lot of new textbooks that supported Apple's vision. But with the backing of such prominent textbook publishers as Houghton Mifflin Harcourt, McGraw-Hill, and Pearson, it would appear to be only a matter of time. What's more, it's worth noting that some third-party publishers such as Kno and Inkling are also producing some very interesting interactive textbooks.

According to Apple, hundreds of thousands of books in the iBookstore can be used in school curriculums, including novels for English or social studies. It's also worth noting that some of the books are accessible via the iTunes U app.

As you consider these various efforts, we understand if you wish you had owned an iPad with digital textbooks back when you were in school.

We should also point out that although educational materials are the main impetus behind iBooks 2 and iBooks 3 for iPad, other books rich in audio, video, and other interactive materials take full advantage of Apple's latest software. One example: *George Harrison Living In the Material World,* a handsome $14.99 book written by the ex-Beatle's widow, Olivia Harrison. You can view it only on an iPad with iBooks 2 or later software.

Changing the type size, font, and page color
If you want to enlarge the typeface size (or make it smaller), here's how:

1. **Tap the Text Size and Fonts button, labeled earlier, in Figure 10-3, at the upper-right corner of the screen.**

2. **Tap the uppercase *A*.**

The text swells right before your eyes so that you can pick a size that's comfortable for you.

To make the font smaller, tap the lowercase *a* instead.

If you want to change the fonts, tap the Text Size, Themes, and Fonts button, and then tap Fonts and the font style you want to switch to. Your choices at this time are Original (the default), Athelas, Charter, Georgia, Iowan, Palatino, Seravek, and Times New Roman. We don't necessarily expect you to know what these look like just by their font names — fortunately, you get to examine the change right before your eyes. A check mark indicates the selected font style.

To change the page color, tap Theme and pick Normal (the default), Sepia, or Night. While you're there, you can slide the Full Screen button to On if you want more of the content to stretch out across the entire page. As we mention earlier in this chapter, you can also choose tap Themes and then Scroll to scroll while you're reading on a page.

Searching inside and outside a book

If you want to find a passage in a book but just can't remember where it is, try searching for it. Here's how:

1. **Tap the magnifying glass Search icon to enter a search word(s) or page number on the virtual keyboard that slides up from the bottom.**

   All the occurrences in the book turn up in a window under the Search icon, complete with a few lines of text and a page citation.

2. **Tap one of the items to jump to that portion of the book.**

   The words you were searching for are highlighted on that page.

You can also search the web (via Google) or the Wikipedia online encyclopedia by using the corresponding buttons at the bottom of the search results. If you do so, the iBooks app closes, and the Safari browser fires up Google or Wikipedia, with your search term already entered.

 If you search Google or Wikipedia in this fashion, you are, for the moment, closing the iBooks application and opening Safari. To return to the book you're reading, you must reopen the app. Fortunately, you're brought back to the page in the book where you left off.

Shopping for E-Books

We love browsing in a physical bookstore. But the experience of browsing Apple's iBookstore, although certainly different, is equally pleasurable. Apple makes it a cinch to search for books you want to read, and even lets you peruse a sample prior to parting with your hard-earned dollars. To enter the store, tap the Store button in the upper-left corner of your virtual bookshelf or your library List view.

A few things to keep in mind: The iBooks app and iBookstore are available to the United States, Canada, Australia, and 29 European countries, including the U.K., Germany, and France. Apple's iBookstore had more than 700,000 titles for U.S. customers at the time our book was being published, including some works — Jay-Z's memoir *Decoded,* for example — that are enhanced with video. Outside American soil, hundreds of thousands are available, Apple says. Folks can read iBooks in more than 40 languages. Meanwhile, the store includes titles from all six major trade publishers: Hachette Book Group, HarperCollins, Macmillan, Penguin Group, Simon & Schuster, and Random House, as well as several independents. John Wiley & Sons is also represented, of course. Random House had been the only holdout among big-name publishers when Apple first launched the iBookstore, but the largest trade-book publisher in the United States finally came aboard.

Publishers, not Apple, set the prices. Many bestsellers in the joint cost $12.99, though some fetch $9.99 or less. In fact, Apple even has a $9.99-or-less section, the virtual equivalent of the bargain rack. And free selections are available. On the other hand, Walter Isaacson's *Steve Jobs* bio commands $16.99.

Just browsing iBookstore

You have several ways to browse for books in the iBookstore. The top portion of the screen shows ever-changing ads for books that fit a chosen category, such as Children & Teens in the example shown in Figure 10-6, or All Categories. But you can also browse subsections. In the Children & Teens example, you see Recent Releases, New Teen Fiction, or, by scrolling down, Children's Picture Books. You see different choices, of course, in other categories. Choose Mysteries & Thrillers as the underlying category and you'll find the Hard-Boiled section. One subsection under Romance is Paranormal Romance (we won't comment). Tap See All for many more selections in whatever subsections you choose.

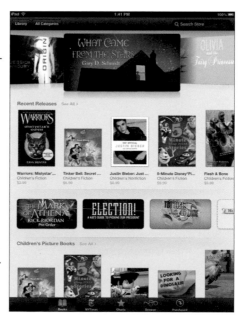

Figure 10-6: The featured Children & Teens page.

Look at the bottom of the screen. You see the following icons:

- **Books:** This is where you've been hanging out so far in this chapter. Featured works are the books being promoted in the store. These may include popular titles or an author spotlight from the likes of *Twilight* writer Stephenie Meyer. Swipe the featured books at the top of the screen for more choices. You can narrow your choices to fiction or non-fiction or tap More to choose by category. Tap See All for more selections.

- **NYTimes:** Short for *The New York Times,* of course. These books make the newspaper's famous bestsellers lists, which are divided into fiction and nonfiction works. The top books in each list are initially shown. Scroll down to see more titles.

- **Top Charts:** Apple shows you the most popular books in the iBookstore. You find a list for paid books and one for free books. Scroll down to see more of the top books in each category.

- **Top Authors:** Are you a fan of Stephen King? Or Barbara Kingsolver? Tapping the Top Authors icon lets you find books by poring through a list of popular authors, shown in a scrollable pane on the left half of the screen. Flick your finger up or down to scroll the list, or tap one of the letters in the margin to jump to authors whose name begins with that letter. When you tap an author's name, a list of his or her available titles appears in a scrollable pane on the right.

- **Purchased:** Tapping here shows you the books you've already bought, which you can download onto your iPad. In this area, you can also check out your iTunes account information, tap a button that transports you to iTunes customer service, and redeem any iTunes gift cards or gift certificates.

Searching iBookstore

In the upper-right corner of the iBookstore is the Search Store field, similar to the Search field you see in iTunes. Using the virtual keyboard, type an author name or title to find the book you seek.

If you like freebies, search for *free* in the iBookstore. You'll find tons of (mostly classic) books that cost nothing, and you don't even have to import them. See the section "Finding free books outside iBookstore," later in this chapter, for more places to find free books. By Apple's count, free content is distributed in 155 countries. Off the top of our heads, we can't remember how many countries are on Planet Earth. But it's fair to say that when it comes to digital books, Apple has most of them covered.

Deciding whether a book is worth it

To find out more about a book that you come across in the iBookstore, you can check out the detail page and other readers' reviews or read a sample of the book:

- ✓ **Find the book's details.** Tap its cover. An information screen appears with Details highlighted by default. You can see when the book was published, read a description, and more.

- ✓ **Find ratings and reviews.** Tap Ratings and Reviews to see the grades and comments bestowed on the book by other readers.

  You can throw in your own two cents, if you've already read it, by tapping Write a Review.

- ✓ **Find other books by the same author.** Tap Related to see the covers of other books written by the author.

- ✓ **Share your interest in a book.** Tap the Action button in the upper-right corner of the information screen. You can then sing the praises of a book by tapping icons for Email, Message, Twitter, and Facebook. You can also tap Copy Link.

Of course, the best thing you can do to determine whether a book is worth buying is to read a sample. Tap Sample, and the book cover almost immediately lands on your bookshelf. You can read it like any book, until that juncture in the book where your free sample ends. Apple has placed a Buy button inside the pages of the book to make it easy to purchase it if you're hooked. The word *Sample* is plastered on the cover on the bookshelf, to remind you that this book isn't quite yours — yet.

Buying a book from iBookstore

Assuming that the book meets or exceeds your lofty standards, and you're ready to purchase it, here's how to do so:

1. **Tap the price shown in the gray button on the book's information page.**

   After you do so, the dollar amount disappears, and the button becomes green and carries the Buy Book label. If you tap a free book instead, the button is labeled Get Book.

2. **Tap the Buy Book/Get Book button.**

3. **Enter your iTunes password to proceed with the transaction.**

   The book appears on your bookshelf in an instant, ready for you to tap it and start reading. You get an e-mail receipt acknowledging your purchase via the same mail account in which you receive other receipts from iTunes for music, movies, and apps.

If you buy another book within 15 minutes of your initial purchase, you aren't prompted for your iTunes password again.

Buying books beyond Apple

The business world is full of examples where one company competes with another on some level only to work with it as a partner on another level. When the iPad first burst onto the scene in early April 2010, pundits immediately compared it to Amazon's Kindle, the market-leading electronic reader. Sure, the iPad had the larger screen and color, but the Kindle had a few bragging points too, including a longer battery life (up to about a month on the latest Kindle versus about 10 hours for the iPad), a lighter weight, and a larger selection of books in its online bookstore.

But Amazon has long said that it wants Kindle books to be available for all sorts of electronic platforms, and the iPad, like the iPhone and iPod touch before it, is no exception. So, we recommend taking a look at the free Kindle app for the iPad, especially if you've already purchased a number of books in Amazon's Kindle Store and want access to that wider selection of titles.

The Barnes & Noble NOOK app is also worth a look. In fact, both Barnes & Noble and Amazon are competing against the iPad mini with smaller-screen (and less expensive) tablets: Nook Tablet and Kindle Fire and Kindle Fire HD, respectively. Google is doing the same with the Nexus 7 tablet (with its Google Play app).

Meanwhile, we haven't tried them all, and we know it's hard enough competing against Apple (or Amazon). But we'd be selling our readers short if we didn't at least mention that you can find several other e-book–type apps for the iPad in the App Store. As this book goes to press, you can have a look at the following apps, just to name a few:

- CloudReaders from Satoshi Nakajima (free)
- Free e-books by Kobo
- Stanza from Lexcycle (free), owned by Amazon
- Bluefire Reader from Bluefire Productions

See Chapter 11 for details about finding and downloading apps.

Finding free books outside iBookstore

Apple supports a technical standard — *ePub,* the underlying technology behind thousands of free public-domain books. You can import these to the iPad without shopping in the iBookstore. Such titles must be *DRM-free,* which means that they're free of digital rights restrictions.

To import an ePub title, you can download it to your Mac or PC (assuming that it isn't already there) and then sync it to the iPad through iTunes. There are other methods. If you have Dropbox, for example, you can bring an ePub into your account, and from Dropbox you can share the title with iBooks. You can also e-mail it as an attachment.

You can find ePub titles at numerous cyberspace destinations, among them

- **Feedbooks:** www.feedbooks.com
- **Google Play:** http://play.google.com/store/books (Not all the books here are free, and Google has a downloadable app.)
- **Project Gutenberg:** www.gutenberg.us
- **Smashwords:** www.smashwords.com
- **Baen:** www.baen.com

Also, check out the free titles that you can find through the apps mentioned in the previous section.

Reading Newspapers and Magazines

People in the newspaper business know that it's been tough sledding in recent years. The Internet, as it has in so many areas, has proved to be a disruptive force in media.

It remains to be seen what role Apple generally, and the iPad specifically, will play in the future of electronic periodicals or in helping to turn around sagging media enterprises. It's also uncertain which pricing models will make the most sense from a business perspective.

What we can tell you is that reading newspapers and magazines on the iPad is not like reading newspapers and magazines in any other electronic form. The experience is slick, but only you can decide whether it's worth paying the tab (in the cases where you do have to pay).

There are two paths you might follow to subscribe to or read a single issue of a newspaper or magazine. The first path includes several fine publishing apps worth checking out, including *USA TODAY* (where Ed works), *The Wall Street Journal*, *TIME* magazine, *The New York Times*, *The New Yorker*, *Reuters News Pro*, *BBC News*, *Vanity Fair*, and *Popular Science*. We also highly recommend fetching the free Zinio app, which offers publications including *Rolling Stone*, *The Economist*, *Macworld*, *Newsweek*, *PC Magazine Digital Edition*, *Car and Driver*, *National Geographic Interactive*, *Spin*, *Bloomberg Businessweek*, and many more. You can buy single issues of a magazine or subscribe, and you can sample and share a certain number of articles without a subscription.

You have to pay handsomely or subscribe to some of these newspapers and magazines, which you find not in the iBookstore but in the regular App Store, which we cover in Chapter 11. You also see ads (somebody has to pay the freight).

The second path is Newsstand. This handy icon on your Home screen purports to gather all your newspaper and magazine subscriptions in a single place. Newsstand is a special type of folder rather than an app.

You purchase subscriptions in a section of the App Store, which you can also get to by tapping Newsstand on your Home screen and then tapping the Store button, which opens the App Store (see Chapter 11) to the new Subscriptions section.

Numerous publications have adopted the Newsstand paradigm, though some choose custom apps or Zinio, and many do both.

Part IV
The iPad mini at Work

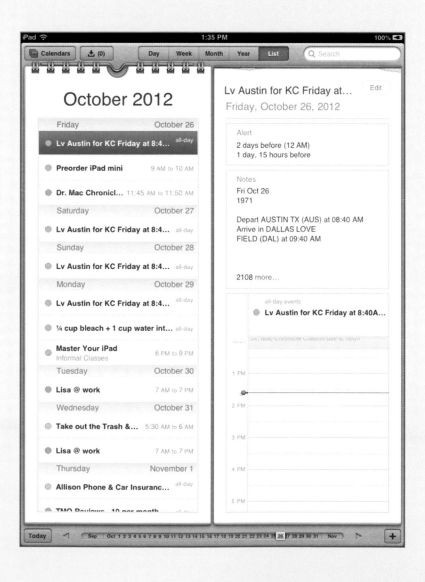

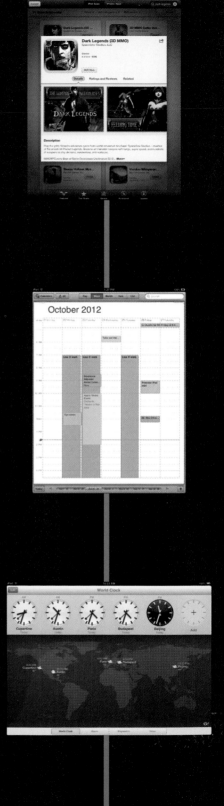

1 n Part IV, we look at some of the less-sexy but nonetheless useful features of your iPad. Indeed, we'd venture to say that few people got their iPad mini exclusively for its Calendar, Contacts, Notes, Reminders, Clock, or Game Center apps. And still, having these programs is awfully handy, and we use them every day.

We love going on a shopping spree as much as the next guy. Chapter 11 is all about finding out how to shop in the App Store, an emporium replete with a gaggle of neat little programs and applications. Best of all, unlike most of the stores you shop in, a good number of the items can be had for free.

Then we'll really get down to business and explore staying on top of your appointments and people with the Calendar and Contacts apps in Chapter 12. In Chapter 13, you discover other useful utilities such as the Reminders, Notes, and Clock apps, Notifications, and the Notification Center. A brief interlude on social media and instructions for using your iPad as an Internet hotspot close out the chapter.

Finally, in Chapter 14, you meet Siri, your (mostly) intelligent assistant. She responds to your voice and can do some amazing things, including sending messages, scheduling appointments and reminders, searching the web, playing a specific song or artist, and so much more.

11

Apply Here (To Find Out about iPad mini Apps)

In This Chapter

▸ Getting a handle on the different types of apps

▸ Searching for specific apps

▸ Getting apps onto your iPad

▸ Managing iPad apps

▸ Deleting and reviewing apps

*O*ne of the best things about the iPad is that you can download and install apps created by third parties, which is to say apps not created by Apple (the first party) or you (the second party). At the time of this writing, more than 700,000 apps are available in the iTunes App Store. Furthermore, iPhone, iPod touch, and iPad owners have downloaded more than 35,000,000,000 (yes, 35 *billion*) apps.

Many apps are free, but others cost money; some apps are useful, but others are lame; and most apps are perfectly well-behaved, but others quit unexpectedly (or worse). The point is that among the many apps, some are better than others.

In this chapter, we take a broad look at apps that you can use with your iPad. You discover how to find apps on your computer or your iPad, and you find some basics for managing your apps. Don't worry: We have plenty to say about specific third-party apps in Chapters 18 and 19.

Tapping the Magic of Apps

Apps enable you to use your iPad as a game console, a streaming Netflix player, a recipe finder, a sketchbook, and much, much more. You can run three categories of apps on your iPad:

✔ **Apps made exclusively for the iPad:** This is the newest kind, so you find fewer of these than the other two types. These apps won't run on an iPhone or iPod touch, so you can't even install them on either device. That said, there are already 275,000 of these puppies, with more arriving every day!

✔ **Apps made to work properly on the iPad, iPhone, or iPod touch:** This type of app can run on any of the three devices at full resolution. What is the full-screen resolution for each device? Glad you asked. For most iPhones and the iPod touch, it's 480 x 320 pixels; for the iPhone 4 or later, it's 960 x 640; for your iPad mini (as well as first- and second-generation iPads,) it's 1024 x 768 pixels; and the Retina display in the third- and fourth-generation iPads is a whopping 2048 x 1536 pixels.

✔ **Apps made for the iPhone and iPod touch:** These apps run on your iPad but only at iPhone/iPod touch resolution (480 x 320) rather than at the full resolution of your iPad (1024 x 768).

You can double the size of an iPhone/iPod touch app by tapping the little 2x button in the lower-right corner of the screen; to return the app to its native size, tap the 1x button. Figure 11-1 shows you what this looks like.

Frankly, most iPhone/iPod apps look pretty good at 2x size, but we've seen a few that have jagged graphics and don't look as nice. Still, with 700,000 or more to choose from, we're sure that you can find a few that make you happy.

You can obtain apps for your iPad in two ways:

✔ On your computer
✔ On your iPad

To use the App Store on your iPad, it must be connected to the Internet. And if you obtain an app on your computer, it isn't available on your iPad until you either sync the iPad with your computer or download the app from iCloud from the Purchased tab, covered later in this chapter. See Chapter 3 for details about syncing.

After you've obtained an app from the App Store on your computer or iPad, you can download it from iCloud to as many as ten iOS devices.

Figure 11-1: iPhone and iPod touch apps run at a smaller size (left), but can be increased to double size (right).

But before you can use the App Store on your iPad or your computer, you first need an iTunes Store account. If you don't already have one, we suggest that you launch iTunes on your computer or the App Store or iTunes app on your iPad. Here's how:

- ✔ **On your computer:** Launch iTunes, click Sign In near the upper-right corner of the iTunes window, click Create New Account, and follow the onscreen instructions.

- ✔ **On your iPad:** Tap Settings➪Store➪Sign In➪Create New Account and follow the onscreen instructions.

If you don't have an iTunes Store account, you can't download a single cool app for your iPad. 'Nuff said.

Using Your Computer to Find Apps

Okay, start by finding cool iPad apps using iTunes on your computer. Follow these steps:

1. **Launch iTunes.**

2. **Click the iTunes Store link in the sidebar on the left.**

3. **Click the App Store link.**

   The iTunes App Store appears, as shown in Figure 11-2.

4. **(Optional) If you want to look only for apps designed to run at the full resolution of your iPad, click the iPad tab at the top of the window.**

   Now you're ready to browse, search, and download apps, as we explain in the following sections.

App Store drop-down menu

App Store link   Search iTunes Store

iTunes Store (in sidebar)   iPad tab

Scroll bar

Figure 11-2: The iTunes App Store, in all its glory (with the iPad tab selected).

Browsing the App Store from your computer

After you have the iTunes App Store on your screen, you have a couple of options for exploring its virtual aisles. Allow us to introduce you to the various "departments" available from the main screen.

The main departments are featured in the middle of the screen, and ancillary departments appear on either side of them. We start with the ones in the middle:

- ✔ The **New and Noteworthy** department has 14 visible icons in Figure 11-2. These represent apps that are — what else? — new and noteworthy.

  Only 14 icons are visible, but the New and Noteworthy department actually has more than that. Look to the right of the words *New and Noteworthy.* See the See All link? Click it to see *all* apps in this department on a single screen. Or you can click and drag the scroll bar to the right to see more icons.

- ✔ The **What's Hot** department displays 14 icons (refer to Figure 11-2), representing apps that are popular with other iPad users. Again, you can see more of these icons by clicking and dragging the scroll bar to the right.

- ✔ The **Staff Favorites** department appears below the What's Hot department and isn't visible in Figure 11-2.

Apple has a habit of redecorating the iTunes Store every so often, so allow us to apologize in advance if things aren't exactly as described here when you visit.

You also see display ads for five featured items between the New and Noteworthy department and the What's Hot department (Games, Cookies, Real Racing 2, Solar Walk, and Education) in Figure 11-2.

Three other departments appear to the right, under the Top Charts heading: Paid Apps; one of our favorite departments, Free Apps; and Top Grossing Apps (which isn't visible in Figure 11-2). The number-one app in each department displays both its icon and its name; the next nine apps show text links only.

The App Store link near the top of the screen is also a drop-down list (as are most of the other department links to its left and right), as shown in Figure 11-2.

Using the Search field in the iTunes Store

Browsing the screen is helpful, but if you know exactly what you're looking for, searching is faster. Follow these steps to search for an app:

1. **Type a word or phrase into the Search field in the upper-right corner of the main iTunes window. Press Return or Enter to initiate the search.**

   In Figure 11-3, we searched for *flashlight*. You see results for the entire iTunes Store, which includes music, television shows, movies, and other stuff in addition to iPad apps.

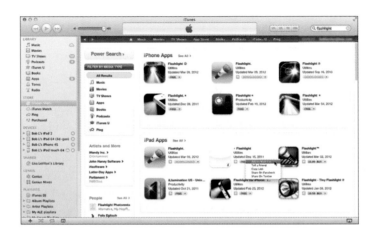

Figure 11-3: We want to use our iPad as a flashlight, so we searched for *flashlight.*

2. **Among your search results, find the category for iPad Apps (refer to Figure 11-3).**

   If you search for a common word such as *twilight* or *rat,* the screen displays choices from Albums, Songs, Movies, TV Shows, Music Videos, and more, so you might have to scroll down to see the iPad Apps section.

   Fortunately, you can also easily filter by media type. Just tap Apps in the Filter by Media Type list near the upper-left corner of the screen, and everything but iPhone and iPad apps disappears from the screen. Sweet!

3. **Click the See All link to the right of the words *iPad Apps* (refer to Figure 11-3).**

   All the iPad apps that match your search word or phrase appear on a single screen.

One last thing: The little triangle to the right of each item's price is another drop-down list, as shown for the Flashlight app in Figure 11-3. This drop-down list lets you give this app to someone as a gift, add it to your wish list (selected in Figure 11-3), send an e-mail to a friend with a link to it, copy the link to this product to the Clipboard so that you can paste it elsewhere, or share this item on Facebook or Twitter.

Getting more information about an app in the iTunes Store

After you know how to find apps in the App Store, this section delves a little deeper and shows you how to find out more about an application that interests you.

To find out more about an app, simply click its icon or text link. A detail screen, like the one shown in Figure 11-4, appears.

This screen tells you most of what you need to know about the application, such as basic product information and a narrative description, what's new in this version, the language it's presented in, and the system requirements to run it. In the following sections, you take a closer look at the various areas on the screen.

Finding the full app description

Notice the blue More link in the lower-right corner of the Description section in Figure 11-4; click it to see a much longer description of the app.

Figure 11-4: The detail screen for SketchBook Pro, a nifty drawing and painting app for your iPad.

Bear in mind that the application description on this screen was written by the application's developer and may be somewhat biased. Never fear, gentle reader: In an upcoming section, we show you how to find reviews of the application — written by people who have used it (and, unfortunately, sometimes people who haven't).

Understanding the app rating

Notice that the SketchBook Pro app is rated 4+, as you can see below the Buy App button in the upper-left corner of the screen (refer to Figure 11-4). The rating indicates that this app contains no objectionable material. Here are the other possible ratings:

- **9+:** May contain mild or infrequent occurrences of cartoon, fantasy, or realistic violence; or infrequent or mild mature, suggestive, or horror-themed content that may not be suitable for children younger than the age of 9.

- ✔ **12+:** May contain infrequent mild language; frequent or intense cartoon, fantasy, or realistic violence; mild or infrequent mature or suggestive themes; or simulated gambling that may not be suitable for children younger than the age of 12.

- ✔ **17+:** May contain frequent and intense offensive language; frequent and intense cartoon, fantasy, or realistic violence; mature, frequent, and intense mature, suggestive, or horror-themed content; sexual content; nudity; or depictions of alcohol, tobacco, or drugs that may not be suitable for children younger than the age of 17. You must be at least 17 years old to purchase games with this rating.

Following related links

Just below the application description, notice the collection of useful links, such as the Autodesk Inc. Web Site link and the SketchBook Pro for iPad Support link. We urge you to explore these links at your leisure.

Checking requirements and device support for the app

Last but not least, remember the three categories of apps we mention earlier in the chapter, in the section "Tapping the Magic of Apps"? If you look below the rating in Figure 11-4 (Rated 4+), you can see the requirements for this particular app. Because it says `Compatible with iPad. Requires iOS 3.2 or later` and doesn't mention the iPhone or iPod touch, this app falls into the first category — apps made exclusively for the iPad. Another clue that it falls into the first category is that it says `iPad Screenshots` above the two pictures shown in Figure 11-4.

If the app belonged to the second or third category — apps made to work properly on an iPad, iPhone, or iPod touch, or apps made for the iPhone or iPod touch — it would say `Compatible with iPhone, iPod touch, and iPad` rather than `Compatible with iPad`.

Now you're probably wondering how you can tell whether an app falls into the second or third category. The first clue is the little gray plus sign (+) next to the price, which appears for many of the apps shown earlier, in Figure 11-3. Apps with this symbol are universal and run at full resolution on iPhones and iPads. Another clue is to look at the screen shots. If you see *two* tabs — iPhone and iPad — after *Screenshots,* the app will work at the full resolution of an iPad, iPhone, or iPod touch. Conversely, if you see only one tab that says `iPhone Screenshots`, the app will run at iPhone/iPod touch resolution on your iPad.

One way to ensure that you look only for apps that take advantage of your iPad's big screen is to click the iPad tab on the front page of the App Store (refer to Figure 11-2). All the apps displayed under the iPad tab are of the first or second type and are designed to take advantage of your iPad's larger screen.

Reading reviews

If you scroll down the detail screen, near the bottom you find a series of customer reviews written by users of this app. You can see the first of these in Figure 11-4. Each review includes a star rating, from zero to five. If an app is rated four or higher, as SketchBook Pro is, the app is well-liked by people who use it.

In Figure 11-4, you can see that this application has an average rating for the current version of 4½ stars based on 52 user ratings. Its average rating for all versions is 4 stars based on 2,910 user ratings. That means it's probably a pretty good app.

You see a few more reviews with star ratings below the review shown in Figure 11-4. If you care to read even more reviews than are shown on the detail page, click the small buttons on the right side of the Customer Reviews section — Back, 1, 2, 3, and Next — to navigate to the second page of comments for this app.

Finally, just above these icons is a pop-up Sort By menu that says Most Helpful in Figure 11-4. This menu lets you sort the customer reviews by your choice of Most Helpful, Most Favorable, Most Critical, or Most Recent.

Don't believe everything you read in reviews. Some people buy an app without reading its description or try to use it without following the included instructions. Then when the app doesn't do what they expected, they give it a low rating. The point is, take the ratings and reviews with a grain of salt.

Downloading an app from the iTunes Store

This part is simple. When you find an app you want to try while browsing the App Store on your computer, simply click the app's Free App or Buy App button. When you do so, you have to log on to your iTunes Store account, even if the app is free.

After you log on, the app begins downloading. When it's finished, it appears in the Apps section of your iTunes library, as shown in Figure 11-5.

If an app costs money, you'll get a receipt for it via e-mail, usually within 24 hours.

Downloading an app to your iTunes library is only the first half of getting it onto your iPad. After you download an app, you can sync your iPad so that the app will be available on it. Chapter 3 covers syncing in detail. You can also get the app via the App Store's Purchased tab (described later in this chapter) or by enabling automatic downloads on the Settings app's Store pane or the iTunes Preferences Store tab on your computer.

Figure 11-5: Apps that you download appear in the Apps section of your iTunes library.

If you want apps to download to your iPad automatically regardless of which device you used to purchase the app, you can set that up:

- **On a computer:** Connect your iPad via either USB cable or Wi-Fi. Launch iTunes and click your iPad's name in the sidebar on the left. Click the Apps tab and select the Automatically Sync New Apps check box.

- **On your iPad:** Tap Settings⇨Store. Then turn on the switch for Apps in the Automatic Downloads section.

You can enable Automatic Downloads for Music and Books on your iPad (but not in iTunes).

By the way, if your iTunes App library doesn't look like ours (with big icons in a grid pattern), click the third icon from the left in the quartet of icons to the left of the Search field, near the top of the iTunes window. Just so you know, the leftmost icon displays your apps in a list; the next one shows them in a list with icons; the third one displays them as a grid; and the rightmost icon displays your apps in Cover Flow view.

Updating an app from the iTunes Store

Every so often, the developer of an iPad app releases an update. Sometimes these updates add new features to the app, sometimes they squash bugs, and sometimes they do both. In any event, updates are usually good for you and your iPad, so it makes sense to check for them every so often.

To do this in iTunes, try any of the following methods:

- ✔ Click the Check for Updates link near the lower-right corner of the Apps screen. Note that if any updates are available, this link tells you how many (eight updates are available in Figure 11-5) instead of Check for Updates.
- ✔ Look at the little number in a circle next to the Apps item in the iTunes sidebar (which is 8 in Figure 11-5).
- ✔ Check the App Store icon on your iPad — it sprouts a little number in a circle in its upper-right corner when updates are waiting.

To grab any available updates, either click the Download All Free Updates button or click the Get Update button next to each individual app. After you download an update this way, it replaces the older version on your iPad automatically the next time you sync. Or if you've enabled automatic downloads for apps as described earlier in this chapter, the new app replaces the old app automatically.

If you click the Get More Apps link, shown in the lower-right corner of Figure 11-5, next to the Check for Updates link, you find yourself back at the main screen of the iTunes App Store (refer to Figure 11-2).

Using Your iPad to Find Apps

Finding apps with your iPad is almost as easy as finding them by using iTunes. The only requirement is that you have an Internet connection of some sort — Wi-Fi or cellular data network — so that you can access the iTunes App Store and browse, search, download, and install apps.

Browsing the App Store on your iPad

To get started, tap the App Store icon on your iPad's Home screen. After you launch the App Store, you see five icons at the bottom of the screen, representing five ways to interact with the store, as shown in Figure 11-6. The first four icons at the bottom of the screen — Featured, Genius, Top Charts, and Purchased — offer four different ways to browse the virtual shelves of the App Store. (The fifth icon we cover a little later, in the section "Updating an app from the App Store.")

Figure 11-6: The icons across the bottom represent the five sections of the App Store.

The first four icons are described in this list:

- ✔ The **Featured** section has five tabs at the top of the screen: All Categories, Games, Education, Newsstand, and More (refer to Figure 11-6) in portrait mode. In landscape mode, the Newsstand category is missing.

- ✔ The **Charts** section offers lists of the Top Paid iPad apps and the Top Free iPad apps. These are, of course, the most popular apps that either cost money or don't.

  In the upper-left corner of the Charts screen is a Categories button. Tap it and you see a list of categories such as Books, Education, Games, Music, News, and Productivity, to name a few. Tap one of these categories to see the Top Paid and Top Free iPad apps for that category.

- ✔ The **Genius** section has two tabs at the top: The iPad Apps tab displays the Genius's app recommendations based on the apps you already own. The iPad Upgrades tab has upgrades to the iPad version of your iPhone apps. Tap the Categories button in the upper-left corner to restrict the results on either tab to a particular category.

- ✔ The **Purchased** section displays all your iPad apps — the ones currently installed on this iPad and any that you've purchased that aren't installed. To the right of each app, you see either *Installed* or *iCloud* (as shown in the margin). To install an uninstalled app, tap its iCloud button and then type your password.

Most pages in the App Store display more apps than can fit on the screen at once. For example, the New and Noteworthy section in Figure 11-6 contains more than the nine apps you can see. A few tools help you navigate the multiple pages of apps:

- ✓ **Swipe from right to left** to see more apps in a category, such as New and Noteworthy.
- ✓ **Swipe up the screen** to see additional categories.
- ✓ **Tap the See All link** (top right of most sections) to see all the apps in that section on a single screen.

Using the Search field in the App Store

If you know exactly what you're looking for (or even approximately what you're looking for), rather than simply browse, you can tap the Search field in the upper-right corner of the iPad screen and type a word or phrase; then tap the Search key on the keyboard to initiate the search.

Finding details about an app in the App Store

Now that you know how to find apps in the App Store, the following sections show you how to find out more about a particular application. After tapping an app icon as you browse the store or in a search result, your iPad displays a detail screen, like the one shown in Figure 11-7.

The app description on this screen was written by the developer and may be somewhat biased.

The information you find on the detail tab for an app on your iPad is similar to that info on the iTunes screen on your computer. The links, rating, and requirements simply appear in slightly different places on your iPad screen. (See the section "Getting more information about an app in the iTunes Store," earlier in this chapter, for explanations of the main onscreen items.)

The Ratings and Reviews section differs most from the computer version. To read reviews from your iPad, tap the Ratings and Reviews button. If you scroll to the bottom of the page and see a More Reviews button, tap it to see (what else?) more reviews.

Figure 11-7: Dark Legends is an awesome, free, 3D Massively Multiplayer Online Role-Playing Game (MMORPG) for the iPad.

Downloading an app from the App Store

To download an app to your iPad (while using your iPad), follow these steps:

1. **Tap the price button near the top of its detail screen.**

   In Figure 11-7, it's the gray Free button. The button is replaced by a green Install App button.

2. **Tap the Install App button.**

3. **When prompted, type your iTunes Store account password.**

   After you do, the App Store closes, and you see the Home screen where the new app's icon will reside. The new app's icon is slightly dimmed and has the word *Loading* beneath it, with a blue progress bar near its bottom to indicate how much of the app remains to be downloaded, as shown in the margin.

Downloading other content on your iPad

You may have noticed that the App Store app on your iPad offers nothing but apps. iTunes on your computer, on the other hand, includes sections for music, movies, TV shows, books, podcasts, and iTunes U.

On your iPad, you obtain music, movies, and TV shows with the iTunes app, and books and magazines with the Newsstand app, which are both included with your iPad. To download podcasts or iTunes U content, however, you'll need the Podcasts or iTunes U apps, which (curiously) are not included with your iPad out of the box.

The good news is that both apps are free in the App Store, so if you want to shop for Podcasts or iTunes U content on your iPad, you should probably go download one or both apps now.

All these apps work much the same, so when you understand how to navigate the App Store app, you also know how to use all of the store apps.

4. **If necessary, if the app is rated 17+, click OK on the warning screen that appears after you type your password — to confirm that you're 17 or older — before the app downloads.**

The app is now on your iPad, but it isn't copied to your iTunes library on your Mac or PC until your next sync unless you've enabled automatic downloads. If your iPad suddenly loses its memory (unlikely) or if you delete the app from your iPad before you sync (as we describe later in this chapter, in the section "Deleting an app"), that app is gone. That's the bad news. The good news is that you can download it again from the Purchased tab, as described earlier in this chapter. Or the app will reappear spontaneously on your iPad if you've enabled automatic downloads.

Updating an app from the App Store

As we mention earlier in this chapter, every so often the developer of an iPad application releases an update. If an update awaits you, a little number in a circle appears on the Updates icon at the bottom of the iPad screen. (That number happens to be 2 in Figures 11-6 and 11-7.) Follow these steps to update your apps from your iPad:

1. **Tap the Updates icon if any of your apps needs updating.**

   If you tap the Updates button and see (in the middle of the screen) a message that says All Apps Are Up to Date, none of the apps on your iPad requires an update at this time. If apps need updating, they appear with Update buttons next to them.

2. **Tap the Update button that appears next to any app to update it.**

If more than one app needs updating, you can update them all at one time by tapping the Update All button in the upper-right corner of the screen.

If you try to update an app purchased from any iTunes Store account except your own, you're prompted for that account's ID and password. If you can't provide them, you can't download the update.

Working with Apps

Most of what you need to know about apps involves simply installing third-party apps on your iPad. However, you might find it helpful to know how to delete and review an app.

Deleting an app

The 20 apps that came with your iPad can't be removed, but you have two ways to delete any other app: in iTunes on your computer or directly from your iPad.

To delete an app in iTunes (that is, from your computer), click Apps in the sidebar and then do one of the following:

- Click the app to select it and press the Delete or Backspace key on the keyboard.
- Click the app to select it and then choose Edit⇨Delete.
- Right-click the app and choose Delete.

After taking any of the actions in this list, you see a dialog that asks whether you're sure that you want to remove the selected app. If you click the Remove button, the app is removed from your iTunes library as well as from any iPad that syncs with your iTunes library.

Here's how to delete an app on your iPad:

1. **Press and hold any icon until all the icons begin to wiggle.**

2. **Tap the little *x* in the upper-left corner of the app that you want to delete.**

   A dialog appears, informing you that deleting this app also deletes all its data, as shown in Figure 11-8.

Figure 11-8: Tap an app's little *x,* and then tap Delete to remove the app from your iPad.

3. **Tap the Delete button.**

   You can't delete any of the bundled apps that came with your iPad.

4. **To stop the icons from wiggling, press the Home or Sleep/Wake button.**

You also make icons wiggle to move them around on the screen or move them from page to page. To rearrange wiggling icons, press and drag them one at a time. If you drag an icon to the left or right edge of the screen, it moves to the next or previous Home screen. You can also drag two additional icons to the Dock (where Safari, Mail, Videos, and Music live) and have six apps available in the Dock that appear on all of your Home screens.

Friendly reminder: Rearranging your icons in iTunes is faster and easier than making them wiggle and move on the iPad. See Chapter 3 to find out how.

Writing an app review

Sometimes you love or hate an app so much that you want to tell the world about it. In that case, you should write a review. You can do this in two ways: in iTunes on your computer or directly from your iPad.

To write a review using iTunes on your computer, follow these steps:

1. **Navigate to the detail page for the app in the iTunes App Store.**

2. **Tap the Ratings and Reviews button and then click the Write a Review button.**

   You may or may not have to type your iTunes Store password.

3. **Click the button for the star rating (1 to 5) you want to give the app.**

4. **In the Title field, type a title for your review, and in the Review field, type your review.**

5. **Click the Submit button when you're finished.**

   The Preview screen appears. If the review looks good to you, you're done. If you want to change something, click the Edit button.

To write a review from your iPad, follow these steps:

1. **Tap the App Store icon to launch the App Store.**

2. **Navigate to the detail screen for the app.**

3. **Scroll down the page and tap the Write a Review link.**

   You probably have to type your iTunes Store password.

4. **Tap one to five of the stars at the top of the Write a Review screen to rate the app.**

5. **In the Title field, type a title for your review, and in the Review field, type your review.**

6. **Tap the Submit button in the upper-right corner of the screen.**

Whichever way you submit your review, Apple reviews your submission. As long as the review doesn't violate the (unpublished) rules of conduct for app reviews, it appears in a day or two in the App Store, in the Reviews section for the particular app.

People, Places, and Appointments

In This Chapter

▶ Understanding the calendar's different views and functions

▶ Mingling with Contacts

*W*e hate to break the news to you, but your iPad isn't all fun and games; it has a serious side. The iPad can remind you of appointments; help you keep all your contacts straight; and if you're willing to purchase iWork apps, deliver eminently usable spreadsheet, word processor, and presentation apps.

In this chapter, we explore Calendar and Contacts, a pair of apps that aren't particularly flashy but can be remarkably useful.

Working with the Calendar

The Calendar program lets you keep on top of your appointments and events (birthdays, anniversaries, and so on). You open it by tapping the Calendar icon on the Home screen. The icon is smart in its own right because it changes daily; the day of the week and date display.

Mac users can sync their calendars with either Calendar (known as iCal before OS X 10.8 Mountain Lion), Microsoft Outlook 2011 for the Mac, or the discontinued Microsoft Entourage; PC users can sync calendars with Microsoft Outlook. See Chapter 3 for more info on how to sync.

If you want to push your corporate calendar to your iPad, you can set it up at the same time you set up your mail. See Chapter 5 for the details.

Choosing a calendar to view

You have five main ways to peek at your calendar(s): Day, Week, Month, Year, and List views. Choosing one is as simple as tapping the Day, Week, Month, Year, or List button at the top of the Calendar screen. From each view, you can always return to the current day by tapping the Today button in the lower-left corner.

From a single calendar view, you can look at appointments from an individual calendar. Or you can consolidate several calendars — like one for home, one for your kid's activities, and one for your job — in a single view.

To pick the calendars you want to display, follow these steps:

1. **Tap the Calendars button at the upper-left corner of the screen.**

   That summons a Show Calendars overlay.

2. **Tap each calendar you want to view by tapping its entry.**

   A check mark appears. Tap an entry again so that a given calendar won't appear, and the check mark disappears. To show all the calendars, tap Show All Calendars. To make them disappear, tap Hide All Calendars. In the example shown in Figure 12-1, all the calendars are selected.

You can also choose to view your calendar(s) in different views:

   ✔ **List view:** List view isn't complicated. As its name indicates, List view, as shown in Figure 12-2, presents a list of current and future events on the left side of the screen, and an hour-by-hour view of the day that's highlighted on the right. About eight hours of the highlighted date are visible in landscape mode; about ten are visible in portrait mode. You can drag the list up or down with your finger or flick to rapidly scroll the list. To switch the day that's shown, tap the right or left arrow at the bottom of the screen, or tap or drag the timeline.

Figure 12-1: The check mark tells you that all of these calendars are visible.

✔ **Day view:** Day view, as shown in Figure 12-3, reveals the appointments of a given 24-hour period (though you have to scroll up or down on the right side of the screen to see an entire day's worth of entries). As in List view, you can drag or tap the timeline to move to a new date or tap the left or right arrows for the same purpose.

✔ **Week view:** As you'd expect, Week view (displayed in Figure 12-4) shows your events over a seven-day period. Again, use the arrows or timeline at the bottom of the screen to change the time frame that you see. Notice that the timeline reflects one-week intervals in Week view, which is the way it should be.

✔ **Month view:** By now, you're getting the hang of these different views. When your iPad is in Month view, as shown in Figure 12-5, you can see events from January to December. In this monthly calendar view, a colored dot (designating a specific calendar) and short description appear on any day that has appointments or events scheduled. Tap that day to see the list of activities the dot represents.

✔ **Year view:** Dates with events associated with them appear in color. The darker the hue, the more events you have on that date.

Figure 12-2: List view.

Figure 12-3: Day view.

Figure 12-4: Week view.   **Figure 12-5:** Month view.

Searching appointments

Consider that you scheduled an appointment with your dentist months ago, but now you can't remember the date or the time. You could pore through your daily, weekly, or monthly calendars or scroll through a List view until you land on the appointment. But that is the very definition of inefficiency. The much faster way is to simply type the name of your dentist in the Search box in the upper-right corner of the various Calendar screens or use the Spotlight search from your Home screen. You're instantly transported to the date and time of the entry from your current calendar view.

You can also use Siri to search for appointments. Use the word *appointment* or *calendar* and include a keyword or proper name or another type of identifying information.

Adding calendar entries

In Chapter 3, you discover pretty much everything there is to know about syncing your iPad, including syncing calendar entries from your Mac (using Calendar, iCal, or Microsoft Entourage) or PC (using Microsoft Outlook).

With the advent of iOS 5, you can create new calendars on your iPad; before, you had to create calendars on your Mac or PC and then sync them.

Of course, in plenty of situations, you enter appointments on the fly. Adding appointments directly to the iPad is easy. Just tap the Calendar app on your Home screen and follow these steps:

1. **Tap the plus sign (+) in the lower-right corner of the screen.**

   The Add Event screen, as shown in Figure 12-6, appears along with the virtual keyboard.

   If you use a Bluetooth keyboard (see Chapter 17), that pesky virtual keyboard stays out of your way so that you see more of whatever is on the screen.

2. **Tap the Title and Location fields, and finger-type as much (or as little) information as you feel is necessary.**

   If you don't type a title, your event is called New Event; the Location field is optional.

3. **Set the time for the entry by tapping the Starts/Ends fields and then proceeding as follows:**

   If your calendar entry has a start time or an end time (or both):

   a. *On the Start & End screen that appears (see Figure 12-7), choose when the event starts and ends.*

      Use your finger to roll separate wheels for the date, hour, and minute (in five-minute intervals) and to specify a.m. or p.m. It's a little like manipulating one of those combination bicycle locks or an old-fashioned date stamp used with an inkpad.

   b. *Tap Done when you're finished.*

   If you're entering a birthday or another all-day milestone:

   a *Tap the All-Day button so that On (rather than Off) displays.*

   b. *Tap Done.*

   Because the time isn't relevant for an all-day entry, note that the bottom half of the screen now has wheels for the month, day, and year, not for hours and minutes.

4. **When everything looks okay, tap Done.**

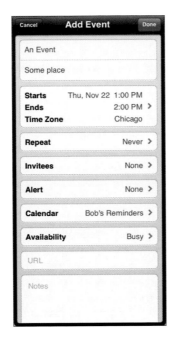

Figure 12-6: You're about to add an event to your iPad.

Figure 12-7: Controlling the Starts and Ends fields is like manipulating a bike lock.

That's the minimum you have to do. But you can do a lot more with your calendar event:

✔ **Set up your event as a recurring entry.** For anything that recurs at a set interval of time, such as an anniversary, tap the Repeat button, tap to indicate how often the event in question recurs, and then tap Done.

The options are Every Day, Every Week, Every 2 Weeks, Every Month, and Every Year.

✔ **Invite others.** Tap Invitees, and an invitation to the event is sent to everyone you specify.

Either type an e-mail address or tap the plus-sign-in-a-blue-circle button to select invitees from your contacts. You can add as many as you like; when you're done, tap Done. Your invitation e-mails are sent immediately (assuming that you've set up Mail properly on your iPad, as we explain in Chapter 5, and you have an active Internet connection, of course).

The invitees receive an invitation, as shown in Figure 12-8, which lets them add the event to their calendars and then accept or decline or say "Maybe" to the invitation.

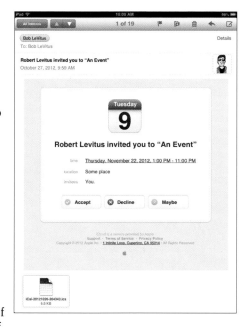

✔ **Set a reminder or an alert.** Tap Alert, tap a time, and then tap Done.

Alerts can be set to arrive on the actual date of an event, 2 days before, 1 day before, 2 hours before, 1 hour before, 30 minutes before, 15 minutes before, or 5 minutes before. When the appointment time rolls around, you hear a sound and see a message like the one shown in Figure 12-9. Tap View Event to check out the details of the appointment, or tap Close if you feel the reminder you just received will suffice.

Figure 12-8: A rather plain invitation, don't you think?

If you're the kind of person who needs an extra nudge, set another reminder by tapping the Second Alert field, which appears only after you've set one alert.

By the way, alerts don't always look like the one shown in Figure 12-9; check out Chapter 13 for details.

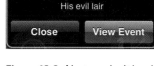

Figure 12-9: Alerts make it hard to forget.

✔ **Assign your event to a particular calendar.** Tap Calendar, and then tap the calendar you have in mind (Home or Work, for example), assuming that you have multiple calendars. Then tap Done.

✔ **Display this time as free.** It's displayed as Busy by default, so tap Availability and then tap Free.

✔ **Add notes or a URL.** If you want to enter a website URL or type some notes about the appointment or event, tap URL or Notes and type your URL or note on the virtual keyboard.

Click Done when you finish to save all your changes.

Setting your default calendar and time zone

Choose a default calendar by tapping Settings⇨Mail, Contacts, Calendars, and then flicking the screen until the Calendar section appears. Tap Default Calendar and select the calendar that you want new events you create on your iPad to appear on.

If you travel long distances for your job, you can also make events appear according to whichever time zone you selected for your calendars. In the Calendar settings, tap Time Zone Support to turn it on and then tap Time Zone. Type the time zone location on the keyboard that appears.

When Time Zone Support is turned off, events display according to the time zone of your current location.

Now that you have the hang of creating calendar entries, check out the following tips for working with your calendars:

- **Turn off calendar alerts** by tapping Settings⇨Notifications⇨Calendar⇨ None (for Alert Style).

- **Modify an existing calendar entry** by tapping the entry and then tapping Edit. The Edit window (which looks just like the Add Event window — refer to Figure 12-6) appears. Make whichever changes you need and then tap Done.

- **Wipe out a calendar entry** by tapping the entry, and then tapping Edit, and then tapping Delete Event. It's the last thing in the Edit window, so you may have to scroll down to see it. You have a chance to confirm your choice by tapping either Delete Event (again) or Cancel. To delete an entry in Day view, simply tap the event and then tap Delete Event. You don't need to tap an Edit button as well.

Responding to invitations

The Invitations button, which you find next to the Calendars button in the upper-left corner of the screen, enables you to see and respond to invitations you've received for events. You can also send an invitation when you create a calendar event, as we explain in the earlier section "Adding calendar entries."

If you don't see the Invitations button, tap Settings⇨Mail, Contacts, Calendars⇨New Invitation Alerts to make its blue On button appear.

You need an Internet connection to respond to an invitation. The following steps walk you through the process:

1. **Tap the Invitations button to view your pending invitations.**

   The Invitations button is next to the Calendars button in the upper-left corner of the screen.

2. **Tap any of the items in the list to see more details.**

   Suppose that a meeting invitation arrives from your boss. You can see who else is attending the shindig (by tapping Invitees); send them an e-mail, if need be; and check scheduling conflicts, among other options.

3. **Choose how to respond by tapping one of these buttons:**

   • *Accept:* Let the meeting organizer know you're attending.

   • *Decline:* Maybe you have something better to do (and aren't worried about upsetting the person who signs your paycheck).

   • *Maybe:* You're waiting for a better offer.

You can also import events from an e-mail. Open the message and tap the calendar file, which adheres to the `.ics` standard. When the events show up, tap Add All, choose the calendar you want to add it to, and then tap Done.

Subscribing to calendars

You can subscribe to calendars that meet the CalDAV and iCalendar (`.ics`) standards, which are supported by the popular Google and Yahoo! calendars, or iCal or Calendar on the Mac. Although you can read entries on the iPad from the calendars you subscribe to, you can't create new entries from the iPad or edit the entries that are already present.

To subscribe to one of these calendars, follow these steps:

1. **Tap Settings⇨Mail, Contacts, Calendars⇨Add Account⇨Other.**

2. **Choose either Add CalDAV Account or Add Subscribed Calendar.**

3. **Enter the URL of the calendar you want to subscribe to.**

4. **If prompted, enter a username, a password, and an optional description.**

   After you subscribe to a calendar, it appears just like any another calendar on your iPad.

   Calendars you subscribe to are *read-only*. In other words, you can't change existing events or add new ones.

Sifting through Contacts

If you read Chapter 3, on syncing, you know how to move the snail-mail addresses, e-mail addresses, and phone numbers that reside on your Mac or PC into the iPad. Assuming that you completed that drill already, all those addresses and phone numbers are hanging out in one place. Their not-so-secret hiding place is revealed when you tap the Contacts icon on the Home screen. The following sections guide you from the main screen to whatever you want to do with your contacts' information.

Adding and viewing contacts

To add contacts from within the Contacts app, tap the + button at the bottom of the screen and type as much or as little profile information as you have for the person. Tap Add Photo to add a picture from your photo albums (or to take a snapshot with your iPad camera). You can edit the information later by tapping the Edit button when a contact's name is highlighted.

A list of your contacts appears on the left panel of the screen, with the one you're viewing shown in blue; see Figure 12-10. On the right, you can see a mug shot of your contact, plus any info you have: phone number, e-mail address, home and another address, and birthday (all blurred in Figure 12-10 to protect Jacob's privacy). You also find an area to scribble notes about a contact.

You have three ways to land on a specific contact:

- **Flick your finger so that the list of contacts on the left side scrolls rapidly up or down,** loosely reminiscent of the spinning Lucky 7s and other pictures on a Las Vegas slot machine. (Think of the payout you'd get with that kind of power on a one-armed bandit.)

- **Slide your thumb or another finger along the alphabet on the left edge of the contacts list, or tap a teeny-tiny letter** to jump to names beginning with that letter.

- **Start to type the name of a contact in the Search field near the top of the contacts list. Or type the name of the place where your contact works.** When you're at or near the appropriate contact name, stop the scrolling by tapping the screen.

When you tap to stop the scrolling, the tap doesn't select an item in the list. This may seem counterintuitive the first few times you try it, but we've gotten used to it, and now we really like it this way.

You can change the way your contacts are displayed. Tap Settings➪Mail, Contacts, Calendars. Then scroll down to Contacts settings on the right side of the screen, if it's not already visible. Tap Sort Order or Display Order, and for each one, choose the First, Last option or the Last, First option to indicate whether you want to sort or display entries by a contact's first name or last name.

Figure 12-10: A view of all contacts.

Searching contacts

You can search contacts by entering a first name or last name in the Search field or by entering a company name.

You can locate people on your iPad without opening the Contacts app. Type a name in the Spotlight Search field (see Chapter 2), and then tap the name in the search results. And you can not only ask Siri to find people for you but also have her compose and send them an e-mail or iMessage or call them on the telephone or via FaceTime video chat.

If you're searching contacts with a Microsoft Exchange account, you may be able to search your employer's *Global Address List* (or GAL, for short). This search typically works in one of two ways:

➤ Tap the Groups button in the upper-left corner of the All Contacts screen and tap the appropriate Exchange server name to find folks. Groups on your computer might reflect, say, different departments in your company, friends from work, friends from school, and so on.

➤ You can search a so-called LDAP *(Lightweight Directory Access Protocol)* server. (It strikes us that nothing is "lightweight" about something called an LDAP server, but we digress.) Similarly, if you have a CardDAV account, you can search for any contacts that have been synced to the iPad.

Contacting and sharing your contacts

You can initiate an e-mail from within Contacts by tapping an e-mail address under a contact's listings. Doing so fires up the Mail program on the iPad, with the person's name already in the To field. For more on the Mail app, we direct you to Chapter 5.

You can also share a contact's profile with another person. Tap the Share Contact button (you may have to scroll down to see it), and once again the Mail program answers the call of duty. This time, the contact's vCard is embedded in the body of a new Mail message. Just address the message and send it on its merry way. A *vCard* is kind of like an electronic business card. You can identify it by its `.vcf` file format.

Finally, you can tap a contact's snail-mail address to launch the Maps app and see the address pinned to a map.

Linking contacts

The people you know most likely have contact entries in more than one account, so you might end up with redundant entries for the same person. The iPad solution is to *link* contacts. Find the contact in question, tap Edit, and tap the Silhouette icon with the + at the lower-right corner of the entry. Choose the related contact entry and then tap Link. It's worth noting that the linked contacts in each account remain separate and aren't merged.

Removing a contact

Hey, it happens. A person falls out of favor. Maybe he's a jilted lover. Or maybe you've moved across the country and no longer will call on the services of your old gardener.

Removing a contact is easy, if unfortunate. Tap a contact and then tap Edit. Scroll to the bottom of the Edit screen and tap Delete Contact. You get one more chance to change your mind.

13

Indispensible iPad mini Utilities

*W*e'd venture to say that no one bought an iPad mini because of Notes, Clock, Reminders, or Game Center. Still, these apps help make the iPad indispensable on a daily basis.

In addition to the indispensable apps described in this chapter, iPad mini owners are in for a treat because we demonstrate how to create a Wi-Fi hotspot no matter where you are — if you bought a Wi-Fi + Cellular model.

Taking Note of Notes

The *Notes* app lets you create text notes that you can save or send through e-mail. To create a note, follow these steps:

1. **Tap the Notes icon on the Home screen.**

2. **Tap the + button in the upper-right corner to start a new note.**

   The virtual keyboard appears.

3. **Type a note, such as the one shown in Figure 13-1.**

You can use Siri to set up your note, or employ dictation, too, which you can hear all about in Chapter 14.

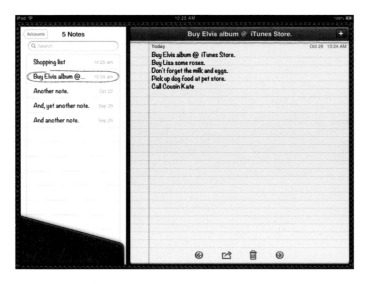

Figure 13-1: The Notes app, revealed.

Other things you can do before you quit the Notes app include

- Tap the Notes button in the upper-left corner of the screen to see a list of all your notes. If you sync notes with more than one account, such as iCloud, Google, or Yahoo!, you see buttons for All Notes as well as buttons for notes synced with each service.

- When the list is onscreen, just tap a note to open and view, edit, or modify it.

- Tap the left- or right-arrow button at the bottom of the screen to read the previous or next note.

- Tap the Action button at the bottom of the screen (it looks like an arrow trying to escape a rectangle) to send the note using the Mail or Messages apps (see Chapter 5 for more about Mail and iMessages), copy the note to the clipboard (see Chapter 2 for the scoop on copy and paste), or print the note (see Chapter 2 for more about printing).

- Tap the Trash icon at the bottom of the screen to delete the note.

Like most iPad apps, your notes are saved automatically while you type them so that you can quit Notes at any time without losing a single character.

We'd be remiss if we didn't remind you that you can sync Notes with your Mac and other devices via iCloud. We'd also be remiss if we didn't mention that unlike using other sync functions, you don't enable Notes syncing in iTunes. Instead, you enable it in Settings⇨iCloud on your iPad and System Preferences⇨iCloud on your Mac.

Finally, visit the Settings app's Notes pane to choose one of the three available fonts: Noteworthy, Helvetica, or Marker Felt.

And that's all she wrote. You now know what you need to know about creating and managing notes with Notes.

Remembering with Reminders

You can find lots of good to-do list apps in the App Store; if you don't believe us, try searching for *to-do list,* and you'll find more than 100 offerings for the iPad. Many of them are free, but others sell (and sell briskly, we might add) at prices up to $30 or $40.

Most of these third-party reminder apps have nothing to worry about from the Reminders app. Although some people may love it, we'd be remiss if we didn't point out your numerous other options in features not available from Reminders.

What you get for free is Reminders, a simple to-do list app for making and organizing lists, with optional "reminders" available for items in your lists.

Tap the Reminders icon on your Home screen, and you'll see something that looks like Figure 13-2.

Figure 13-2: The Reminders app.

Reminders on the right side of the screen in Figure 13-2 belong to the list labeled *Bob's To Dos Important Stuff,* which is highlighted on the left side of the screen.

Working with lists

You can have as many or as few lists as you like. Whatever you decide, you have to tap the Edit button, shown in Figure 13-2, to work with your lists. When you do, the left side of the screen converts to what we like to think of as Edit mode, as shown in Figure 13-3.

Here's a quick rundown of how it all works (after you tap the Edit button):

Figure 13-3: Tap the Edit button to create, delete, or reorder your lists.

- **Create a new list:** Tap Create New List, type a name for the list on the virtual keyboard, and then tap Done.

- **Delete a list:** Tap the red minus sign for the list. The sign rotates 90 degrees, and the Delete button appears next to the list's name (refer to Projects in Figure 13-3).

  You can also delete a list without first tapping the Edit button, by swiping the list from left to right. A red Delete button appears next to the list's name. Tap the button to delete the list, or tap anywhere else to cancel and not delete it.

- **Reorder (move up or down) lists:** Press and hold your finger on the three horizontal rectangles (shown in the margin) to the right of a list's name and drag the list up or down. When the list is where you want it to be, lift your finger.

Setting up reminders

Reminders is a simple app, and the steps for managing reminders are equally simple. Here's how to remind yourself of events with the Reminders app:

1. **To create a new reminder, tap the + button in the upper-right corner (refer to Figure 13-2) or tap the first blank item in the Reminder list.**

   The virtual keyboard appears.

2. **Type a title for the new reminder and then tap the Return key.**

   You can dictate your reminder rather than type it, if you prefer. You can find out more about dictation in Chapter 14.

The item appears in the current Reminders list.

At this point, your reminder is bare bones, and its date, repeat, and priority options have not been activated.

3. **To activate any or all of these options, tap the reminder, and in the Details overlay that appears, tap Show More to see all the options.**

All options are shown in Figure 13-4, which is why you don't see the Show More button. Rest assured that if there were more to see, you'd see *Show More* below Notes and above Delete.

Your options include

- **Remind Me:** Tap it if you want to specify a day and time for this reminder.

  If you have an iPad with 3G or 4G, you can also set a location-based reminder. Just tap the At a Location switch to enable it, specify the location, and then choose When I Arrive or When I Leave.

Figure 13-4: Details for our shiny new reminder.

Location-based reminders will suck your iPad battery dry faster than almost anything else. Remember to mark location-based reminders as completed by tapping their check boxes when you finish them or else you'll be reminded of something you've already done every time you pass that location — and drain your iPad battery unnecessarily.

If you set a location-based reminder with an iPhone or any iPad with cellular, or with the Reminders app in OS X Mountain Lion, the reminder syncs with your Wi-Fi–only iPad mini, but without the location. In fact, you don't even see the At a Location switch if your iPad is Wi-Fi–only.

- **The Repeat button:** It wasn't there earlier, but it's there now. Tap it to set a second reminder for a different day or time.

- **Priority:** To specify a priority for this reminder, tap Priority. Select None, Low, Medium, or High.

- **List:** Tap it if you want this reminder to appear in a list other than the one it now appears in. Tap the list you want to move this reminder to.

4. **Tap the Done button in the upper-right corner after you've set all your options.**

Choose the list you want your new reminder to appear on *before* you create it.

Viewing and checking off reminders

After you create reminders, the app helps you see what you have and haven't done and offers a few other tools that are good to know about:

- **Check off reminders.** You've probably noticed that every reminder you create includes a check box to its left. You may have also noticed a list named Completed above all the other lists. In fact, if you harken back to Figure 13-3, you can see that unlike other lists, *it cannot be deleted* — your Reminders app keeps track of completed tasks for you, moving them from the list you put them on to the Completed list.

  So that's what happens when you select that little check box. Furthermore, if you deselect that box, your reminder jumps right back onto the list it came from.

- **Search reminders.** To search for a word or phrase in all your reminders, completed or not, tap the Search field at the upper left, type your word or phrase, and then tap the Search key. Or from the Home screen, swipe right to search for it with Spotlight.

- **Keep reminders on your Mac or PC.** You can create reminders on your Mac or PC with to-do items in iCal (Lion) or Reminders (Mountain Lion) or Tasks in Outlook. And if you're using iCloud, your reminders will always be up to date on all your devices.

That's about it. The Reminders app isn't a bad effort. If it lacks a feature or two that you desire, we remind you to check out the myriad third-party to-do list apps in the App Store.

Negotiating the Notification Center

The Notification Center, shown in Figure 13-5, drops down over whatever you're doing at the time so that you can easily see calendar entries, reminders, and new e-mail messages. The Notification Center works regardless of which app you're using. To summon the Notification Center to the forefront of your iPad screen, all you need is the magical incantation — that is, a swipe from the top of the screen downward. Go ahead and give it a try. We'll wait.

iOS 5 also introduced an alternative notification style, known as the *banner,* shown from the Lock screen in Figure 13-6.

Banner notifications are sweet, and we're particularly fond of sliding our finger to view a particular item. But we digress. You find out how to enable or disable banner notifications in Chapter 15.

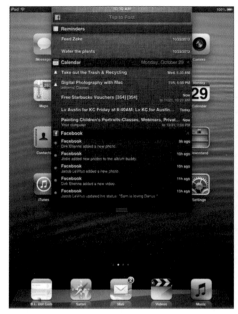
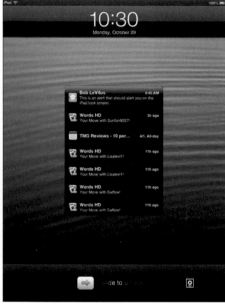

Figure 13-5: The Notification Center, in all its splendor.

Figure 13-6: Banner notifications on the Lock screen; slide your finger on one to open it.

Here's what you need to know about navigating the Notification Center:

- ✔ **Close the Notification Center.** Either drag the three little gray lines (at the bottom of the list) upward or tap anywhere outside the list.
- ✔ **Open a notification.** Tap it, and it opens in the appropriate program.
- ✔ **Clear all notifications from a particular app.** Tap the little *x* in a circle to the right of the app's name. (Refer to Calendar and Reminders in Figure 13-5.) Tapping the *x* turns it into a Clear button. (Look at Mail in Figure 13-5.)

  Tap the Clear button, and all the notifications from that app are cleared. The app's name then disappears from the Notification Center, though it reappears if and when the app needs to notify you.

That's how to summon and use the Notification Center. There's still a bit more — including how to change the notification settings for individual apps — see the Settings chapter (which happens to be Chapter 15).

Punching the Clock

We hear you: "So the iPad now has a clock. Big whoop. Doesn't every tablet have a clock?"

Well, yes, most tablets do have clocks. But not every tablet has a *world clock* that lets you display the time in multiple cities on multiple continents. And not every device also has an alarm, a stopwatch, and a timer to boot.

Let's take a look at the time functions on your iPad.

World clock

Want to know the time in Beijing or Bogota? Tapping World Clock (inside the Clock app) lets you display the time in numerous cities around the globe, as shown in Figure 13-7. When the clock face is dark, it's nighttime in the city you chose; if the face is white, it's daytime outside.

Figure 13-7: What time is it in Budapest?

Tap the + in the middle of the clock in the upper-right corner of the screen (the one that says *Add*) to add a new city, and then use the virtual keyboard to start typing a city name, as shown in Figure 13-8.

If there isn't a clock with a + in the upper-right corner, you probably have six or more clocks already. To see the rest of the clocks and the clock with the + button, swipe the clocks from left to right.

The moment you press the first letter, the iPad displays a list of cities or countries that begin with that letter. So, as Figure 13-8 shows, typing V brings up Andorra la Vella, Andora; Bantam Village, Cocos (Keeling) Islands; and Boa Vista, Brazil, among myriad other possibilities. You can create clocks for as many cities as you like, though only six cities at a time appear onscreen.

To remove a city from the list, tap Edit and then tap the red circle with the white horizontal line that appears to the left of the city you want to drop. Then tap Delete.

You can also rearrange the order of the cities displaying the time. Tap Edit, and then press your finger against the symbol with three horizontal lines to the right of the city you want to move up or down in the list. Then drag the city to its new spot.

Figure 13-8: Clocking in around the world.

Alarm

Ever try to set the alarm in a hotel room? It's remarkable how complicated setting an alarm can be, on even the most inexpensive clock radio. Like almost everything else, the procedure is dirt-simple on the iPad:

1. **Tap Clock on the Home screen to display the Clock app.**
2. **Tap the Alarm icon at the bottom of the screen.**
3. **Tap the + button in the upper-right corner of the screen.**
4. **Choose the time of the alarm by rotating the wheel in the bottom half of the screen.**

   This step is similar to the action required to set the time that an event starts or ends on your calendar.

5. **Tap Save when the alarm settings are to your liking.**

That's what you can do with a regular alarm clock. What's the big deal, you say? Well, you can do even more with your iPad alarm:

- **Set the alarm to go off on other days.** Tap Repeat and then tell the iPad the days you want the alarm to be repeated, as in Every Monday, Every Tuesday, Every Wednesday, and so on.

- **Choose your own sound.** Tap Sound to choose the tone that will wake you up. You can even use custom ringtones.

  Your choice is a matter of personal preference, but we can tell you that the ringtone for the appropriately named Alarm managed to wake Ed from a deep sleep.

✔ **Set the snooze to sleep in.** Tap Snooze to display a Snooze button along with the alarm. Tap the Snooze button to shut down the alarm for nine minutes.

✔ **Name your alarm.** If you want to call the alarm something other than, um, Alarm, tap the Label field and use the virtual keyboard to type another descriptor.

Simple stuff, really. But if you want really simple, you can ask Siri to set the alarm for you. See Chapter 14 to use Siri.

You know that an alarm has been set and activated because of the tiny status icon (surprise, surprise — it looks like a clock) that appears on the status bar in the upper-right corner of the screen.

An alarm takes precedence over any tracks you're listening to on your iPod. Songs momentarily pause when an alarm goes off, and they resume when you turn off the alarm (or press the Snooze button).

When your ring/silent switch is set to Silent, your iPad doesn't ring, play alert effects, or make iPod sounds. But it _will_ play alarms from the Clock app. And, although it seems obvious, if you want to _hear_ an alarm, you have to make sure that the iPad volume is turned up.

Stopwatch

If you're helping a loved one train for a marathon, the iPad Stopwatch function can provide an assist. Open it by tapping Stopwatch in the Clock app.

Just tap Start to begin the count, and then tap Stop when your trainee arrives at the finish line. You can also tap the Lap button to time individual laps.

Timer

Cooking a hard-boiled egg or Thanksgiving turkey? Again, the iPad comes to the rescue. Tap Timer (in the Clock app) and then rotate the Hour and Minute wheels until the time you have in mind is highlighted. Tap the Sounds button in the upper-left corner to choose the ringtone that will signify "time's up."

After you set up the length of the timer, tap Start when you're ready to begin. You can watch the minutes and seconds wind down on the screen, if you have nothing better to do. Or tap Pause to pause the countdown temporarily.

If you're doing anything else on the iPad — admiring photos, say — you hear the ringtone and see a Timer Done message on the screen at the appropriate moment. Tap OK to silence the ringtone.

Socializing with Social Media Apps

At first glance, it appears the iPad is light on social media support. What we mean is that Game Center is really the only sign of social media on a brand-new iPad.

Still, your iPad mini is much more friendly to social media than it appears at first glance. Although your iPad doesn't come supplied with official Facebook or Twitter apps, support for the two most popular social networks is baked right into iOS 6.

You can find free apps for these social media networks (and many others) in the App Store, but iOS 6 lets you install the Facebook and Twitter apps without even having to visit the App Store. Just tap Settings⇨Facebook (or Twitter), and then tap the Install button to install the app.

You don't necessarily need an app to participate in social networking. The networks we talk about in this section can be fully utilized using Safari on your iPad. And frankly, unlike the iPhone, where the Safari experience is hampered by the tiny screen and keyboard, the websites are eminently usable on your iPad. So, if you want to check them out and don't feel like downloading their apps, here are their URLs:

- **Facebook:** www.facebook.com
- **Twitter:** http://twitter.com

We'd be remiss if we didn't at least point out some of the niceties you get when you access one of these social media networks using an app instead of a browser, so the following sections offer a few of our insights.

The first thing to do, regardless of whether you intend to use the apps, is to tap Settings⇨Facebook and Settings⇨Twitter and provide your username and password for each service you intend to use. This will let you share photos, maps and directions, videos, URLs, and much more by tapping the Share button (shown in the margin) and then tapping the icon for Facebook or Twitter.

Facebook

The Facebook iPad app, as shown in Figure 13-9, makes it easy to access the most popular Facebook features with a single finger tap.

Note that the Facebook app has a slick interface with quick access to many popular Facebook features, as shown on the left in Figure 13-9.

On the other hand, Safari can't provide push notifications for Facebook events such as messages, Wall and Timeline posts, friend requests and confirmations, photo tags, events, or comments, whereas the iPad app does all that and more.

Figure 13-9: Bob's Facebook News Feed, as shown in the Facebook iPad app (left) and Safari (right); you can use either (or both) to get your Facebook fix.

The bottom line is that there's nothing to prevent having the best of both worlds. So if you're a heavy Facebook user, consider using the Facebook iPad app for some things (such as push notifications and status updates) and Safari for others (such as reading your Wall or News Feeds).

Twitter

Twitter puts a slightly different spin on social networking. Unlike Facebook, it doesn't try to be all-encompassing or offer dozens of features, hoping that some of them will appeal to you. Instead, Twitter does one thing and does it well: lets its users post short messages, or *tweets,* quickly and easily from a variety of platforms, including web browsers, mobile phones, smartphones, and other devices.

Twitter users then have the option of following any other Twitter user's tweets. The result is a stream of short messages, like the ones shown in Figure 13-10.

A tweet is 140 characters or fewer (including spaces). This tip, for example, is precisely 140 characters. Bottom line: Omit needless words.

Game Center

Game Center is the odd duck of the bunch. Unlike the other apps we cover in this section, Game Center has no website; you have to use the Game Center app that comes with your iPad. And unlike the others, which are broad-based and aimed at anyone and everyone, Game Center is designed for a specific segment of the iPad (and iPhone and iPod touch) universe — namely, users who have one or more games on their iPads (or other devices).

Mac users can get in on the fun, too, as long as they're using Mountain Lion, which includes a Game Center app that's similar to the one on your iPad.

Game Center acts as a match-up service, letting you challenge your friends or use its Auto-Match Invite Friend button to challenge a stranger who also happens to be looking for someone to play against.

Figure 13-10: The official Twitter iPad app, through the eyes of Bob (@LeVitus).

Game Center supports thousands upon thousands of games these days, some of which are shown in Figure 13-11.

Figure 13-11: Some of the games with Game Center support.

The games include many top sellers, such as *Angry Birds, Real Racing 2 HD, Fairway Solitaire,* and Bob's latest game obsession, the stunning *Infinity Blade II.*

Sharing Your Connection (Personal Hotspot)

The personal hotspot feature lets iPads with Cellular share their cellular high-speed data connections with other devices, including notebook computers, iPod touches, and other iPads.

To enable your personal hotspot and share your cellular data connection with others:

1. **Tap Settings on your Home screen.**

2. **Tap Personal Hotspot (or General⇨Network⇨Personal Hotspot).**

3. **Tap the Personal Hotspot switch to enable it.**

4. **Tap Wi-Fi Password to create or change the password for the Wi-Fi network you create.**

Now Wi-Fi, Bluetooth, or USB-enabled devices can join your hotspot network and share your iPad's cellular data connection.

Your personal hotspot network adopts your iPad's name, which is Bob L's iPad 64 (3d-gen) in Figure 13-12.

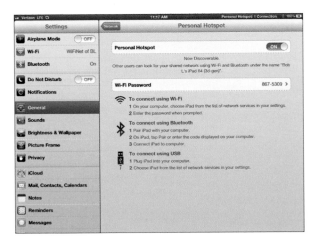

Figure 13-12: Devices can join this network via Wi-Fi, Bluetooth, or USB by following the appropriate connection instructions.

At the time we wrote this section, Apple hadn't released the iPad mini with Cellular. Our expectation is that the three wireless carriers selling the tablet (AT&T, Sprint, and Verizon) would offer the personal hotspot in the USA. But check with your carrier to make sure.

On the full-size iPad, Verizon doesn't charge extra for this feature, but the data used by connected devices counts as part of your monthly data plan allotment.

To see how much data you're using, tap Settings➪General➪Usage➪ Cellular Usage.

14

Taking the iPad mini Siri-ously

In This Chapter

▶ Calling Siri

▶ Determining what you can say

▶ Editing mistakes

▶ Using Dictation

▶ Making Siri better

How could you not love Siri? The intelligent, voice-activated, virtual personal assistant living like a genie inside the latest iPad not only *hears* what you have to say but also attempts to figure out the intent of your words. Siri then does her darnedest to respond to your wishes. She — yes, it's a female voice, at least when you choose U.S. English as your language — can help you dictate and send a message, get directions, tell you who won the ballgame, alert you when the movie is playing, search the web, find a decent place to eat, and lots more. Siri talks back, too, sometimes with humor and other times with attitude. When Ed once told Siri he was tired, she responded with, "That's fine. I just hope you're not doing anything dangerous."

Siri used to be available as a free third-party app on the iPad's cousin, the iPhone. Apple ended up buying the start-up company behind this neat technology and incorporating the magic inside the iPhone 4S. With iOS 6, Siri moved to iPad (third generation and later). And of course she's ready to serve you on your mini.

Apple concedes that Siri isn't perfect. In our experience, when Siri mishears us — sometimes more often than we'd like — it's because she didn't quite know what we had in mind. She also requires an Internet connection. But blemishes and all, we think she's pretty special, and we think you'll agree.

Summoning Siri

When you first set up the iPad mini, you have the option of turning on Siri. If you did so, you're good to go. If you didn't, tap Settings⇨General⇨Siri and flip the switch so that On is showing.

To call Siri into action, press and hold the Home button until you hear a tone, and then start talking. Pretty simple, eh? On the right side of the screen, you see a picture of a microphone inside a circle, as shown in Figure 14-1. The question "What can I help you with?" appears on the screen.

Tap here to see sample Siri queries.

Figure 14-1: Siri is eager to respond.

Siri also responds when you press a button on a Bluetooth headset.

What happens next is up to you. You can ask a wide range of questions or issue voice commands. If you didn't get your words out fast enough or you were misunderstood, tap the Microphone icon and try again.

Siri relies on voice recognition and artificial intelligence (hers, not yours). She'll respond in a conversational (if still ever-so slightly robotic) manner. But using Siri isn't entirely a hands-free experience. Spoken words are supplemented by information on the iPad screen (as you see in the next section).

Just where does Siri get that information? She seeks answers from the web, using sources such as Yelp, Yahoo!, OpenTable, and WolframAlpha, which you can read more about in the later sidebar. She taps into Location Services on the mini.

Siri on the iPad can open apps — Apple's own as well as third-party apps. Indeed, from your contacts, Siri might be able to determine who your spouse, co-workers, and friends are, and even know where you live. You might ask, "How do I get home from here?" and Siri will fire up Maps to help you on your way. Or you can specify, "Find a good Italian restaurant near Barbara's house," and Siri will serve up a list, sorted by Yelp rating.

Siri requires Internet access. A lot of factors go into her accuracy, including surrounding noises and unfamiliar accents. You also need to be comfortable with the fact that Apple is recording what you say.

Making your iPad (and other computers) really smart

Chances are you haven't heard of WolframAlpha. But if you want to know the gross domestic product of France or find events that happened on the day you were born, WolframAlpha can deliver such facts. You don't search the web *per se* on WolframAlpha as you would using a service such as Google. WolphramAlpha describes itself as a "new way to get knowledge . . . by doing dynamic computations based on a vast collection of built-in data, algorithms, and methods." It taps into knowledge curated by human "experts." So you can get nutritional information for peanut M&Ms or compute a growth chart for your 4-foot, 7-inch ten-year old daughter.

There's a reason that Siri relies on this "computational knowledge engine," which was driven over a period of nearly 30 years by supersmart guy Stephen Wolfram. We also recommend checking out the $1.99 WolframAlpha app for your iPad.

Figuring Out What to Ask

The beauty of Siri is that there's no designated protocol you must follow when talking to her. Asking, "Will I need an umbrella tomorrow?" as shown in Figure 14-2, produces the same result as "What is the weather forecast around here for tomorrow?"

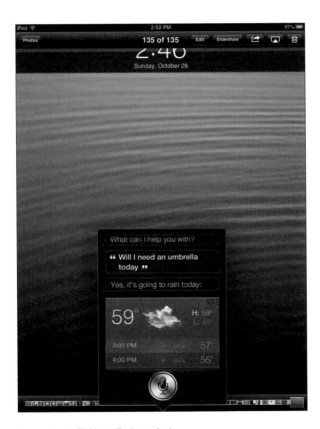

Figure 14-2: Siri can find you help.

If you're not sure what to ask, tap the circled *i* to list sample questions or commands, as shown in Figure 14-3. You can tap on any of these examples to see even more samples.

Figure 14-3: Siri can help out in many ways.

Here are some ways Siri can lend a hand — um, we mean *voice:*

- **FaceTime:** "FaceTime *phone number* my wife."
- **Music:** "Play Frank Sinatra."
- **Messages:** "Send a message to Nancy to reschedule lunch."
- **Calendar:** "Set up a meeting for 9 a.m. to discuss funding."
- **Reminders:** "Remind me to take my medicine at 8 A.M. tomorrow."
- **Maps:** "Find an ATM near here."
- **Mail:** "Mail the tenant about the recent check."
- **Stocks:** "What's Apple's stock price?"
- **Web search:** "Who was the 19th president of the United States?"

- ✔ **WolframAlpha:** "How many calories are in a blueberry muffin?"
- ✔ **Clock:** "Wake me up at 8:30 in the morning."
- ✔ **Sports:** "Who is pitching for the Yankees tonight?
- ✔ **Trivia:** "Who won the Academy Award for Best Actor in 2003?"
- ✔ **Twitter:** "Send tweet, `Going on vacation,' smiley-face emoticon.'"

Correcting Mistakes

As we point out, as good as Siri is, she sometimes needs to be put in her place. Fortunately, you can correct her mistakes fairly easily. The simplest way is to tap the Microphone icon and try your query again. You can say something along the lines of, "I meant Botswana."

You can also tap the bubble showing what Siri thinks you said, and make edits by using the virtual keyboard or by voice. If a word is underlined, you can use the keyboard to make a correction.

Before Siri sends a dictated message, she seeks your permission first. That's a safeguard you'll come to appreciate. If you need to modify the message, you can do so by saying such things as, "Change Tuesday to Wednesday" or "Add: I'm excited to see you, exclamation mark" — indeed, the phrase *I'm excited to see you* and an *!* will be added.

Using Dictation

The iPad mini offers a dictation function, so you can speak to your iPad and have the words you say translated into text. It's easy, and it usually works well. Even if you're a pretty good virtual-keyboard typist or you use a Bluetooth keyboard (see Chapter 17), dictation is often the fastest way to get your words into your iPad.

If you didn't enable dictation when setting up your iPad, here's how to enable it now:

1. **Tap Settings on your Home screen.**
2. **Tap General, and then scroll down and tap Keyboard.**
3. **Tap the Dictation switch to turn it on.**

When this feature is enabled, you can use dictation instead of typing whenever the virtual keyboard appears on the screen. Just tap the Microphone key on the keyboard and begin speaking when the Microphone icon pops out of the key, as shown in Figure 14-4.

Dictation works only if you're connected to the Internet. If you're not connected, the Microphone key is grayed-out.

Most apps display the Microphone key on the keyboard, but several, including Safari, don't. If you don't see the Microphone key, the app doesn't accept dictated input.

Figure 14-4: Tap the Microphone key to begin dictation; tap anywhere onscreen to end it.

Tap anywhere on the screen to end the dictation. Your iPad cogitates for a moment, displaying a purple ellipsis (three dots) where your words will be in a few more seconds. Then your words magically appear.

The purple filling inside the ellipsis denotes the relative loudness of your voice. If you're not getting good results, make sure you're not speaking too loudly (the icon fills up to the top with purple) or too softly (the icon shows little or no purple filling). If you see no purple filling, your microphone may not be working.

Here are a couple of ways you can improve your dictation experience:

✔ You can speak punctuation by saying it. Remember to say, "period," "question mark," or whatever at the end of your sentences. You can also insert commas, semicolons, dashes, and other punctuation symbols by saying their names.

✔ The better your iPad hears you, the better your results:

• A wired headset with a microphone is helpful when you have a lot of ambient noise nearby.

• A Bluetooth headset may be better than the built-in microphone.

• If you use the iPad's built-in mic, make sure the iPad case or your fingers aren't covering it.

Making Siri Smarter

From Settings, you can tell Siri which language you want to converse in. As of this writing, Siri was available in English (United States, Canada, United Kingdom, or Australia), as well as versions of Chinese, French, German, Italian, Japanese, Korean, and Spanish.

You can also request voice feedback from Siri all the time, or just when you're using a hands-free headset.

In the My Info field under Settings (tap General⇨Siri⇨My Info), you can tell Siri who you are. When you tap My Info, your Contacts list appears. Tap your own name in Contacts.

You can call upon Siri even from the Lock screen. That's the default setting, anyway. Consider this feature a mixed blessing. Not having to type a passcode to get Siri to do her thing is convenient. On the other hand, if your iPad ends up with the wrong person, that person can use Siri to send an e-mail, send a message in your name, post to Facebook, or tweet — bypassing whatever passcode security you thought was in place. If you find this potential scenario scary, tap Settings⇨General⇨Passcode Lock. Then enter your passcode and switch the Siri option under Allow Access When Locked from On to Off. For more on Settings, read Chapter 15.

Part V
The Undiscovered iPad mini

The 5th Wave   By Rich Tennant

"What I'm doing should clear your sinuses, take away your headache, and charge your iPad mini."

*T*his part is where we show you what's under the hood and how to configure your iPad mini to your liking. Then we look at the things to do if your iPad ever becomes recalcitrant.

In Chapter 15, we explore every single iPad setting that's not discussed in depth elsewhere in the book. The iPad offers dozens of different preferences and settings to make your iPad your very own; by the time you finish with Chapter 15, you'll know how to customize every part of your iPad that can be customized.

iPads are well-behaved little beasts for the most part, except when they're not. Like the little girl with the little curl, when they're good, they're very, very good, but when they're bad, they're horrid. So Chapter 16 is your comprehensive guide to troubleshooting the iPad. It details what to do when almost anything goes wrong, offering step-by-step instructions for specific situations as well as describing a plethora of tips and techniques you can try if something else goes awry. You may never need Chapter 16 (and we hope you won't), but you'll be very glad we put it here if your iPad ever goes wonky on you.

Finally, in Chapter 17, we take a look at some iPad accessories that we use and recommend including carrying cases, physical keyboards, earphones and headphones, speakers, and more. No, this stuff's not included with your iPad, but we consider most of it essential just the same.

Setting You Straight on Settings

In This Chapter

▶ Getting the lowdown on Settings

▶ Taking off in Airplane mode

▶ Preparing networks

▶ Brushing up on Bluetooth

▶ Uncovering usage statistics

▶ Setting up notifications

▶ Figuring out your location

▶ Seeking sensible sounds and screen brightness

▶ Finding a lost iPad

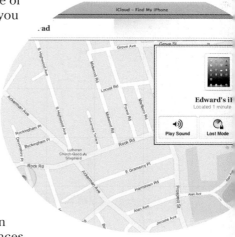

*D*o you consider yourself a control freak? The type of person who has to have it your way? Boy, have you landed in the right chapter.

Settings is kind of the makeover factory for the iPad mini. You open Settings by tapping its Home screen icon, and from there you can do things like change the tablet's background or wallpaper and specify Google, Yahoo!, or Bing as the search engine of choice. You can also alter security settings in Safari, tailor e-mail to your liking (among other modifications), and get a handle on how to fetch or push new data.

The Settings area on the iPad is roughly analogous to System Preferences on a Mac or the Control Panel in Windows, with a hearty serving of application preferences thrown in for good measure.

Because we cover some settings elsewhere in this book, we don't dwell on every setting here. But you still have plenty to digest to help you make the iPad your own.

Checking Out the Settings Screen

When you first open Settings, you see a display that looks something like Figure 15-1, with a scrollable list on the left side of the screen and a pane on the right that corresponds to whichever setting is highlighted in blue. We say "something like this" because the Settings on your iPad may differ slightly from those of your neighbor's.

Figure 15-1: Your list of settings.

One other general thought to keep in mind: If you see a greater-than symbol (>) appear to the right of a listing, the listing has a bunch of options. Throughout this chapter, you tap the > symbol to check out those options.

As you scroll to the bottom of the list on the left, you come to all the settings that pertain to some of the specific third-party apps you've added to the iPad (see Chapter 11). Everybody has a different collection of apps on his iPad, so any settings related to those programs will also obviously be different.

Flying with Sky-High Settings

Your iPad offers settings to keep you on the good side of air-traffic communications systems. However, the settings for the iPad mini Wi-Fi + Cellular models differ from those of the Wi-Fi–only model. Using a cellular radio on an airplane is a no-no. Wi-Fi is too, some of the time. But nothing is verboten about using an iPad on a plane to listen to music, watch videos, and peek at pictures — at least, after the craft has reached cruising altitude.

So how do you take advantage of the iPad's built-in iPod (among other capabilities) at 30,000 feet, while temporarily turning off your wireless gateway to e-mail and Internet functions? The answer is that you turn on Airplane mode.

To do so, merely tap Airplane Mode on the Settings screen to display On (rather than Off).

That act disables each of the iPad's wireless radios (depending on the model): Wi-Fi, cellular, and Bluetooth. While your iPad is in Airplane mode, you can't surf the web, get a map location, send or receive e-mails, sync through iCloud, use iTunes or the App Store, take advantage of Siri or dictation or do anything else that requires an Internet connection. If a silver lining exists here, it's that the iPad's long-lasting battery ought to last even longer — good news if the flight you're on is taking you halfway around the planet.

 The appearance of a tiny Airplane icon on the status bar at the upper-left corner of the screen reminds you that Airplane mode is turned on. Just remember to turn it off when you're back on the ground.

 If in-flight Wi-Fi is available on your flight, you can turn on Wi-Fi independently, leaving the rest of your iPad's wireless radio safely disabled.

Controlling Wi-Fi Connections

As we mention in Chapter 4, Wi-Fi is typically the fastest wireless network that you can use to surf the web, send e-mail, and perform other Internet tricks on the iPad. You use the Wi-Fi setting to determine which Wi-Fi networks are available to you and which one to exploit based on its signal.

Tap Wi-Fi so that the setting is on and all Wi-Fi networks in range display, as shown in Figure 15-2.

 Tap the Wi-Fi switch to Off whenever you don't have access to a network and don't want to drain the battery.

A signal-strength indicator can help you choose the network to connect to if more than one is listed; tap the appropriate Wi-Fi network when you reach a decision. If a network is password-protected, you see a Lock icon and you need the passcode to access it.

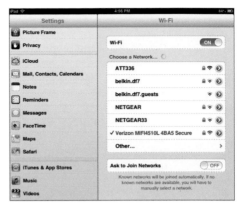

You can also turn the Ask to Join Networks setting on or off. Networks that the iPad is already familiar with are joined automatically, regardless of which one you choose. If the Ask feature is off and no known networks are available, you have to manually select a new network. If the Ask feature is on, you're asked before joining a new network. Either way, you see a list with the same Wi-Fi networks in range.

Figure 15-2: Check out your Wi-Fi options.

If you used a particular network automatically in the past but you no longer want your iPad to join it, tap the > symbol next to the network in question (within Wi-Fi settings) and then tap Forget This Network. The iPad develops a quick case of selective amnesia.

In some instances, you have to supply other technical information about a network you hope to glom on to. You encounter a bunch of nasty-sounding terms: DHCP, BootP, Static IP Address, Subnet Mask, Router, DNS, Search Domains, Client ID, HTTP Proxy, and Renew Lease. (At least this last one has nothing to do with renting an apartment or the vehicle you're driving.) Chances are good that none of this info is on the tip of your tongue — but that's okay. For one thing, it's a good bet that you'll never need to know this stuff. What's more, even if you *do* have to fill in or adjust these settings, a network administrator or techie friend can probably help you.

Sometimes, you may want to connect to a network that's closed and not shown on the Wi-Fi list. If that's the case, tap Other and use the keyboard to enter the network name. Then tap to choose the type of security setting the network is using (if any). Your choices are WEP, WPA, WPA2, WPA Enterprise, and WPA2 Enterprise. Again, it's not exactly the friendliest terminology in the world, but we figure that someone nearby can lend a hand.

If no Wi-Fi network is available, you have to rely on 4G, 3G, or a slower cellular connection if you have capable models. If you don't or you're out of reach of a cellular network, you can't rocket into cyberspace until you regain access to a network.

Getting Fired Up over Bluetooth

Of all the peculiar terms you may encounter in techdom, *Bluetooth* is one of our favorites. The name is derived from Harald Blåtand, a tenth-century Danish monarch, who, the story goes, helped unite warring factions. And, we're told, *Blåtand* translates to *Bluetooth* in English. (Bluetooth is all about collaboration between different types of devices — get it?)

Blåtand was obviously ahead of his time. Although we can't imagine that he ever used a tablet computer, he now has an entire short-range wireless technology named in his honor. On the iPad, you can use Bluetooth to communicate wirelessly with a compatible Bluetooth headset or to use an optional wireless keyboard. Such accessories are made by Apple and many others.

To ensure that the iPad works with a device, it has to be wirelessly *paired,* or coupled, with the chosen device. If you're using a third-party accessory, follow the instructions supplied with that headset or keyboard so that it becomes *discoverable,* or ready to be paired with your iPad. Then turn on Bluetooth (on the Settings screen) so that the iPad can find such nearby devices and the device can find the iPad.

In Figure 15-3, an Apple Wireless Keyboard and the iPad are successfully paired when you enter a designated passkey on the keyboard. Bluetooth works to a range of about 30 feet.

You know Bluetooth is turned on when you see the Bluetooth icon on the status bar. If the symbol is white, the iPad is communicating wirelessly with a connected device. If the symbol is gray, Bluetooth is turned on in the iPad *but* a paired device isn't nearby or isn't turned on. If you don't see a Bluetooth icon, the setting is turned off.

Bluetooth icon

PIN code

To unpair a device, select it from the device list and tap Unpair. We guess breaking up *isn't* hard to do.

Figure 15-3: Pairing an Apple Wireless Keyboard with the iPad.

The iPad supports *stereo* Bluetooth headphones, so you can now stream stereo audio from the iPad to those devices.

The iPad can tap into Bluetooth in other ways. One is through *peer-to-peer* connectivity, so you can engage in multiplayer games with other nearby iPad, iPhone, or iPod touch users. You can also do such things as exchange business cards, share pictures, and send short notes. And you don't even have to pair the devices as you do with a headset or wireless keyboard.

You can't use Bluetooth to exchange files or sync between an iPad and a computer. Nor can you use it to print stuff from the iPad on a Bluetooth printer (though the AirPrint feature added handles that chore in some instances). That's because the iPad doesn't support any of the Bluetooth profiles (or specifications) required to allow such wireless stunts to take place — at least not as of this writing. We think that's a shame.

Roaming among Cellular Data Options

You see another set of settings only if you have the Wi-Fi + Cellular iPad. These options appear on the right pane of the Settings screen when you highlight Cellular Data on the left:

- **Data Roaming:** You may unwittingly rack up lofty roaming fees when exchanging e-mail, surfing with Safari, or engaging in other data-heavy activities while traveling abroad. Turn off Data Roaming to avoid these potential charges.

- **Cellular Data:** If you know you don't need the cellular network when you're out and about or you're in an area where you don't have access to the network, turn it off. Your battery will thank you later. But even if you have access to a speedy cellular network, be prudent; in a 4G environment where you can easily consume gobs of data, the charges can rack up fast.

- **Account Information:** Tap View Account to see or edit your account information or to add more data.

- **Add a SIM PIN:** The tiny *SIM,* or *Subscriber Identity Module,* card inside your iPad holds important data about your account. To add a PIN or a passcode to lock your SIM card, tap SIM PIN. That way, if someone gets hold of your SIM, she can't use it in another iPad without the passcode.

If you assign a PIN to your SIM, you have to enter it to turn the iPad on or off, which some might consider a minor hassle. And be aware that the SIM PIN is different from, and may be in addition to, any passcode you set for the iPad, as described later in this chapter.

- **Personal Hotspot:** Tap Personal Hotspot to share your iPad's data connection with any other devices you carry, perhaps a computer or smartphone. Just know that extra charges apply. Either you, or the owner of the device that's piggybacking on your Internet connection, have to enter the designated password generated by the iPad for the Hotspot connection to work. You can use the Hotspot feature via Wi-Fi

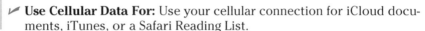

or Bluetooth or by connecting a USB cable. See Chapter 13 to find out how to use Personal Hotspot.

✔ **Enable LTE:** LTE stands for Long Term Evolution. What it really stands for is speed. Turn Enable LTE on for the fastest possible cellular data connection if you're in range. The biggest downside is, you can eat up your data allocation awfully fast.

✔ **Use Cellular Data For:** Use your cellular connection for iCloud documents, iTunes, or a Safari Reading List.

Managing Notifications

Through Apple's Push Notification service, app developers can send you alerts related to programs you've installed on your iPad. Such alerts are typically in text form but may include sounds as well. The idea is that you'll receive notifications even when the app they apply to isn't running. Notifications may also appear as numbered "badges" on their corresponding Home screen icons.

The downside to keeping push notifications turned on is that they can curtail battery life (though, honestly, we've been pretty satisfied with the iPad's staying power, even when push notifications are active). And you may find notifications distracting at times.

There's no global On/Off switch for notifications; iOS 6 requires you to manage them on an app-by-app basis. To do so, tap Notifications on the left side of the Settings screen, as shown in Figure 15-4, and then tap the app you want to manage.

Figure 15-4: Notify the iPad of your notification intentions.

All installed apps that take advantage of Notification Center (see Chapter 13) appear on the right side of the Notification Settings panel, as shown in Figure 15-4, with the enabled apps displayed in the upper section (In Notification Center) and disabled apps in the lower section (Not in Notification Center).

Tap any app to adjust its settings, as shown in Figure 15-5.

Figure 15-5 shows the Notification settings for the Mail app and, more specifically, Gmail. Some apps offer other options, including sound alerts, and other apps may offer fewer options, but we think you'll figure it out. To help you get started, here's a rundown of the options shown in Figure 15-5, starting at the top:

Figure 15-5: The Notification settings for the Mail app.

- **Notification Center:** Tap the switch to enable or disable notifications for this app.

- **Alert Style:** Tap to select the style of alert you want to see:

  - *None:* Choose None, and notifications won't appear spontaneously. They'll still be available in the Notification Center (swipe down from the top of the screen; see Chapter 13) but won't interrupt your work (or play).

  - *Banners:* Choose Banners to display alerts as banners at the top of the screen and have them go away automatically, as opposed to . . .

  - *Alerts:* Choose Alerts to display alerts that require action before proceeding.

- **Badge App Icon:** Enable this to display the number of pending alerts on the app's icon on your Home screen.

- **New Mail Sound:** Tap this setting to choose the sound that accompanies notifications of new mail messages. The Ding sound is selected earlier, in Figure 15-5. But you can pick from a lengthy list of sound and ringtone alternatives and tap each possible choice to hear what the sound snippet sounds like. Or select None if you're in the mood for total quiet.

- **Show Preview:** Enable this to see the first part of the mail or iMessage as part of the notification.

- **View in Lock Screen:** Enable this option if you want to see notifications for this app when your iPad screen is locked.

Apps that don't take advantage of the iOS Notification Center can still offer notifications, but you'll have to scroll down to the Apps section on the left side of Settings and tap the app you want to alter. Note that the app you hope to fiddle with doesn't always appear in the Apps section of Settings. For that matter, many of the apps that appear in the list don't offer notifications anyway.

On the other hand, many apps do. One that has a broad variety of notification options is Facebook. You can choose to have the giant social network push notifications related to Wall or Timeline posts, friend requests, photo tags, events, and more. Or choose not to be notified about any or all of these.

The broader point we're trying to make is that we urge you to check out the settings for *all* the apps you see in this list. You'll never know about many useful options if you don't.

If you find you went overboard with notifications at first, to the point where they become annoying or distracting, don't fret. You can always go back and redo some or all of the notifications that you've set up.

Apple understands that sometimes you don't want to be bothered by notifications or other distractions, no matter how unobtrusive they might be. The result is a feature aptly named Do Not Disturb. Flip the switch so the global setting is turned to On and a Moon icon appears to the left of the clock in the status bar. And rest assured, your alerts are silenced until you turn the setting back to the Off position. Under the Notifications setting, you can refine the Do Not Disturb option to your liking, by scheduling when the feature is enabled, defining who can get in touch via FaceTime and so on.

Location, Location, Location Services

By using the onboard Maps or Camera apps or any number of third-party apps, the iPad makes good use of knowing where you are. The iPads with 3G or 4G cellular exploit built-in GPS. The Wi-Fi–only iPad can find your general whereabouts (by *triangulating* signals from Wi-Fi base stations and cellular towers).

If that statement creeps you out a little, don't fret. To protect your right to privacy, individual apps pop up quick messages (similar to the one shown in Figure 15-6) asking whether you want them to use your current location. But you can also turn off Location Services in Settings. Tap Privacy and then tap Locations Services to turn the setting off. Not only is your privacy shielded, but you also keep your iPad battery juiced a little longer.

Figure 15-6: The iHeartRadio app wants to know where you are.

While visiting the Privacy setting, you may want to consult the Privacy listings for individual apps on your iPad — Contacts, Calendars, Reminders, and Photos. If any third-party apps request access to these apps, they show up here.

From time to time on the iPad, you can land in the same destination in multiple ways. So you can access the same Privacy settings via the Restrictions settings that we address later in this chapter.

Settings for Your Senses

The next bunch of settings control what the iPad looks like and sounds like.

Brightening your day

Who doesn't want a bright, vibrant screen? Alas, the brightest screens exact a trade-off: Before you drag the Brightness slider (shown in Figure 15-7) to the max, remember that brighter screens sap the life from your battery more quickly. The control appears when Brightness & Wallpaper is highlighted.

Figure 15-7: Sliding this control adjusts screen brightness.

That's why we recommend tapping the Auto-Brightness control so that it's on. The control automatically adjusts the screen according to the lighting environment in which you're using the iPad while being considerate of your battery.

Wallpaper

Choosing wallpaper is a neat way to dress up the iPad according to your aesthetic preferences. You can sample the pretty patterns and designs that the iPad has already chosen for you as follows:

1. **Tap Brightness & Wallpaper and then tap the two iPads below the word *Wallpaper*.**

   A list of photo albums appears with Wallpaper, a photo album of lovely images included with your iPad, as shown in Figure 15-8.

Figure 15-8: Choosing a majestic background.

2. **Tap Wallpaper or one of your own photo albums in the list.**

   Thumbnails of the images in that album appear (refer to Figure 15-8).

3. **Tap a thumbnail image.**

   That image fills the screen.

4. **When an image is full-screen, choose one of the options that appear at the top of the screen:**

   - *Set Lock Screen* makes your selected image the wallpaper of choice when the iPad is locked.

   - *Set Home Screen* makes the wallpaper decorate only your Home screen.

   - *Set Both* makes your image the wallpaper for locked and Home screens.

   - *Cancel* takes you back to the thumbnail page without changing your Home screen or Lock screen.

From Settings, you can also turn your iPad into an animated picture frame. See Chapter 9 for more on the Picture Frame feature and the settings to make it look just the way you like it.

Sounds

Consider the Sounds settings area the iPad's soundstage. There, you can turn audio alerts on or off for a variety of functions: new e-mail, sent mail, calendar and reminder alerts, Facebook posts, and tweets. You can also decide whether you want to hear lock sounds and keyboard clicks.

You can also alter the ringtone you hear for FaceTime calls and the text tones you hear for iMessages, and tap a button and visit the iTunes store to buy more text tones or ringtones if you're not satisfied with those that Apple supplies, for 99 cents and $1.29 a pop, respectively. (Mac owners can create their own by using GarageBand. Other third-party options are available for folks with Macs or PCs.) To set a custom tone for individuals in the Contacts app, tap the Edit button and then either the Ringtone or Text Tone option.

To raise the decibel level of alerts, drag the volume slider to the right. Drag in the opposite direction to bring down the noise. An alternative way to adjust sound levels is to use the physical Volume buttons on the side of the iPad for this purpose, as long as you're not already using the iPad's iPod to listen to music or watch video.

You can enable and disable this feature with the Change with Buttons switch, right below the volume slider.

Exploring Settings in General

Certain miscellaneous settings are difficult to pigeonhole. Apple wisely lumped these under the General settings moniker. Here's a closer look at your options.

About About

You aren't seeing double. This section, as shown in Figure 15-9, is all about the About setting. And About is full of trivial (and not-so-trivial) information *about* the device.

Figure 15-9: You find info about your iPad under About.

What you find there is straightforward:

- ✓ **Network you use (Cellular model only):** AT&T, Sprint, or Verizon
- ✓ **Number of songs stored on the device**

✔ **Number of videos**

✔ **Number of photos**

✔ **Number of apps**

✔ **Storage capacity used and available:** Because of the way the device is formatted, you always have a little less storage than the advertised amount of flash memory.

✔ **Software version:** As this book goes to press, we're up to version 6.0. But as the software is tweaked and updated, your device takes on a new build identifier, indicating that it's just a little bit further along than a previous build. So you see, in parentheses next to the version number, a string of numbers and letters that looks like `10A406` and tells you more precisely what software version you have. The number/letter string changes whenever the iPad's software is updated and is potentially useful to the tech support person who might need to know the precise version you're working with.

✔ **Carrier and cellular data (Wi-Fi + Cellular versions only):** Yep, that's AT&T, Sprint, or Verizon in the United States.

✔ **Serial and model numbers**

✔ **Cellular data number**

✔ **Wi-Fi address**

✔ **Bluetooth address:** See the earlier section "Getting Fired Up over Bluetooth" to find out more about Bluetooth.

✔ **IMEI, ICCID, and MEID:** These stand for International Mobile Equipment Identifier, International Circuit Card Identifier, and Mobile Equipment Identifier, respectively. They live up to their geeky acronyms by helping to identify your specific device.

✔ **Advertising:** You get to choose whether to limit ad tracking.

✔ **Diagnostics & Usage:** Choose whether to automatically send diagnostic data to Apple.

✔ **Legal Notices, License, Warranty, Regulatory and RF Exposure:** You had to know that the lawyers would get in their two cents somehow. You find all the fine print here. And *fine print* it is because you can't unpinch to enlarge the text (not that we can imagine more than a handful will bother to read this legal mumbo-jumbo).

Usage settings

The About setting we cover in the preceding section gives you a lot of information about your device. But after you back out of About and return to the main General settings, you can find other settings for statistics on iPad usage:

- **Battery percentage:** You almost always see a little battery meter in the upper-right corner of the screen, except in those instances when you watch videos and the whole top bar disappears. If you also want to see your iPad mini's battery life presented in percentage terms, make sure that the Battery Percentage setting is turned on.

- **Cellular usage (Cellular models only):** This setting showing the amount of network data you sent and received over the AT&T, Sprint, or Verizon network appears only if you have a Wi-Fi + Cellular iPad. You can reset these statistics by tapping the Reset Statistics button.

  The Cellular Usage option is where you find out how close you are to using up your monthly data allotment.

- **iCloud:** See the amount of total and available storage. Tap Manage Storage to, well, manage your iCloud storage, and (if need be) to buy more storage. The 20GB, $40-a-year plan gives you 25GB of storage; the 50GB, $100-a-year plan gives you 55GB. You can also downgrade to a free 5GB plan or pay $20 a year for a 15GB plan.

- **Storage (for the device):** Lets you check out which apps on your iPad are hogging the most storage.

Siri

We love knowing that Siri — the chatty, personal digital assistant who can remind you whether to take an umbrella or clue you in on how the Giants are faring in the NFL — has found her way to the iPad mini from the iPhone 4S, iPhone 5, and the most recent, larger iPads, too. You can talk to her by pressing and holding the Home button and speaking out loud. She will talk back.

But sometimes, well — there's no way to say this kindly — you want to shut her up. To do that, just turn the Siri setting from On to Off. If you disable Siri, be aware that the information she uses to respond to your requests is removed from Apple's servers. So if you call her back into duty later, it may take a little bit of time for her to resend information. Don't fret if you don't remember any of this. Apple reminds you before you silence Siri.

Other Siri settings to take note of:

- **Default language:** You can choose the language in which she speaks to you. The default is U.S. English.

- **Voice feedback:** You can select whether to always get voice feedback from Siri as opposed to only when you're in a "hands-free" situation.

- **Your info:** And you can let Siri know who you are by choosing your name (if it's not already shown) in the My Info section of Siri settings. If for some reason you want to pick another name, you can do so from your list of Contacts.

VPN settings

After you tap Network on the General settings screen, you see a control for VPN.

A *virtual private network,* or *VPN,* is a way for you to securely access your company's network behind the firewall — using an encrypted Internet connection that acts as a secure "tunnel" for data.

You can configure a VPN on the iPad by following these steps:

1. **Tap Settings⇨General⇨VPN⇨Add VPN Configuration.**

2. **Tap one of the protocol options.**

   The iPad software supports the protocols L2TP (Layer 2 Tunneling Protocol), PPTP (Point-to-Point Tunneling Protocol), and IPSec, which apparently provides the kind of security that satisfies network administrators.

3. **Using configuration settings provided by your company, fill in the appropriate server information, account, password, and other information.**

4. **Choose whether to turn on RSA SecurID authentication.**

   Better yet, lend your iPad to the techies where you work and let them fill in the blanks on your behalf.

After you configure your iPad for VPN usage, you can turn that capability on or off by tapping (yep) the VPN On or Off switch inside Settings.

iTunes Wi-Fi Sync

We spend an entire chapter (Chapter 3, to be precise) on syncing. Just know that if you want to sync with iTunes on your computer when you're plugged into power and tapping into Wi-Fi, you can do it there.

Spotlight search

Tell the iPad the apps that you want to search. Touch the three horizontal lines next to an app that you want to include in your search, and drag it up or down to rearrange the search order.

Auto-Lock

Tap Auto-Lock in the General settings pane, and you can set the amount of time that elapses before the iPad automatically locks or turns off the display. Your choices are 15 minutes before, 10 minutes, 5 minutes, or 2 minutes. Or you can set it so that the iPad never locks automatically.

If you work for a company that insists on a passcode (see the next section), the Never Auto-Lock option isn't in the list that your iPad shows you.

Don't worry about whether the iPad is locked. You can still receive notification alerts and adjust the volume.

Passcode Lock

If you want to prevent others from using your iPad, you can set a passcode by tapping Passcode Lock and then tapping Turn Passcode On. By default, you use the virtual keypad to enter and confirm a four-digit passcode. If you prefer a longer, stronger passcode, tap the Simple Passcode switch to Off. Now provide your current passcode, and then enter and confirm your new passcode, which can be almost any combination of the letters, numbers, and symbols that are available on the standard virtual keyboard.

You can also determine whether a passcode is required immediately, after 1 minute, after 5 minutes, 15 minutes, 1 hour, or 4 hours. Shorter times are more secure, of course. On the topic of security, the iPad can be set to automatically erase your data if someone makes ten failed passcode attempts.

On a lighter note, you can choose to turn the Picture Frame setting on or off. Find out how to turn your iPad into a picture frame in Chapter 9.

You can also change the passcode or turn it off later (unless your employer dictates otherwise), but you need to know the present passcode to apply any changes. If you forget the passcode, you have to restore the iPad software, as we describe in Chapter 16.

Cover Lock/Unlock

The iPad mini gives you the choice to automatically lock and unlock your iPad when you close and open the clever iPad mini Smart Cover, or other covers. If you set a passcode, you still have to enter it to wake the iPad from siesta-land.

Restrictions

Parents and bosses may love the Restrictions tools, but kids and employees usually think otherwise. You can clamp down, er, provide proper parental guidance to your children by preventing them, at least some of the time, from using the Safari browser, Camera, FaceTime, iTunes, Ping, iBookstore, Siri, or Game Center. Or you might not let them install new apps or make purchases inside the apps you do allow. Or, conversely, delete apps. When restrictions are in place, icons for off-limit functions can no longer be seen. Tap Enable Restrictions, set or enter your passcode — you have to enter it twice if you are setting up the passcode — and tap the button next to each item in the

Allow or Allowed Content lists that you plan to restrict. Their corresponding settings show Off.

You can also restrict the use of explicit language when you dictate text. (An asterisk (*) replaces a naughty word.)

Moreover, parents have more controls to work with. For instance, you can allow Junior to watch a movie on the iPad but prevent him from watching a flick that carries an R or NC-17 rating. You can also restrict access to certain TV shows, explicit songs and podcasts, and apps based on age-appropriate ratings. In Game Center, you can decide whether your kid can play a multi-player game or add friends. And Apple lets you choose whether to let the kids read books with explicit sexual content. Stop feeling guilty: You have your users' best interests at heart.

If guilt gets the better of you, you can turn off Restrictions. Open the Restrictions setting by again typing your passcode. Then switch the On/Off setting back to On for each setting you free up. Tap Disable Restrictions. You have to enter your passcode one more time before your kids and office underlings return you to their good graces.

Side Switch

You can use the side switch for one of two purposes: Lock the rotation so that the screen orientation doesn't change when you turn the iPad to the side, or mute certain sounds. Here's where you get to make that choice.

Multitasking gestures

Enable this option if you want to use four or five fingers to

- ✔ Pinch to the Home screen
- ✔ Swipe up to reveal the multitasking bar
- ✔ Swipe left or right to switch among open apps

By all means, enable this option if it isn't enabled. The gestures truly improve the multitasking experience, and we recommend you give them a try. If, for some reason, you hate them, you know where to go to turn them off.

Date & Time

In our neck of the woods, the time is reported as 11:32 p.m. (or whatever time it happens to be). But in some circles, it's reported as 23:32. If you prefer the latter format on the iPad's status bar, tap the 24-Hour Time setting (under Date & Time) so that it's on.

This setting is just one that you can adjust under Date & Time. You can also have the iPad set the time in your time zone. Here's how:

1. **Tap Date & Time.**

   You see fields for setting the time zone and the date and time.

2. **Tap the Time Zone field and make sure Set Automatically is turned off.**

   The current time zone and virtual keyboard are shown.

3. **Tap X to remove the city that's showing, and tap the letters of the city or country whose time zone you want to enter until the one you have in mind appears. Then tap the name of that city or country.**

   The Time Zone field is automatically filled in for that city.

4. **Tap the Set Date & Time field so that the time is shown; then roll the bicycle-lock-like controls until the proper time displays.**

5. **Tap the date that's shown so that the bicycle-lock-like controls pop up for the date; then roll the wheels for the month, day, and year until the correct date appears.**

6. **Tap the Set Date & Time button to return to the main Date & Time settings screen.**

You can also dispense with these settings and just have the iPad set the time automatically based on its knowledge of where you happen to be. Make sure the Set Automatically option is set to On.

Keyboard

Under Keyboard settings, you have the following options:

- **Auto-Capitalization:** You can turn Auto-Capitalization on or off.

  Auto-Capitalization, which the iPad turns on by default, capitalizes the first letter of the first word you type after ending the preceding sentence with a period, a question mark, or an exclamation point.

- **Auto-Correction:** When turned on, the iPad takes a stab at what it thinks you meant to type.

- **Check Spelling:** When on, the keyboard can check spelling while you type.

- **Caps Lock:** If Caps Lock is enabled, all letters are uppercased LIKE THIS if you double-tap the Shift key. (The Shift key is the one with the arrow pointing up.) Tap Shift again to exit Caps Lock.

- **"." Shortcut:** You can also turn on this keyboard setting, which inserts a period followed by a space when you double-tap the spacebar. This setting is turned on by default, so if you've never tried it, give it a shot.

You can choose to use an international keyboard (as we discuss in Chapter 2), which you choose from Keyboard settings or the International setting — the next setting after Keyboard in the General settings area.

International

The iPad is an international sensation just as it is in the United States. In the International section, you can set the language you type (by using a custom virtual keyboard), the language in which the iPad displays text, and the date, time, and telephone format for the region in question. You can choose a Gregorian, Japanese, or Buddhist calendar, too.

Accessibility

The Accessibility or Universal Access Features tools on your iPad are targeted at helping people with certain disabilities. The following sections explain each one in turn.

VoiceOver

This screen reader describes aloud what's on the screen. It can read e-mail messages, web pages, and more. With VoiceOver active, you tap an item on the screen to select it. VoiceOver places a black rectangle around it and either speaks the name or describes an item. If you tap, say, Brightness & Wallpaper, the VoiceOver voice speaks the words "Brightness & Wallpaper button." VoiceOver even lets you know when you alternately position the iPad in landscape or portrait mode or when your screen is locked or unlocked.

Within the VoiceOver setting, you have several options. For instance, if you turn on Speak Hints, VoiceOver may provide instructions on what to do next, along the lines of "Double-tap to open." You can drag a Speaking Rate slider to speed up or slow down the speech. You can also determine the kind of typing feedback you get, from among characters, words, characters and words, or no feedback. Additional controls let you turn on Phonetics and Pitch Change and choose the voice.

The voice you hear speaks in the language you specified in International settings, which we explain earlier.

You have to know a whole new set of finger gestures when VoiceOver is on, which may seem difficult, especially when you first start using VoiceOver. When you stop to think about it, this makes a lot of sense. You want to be able to hear descriptions on the screen before you activate buttons. Different VoiceOver gestures use different numbers of fingers. Here's a rundown on many of these:

- **Tap:** Speak the item.

- **Flick right or left:** Select the next or previous item.

- **Flick up or down:** This gesture has multiple outcomes that depend on how you set the so-called "rotor control" gesture. Think of the rotor control as you think about turning a dial: You rotate two fingers on the screen. The purpose is to switch to a different set of commands or features. This leads us back to the flick up or down gestures. Say that you're reading text in an e-mail. By alternately spinning the rotor, you can switch between hearing the body of a message read aloud word by word or character by character. After you set the parameters, flick up or down to hear stuff read back. The flicking up or down gestures serve a different purpose when you type an e-mail: The gestures move the cursor left or right within the text.

- **Two-finger tap:** Stop speaking.

- **Two-finger flick up:** Read everything from the top of the screen.

- **Two-finger flick down:** Read everything from your current position on the screen.

- **Three-finger flick up or down:** Scroll a page.

- **Three-finger flick right or left:** Go to the next or previous page.

- **Three-finger tap:** Know which page or rows are on the screen.

- **Four-finger flick up or down:** Go to the first or last part of the page.

- **Four-finger flick right or left:** Go to the next or previous section.

- **Double-tap:** Activate a selected icon or button to launch an app, turn a switch from On to Off, and more.

- **Touch an item with one finger and tap the screen with another:** Otherwise known as *split-tapping*, when you touch an item, a voice identifies what you touched (for example, "Safari button" or "Notifications On button"). A tap with the second finger selects whatever was identified with the first finger (that is, "Safari button selected" or "Notifications On button selected"). Now you can double-tap to launch the button or whatever else was selected.

- **Double-tap, hold for a second, and then add a standard gesture:** Tell the iPad to go back to using standard gestures for your next move. You can also use standard gestures with VoiceOver by double-tapping and holding the screen. You hear tones that remind you that standard gestures are now in effect. They stay that way until you lift your finger.

- **Two-finger double-tap:** Play or pause. You use the double-tap in the Music, YouTube, and Photos apps.

- **Three-finger double-tap:** Mute or unmute the voice.

- **Three-finger triple-tap:** Turn the display on or off.

Apple lets you use VoiceOver in Maps, Assistive Touch, and Zoom.

Zoom

The Zoom feature offers a screen magnifier for those who are visually challenged. To zoom by 200 percent, double-tap the screen with *three* fingers. Drag three fingers to move around the screen. To increase magnification, use three fingers to tap and drag up. Tap with three fingers and drag down to decrease magnification.

The Zoom feature does have a downside: When magnified, the characters on the screen aren't as crisp (though the Retina display on the third-generation iPad is still pretty sharp), and you can't display as much in a single view.

Large Text

You can make text larger in the Mail, Contacts, Calendars, Messages, and Notes apps. You have the choice of six point sizes (from 20pt to 56pt) in addition to the default, which is Off.

Invert Colors

The colors on the iPad can be reversed to provide a higher contrast for people with poor eyesight. The screen resembles a film negative.

Mono Audio

If you suffer hearing loss in one ear, the iPad can combine the right and left audio channels so that both channels can be heard in either earbud of any headset you plug in. A slider control can adjust how much audio is combined and to which ear it is directed.

The iPad, unlike its cousins the iPhone and the iPod touch, doesn't come with earbuds or headphones. You have to supply your own.

Speak Selection

When this setting is on, the iPad speaks any text you select. You also find a slider control to adjust the speaking rate. And you can highlight words as they are spoken.

Speak Auto-Text

When this setting is on, the iPad automatically speaks auto-corrections and capitalizations.

Guided Access

Parents of autistic kids know how challenging it can be to keep the child focused on a given task. The Guided Access setting can limit iPad usage to a single app and also restrict touch input on certain areas of the screen. You can turn the feature on or off by employing Triple-Click Home, the very next setting.

Triple-Click Home

Set the Triple-Click Home feature to summon the following accessibility tools. Clicking Home three times rapidly can be used to toggle VoiceOver on or off, toggle Invert Colors on or off, or toggle Zoom on or off. You can also set up a prompt to be asked which of these functions you want to accomplish.

In addition, Triple-Click Home can be used to summon Assistive Touch, which lends an assist to people who rely on a joystick or another adaptive accessory because they have difficulty touching the screen.

Still another Accessibility setting in iOS 6 lets you change the home-click speed for activating Double and Triple-Click Home. You can stick with the default or choose a Slow or Slowest setting.

Closed Captioning

To turn on closed captioning subtitles for a movie or video in which they're available, tap Videos Settings and turn on the feature.

Brief diversion: While you're in the Videos Settings area, incidentally, you can also turn on Home Sharing by entering your Apple ID and password. With this feature enabled, you can play movies, TV shows, or music on your iPad that are housed in the iTunes Library on your Mac or PC. You need to be connected to Wi-Fi and be on the same home network.

Reset

As little kids playing sports, we often ended an argument by agreeing to a do-over. Well, the Reset settings on the iPad are one big do-over. Now that you're (presumably) grown up, think long and hard about the consequences before implementing do-over settings. Regardless, you may encounter good reasons for starting over; some of these are addressed in Chapter 16.

Here are your reset options:

- **Reset All Settings:** Resets all settings, but no data or media is deleted.
- **Erase All Content and Settings:** Resets all settings *and* wipes out all your data.
- **Reset Network Settings:** Deletes the current network settings and restores them to their factory defaults.
- **Subscriber Services:** Provides options to reprovision your account and reset your authentication code.

✔ **Reset Keyboard Dictionary:** Removes added words from the dictionary. Remember that the iPad keyboard is intelligent. And, one reason it's so smart is that it learns from you. So when you reject words that the iPad keyboard suggests, it figures that the words you specifically banged out ought to be added to the keyboard dictionary.

✔ **Reset Home Screen Layout:** Reverts all icons to the way they were at the factory.

✔ **Reset Location & Privacy:** Restores factory defaults.

Find My iPad

We hope you never have to use the Find My iPad feature — though we have to say that it's pretty darn cool. If you inadvertently leave your iPad in a taxi or restaurant, Find My iPad may just help you retrieve it. All it takes is a free iCloud account.

Well, that's *almost* all it takes. You'll have to turn it on, though, so tap Settings↪ Mail, Contacts, Calendars, and then tap your iCloud account. Or tap Settings↪iCloud. Either way, make sure Find My iPad is switched to On.

Now suppose that you lost your tablet — and we can only assume that you're beside yourself. Follow these steps to see whether the Find My iPad feature can help you:

1. **Log on to your iCloud account at** `https://www.icloud.com` **from any browser on your computer.**

2. **Click the Find My iPhone icon.**

   If you don't see it, click the icon with a cloud in it that appears in the upper-left corner of the iCloud site. You see a panel with icons that are tied to various iCloud services, including Find My iPhone. (Yes, even though the feature is Find My iPad on the iPad, it shows up as Find My iPhone on the iCloud site. Don't worry: It'll still locate your iPad and, for that matter, a lost Mac — or a lost iPhone or iPod touch.)

   Assuming that your tablet is turned on and in the coverage area, its general whereabouts turn up on a map (as shown in Figure 15-10), in Satellite view, or a hybrid of the two. In our tests, Find My iPad found our iPads quickly.

   The truth is that even seeing your iPad on a map may not help you much, especially if the device is lost somewhere in midtown Manhattan. Take heart.

Figure 15-10: Locate a lost iPad.

3. **At the iCloud site, click the Play Sound button or Lost Mode button (or both).**

4. **(Optional) Enter a phone number where the good samaritan who picked up your iPad (you hope) can find you, and type a message to ask for the return of the device.**

The message appears on the lost iPad's screen, as shown in Figure 15-11.

To get someone's attention, you can also sound an alarm that plays for two minutes, even if the volume is off. Hey, that alarm may come in handy if the iPad turns up under a couch in your house. Stranger things have happened.

> This iPad has been lost.
> Please call me.
> (212) 555-1111

Figure 15-11: An appeal to return the iPad.

Find My iPhone (which finds any iOS device and Macs too) is now available as a free app in the App Store. Another free app, Find My Friends, as the name suggests, locates your friends on a map. Just hope when you find a particular pal that he's not the one who snatched your missing iPad.

After all this labor, if the iPad is seemingly gone for good, click Wipe at the iCloud site to delete your personal data from afar and return the iPad to its factory settings. (A somewhat less drastic measure is to remotely lock your iPad by using a four-digit passcode.) And if you ever get your iPad back, you can always restore the information from an iTunes backup on your Mac or PC or iCloud.

When Good iPad minis Go Bad

In This Chapter

▶ Fixing iPad issues

▶ Dealing with network problems

▶ Eliminating that sinking feeling when you can't sync

▶ Perusing the Apple website and discussion forums

▶ Sending your iPad to an Apple Store

▶ Finding your stuff on a repaired iPad

*I*n our experience, all Apple iOS devices — namely, the iPad, iPhone, and iPod touch — are fairly reliable. But every so often, a good iPad might just go bad. We don't expect it to be a common occurrence, but it does happen occasionally. So, in this chapter, we look at the types of bad things that can happen, along with suggestions for fixing them.

What kind of bad things are we talking about? Well, we're referring to problems involving

✔ Frozen or dead iPads

✔ Wireless networks

✔ Synchronization of computers (both Mac and PC) or iTunes

After we describe all the troubleshooting, we tell you how to get even more help if nothing we suggest does the trick. Finally, if your iPad is so badly hosed that it needs to go back to the mothership for repairs, we offer ways to survive the experience with a minimum of stress or fuss, including how to restore your stuff from an iTunes or iCloud backup.

Resuscitating an iPad with Issues

Our first category of troubleshooting techniques applies to an iPad that's frozen or otherwise acting up. The recommended procedure when this happens is to perform the seven *R*s in sequence:

1. Recharge

2. Restart

3. Reset your iPad

4. Remove your content

5. Reset settings and content

6. Restore

7. Recovery mode

But before you even start those procedures, Apple recommends you take these steps:

1. **Verify that you have the current version of iTunes installed on your Mac or PC.**

   You can always download the latest-and-greatest version here: www.apple.com/itunes/download.

2. **Verify that you're connecting your iPad to your computer using a USB 2.0 or 3.0 port.**

   If you encounter difficulties here, we implore you to read the paragraph in the next section that begins with this sentence:

   "Don't plug the iPad mini's Lightning connector–to–USB cable into a USB port on your keyboard, monitor, or unpowered USB hub."

3. **Make sure that your iPad software is up to date.**

   To check with iTunes on your Mac or PC:

   a. *Connect your iPad to your computer, launch iTunes (if necessary), and then click your iPad in the iTunes sidebar.*

   b. *Click the Summary tab and then click the Check for Update button.*

   To check with your iPad:

   a. *Tap Settings on your Home screen.*

   b. *Tap General in the Settings list on the left side of the screen.*

   c. *Tap Software Update on the right side of the screen.*

If your iPad requires an update, you receive instructions for doing so. Otherwise, please continue.

If those three easy steps don't get you back up and running and your iPad is still acting up — if it freezes, doesn't wake up from sleep, doesn't do something it used to do, or in any other way acts improperly — don't panic. The following sections describe the things you should try, in the order that we (and Apple) recommend.

If the first technique doesn't do the trick, go on to the second. If the second one doesn't work, try the third. And so on.

Recharge

If your iPad acts up in any way, shape, or form, the first thing you should try is to give its battery a full recharge before you proceed.

Don't plug the iPad mini's Lightning–connector–to–USB cable into a USB port on your keyboard, monitor, or USB hub. Plug it into one of the USB ports on your computer itself. That's because the USB ports on your computer supply more power than the other ports. Although other USB ports *may* do the trick, you're better off using the built-in ones on your computer.

Most *powered* USB hubs (the kind you plug into an AC outlet) will charge your iPad just fine. But *unpowered,* or *passive,* hubs (ones that don't plug into the wall for power) don't cut it when it comes to charging your iPad.

If your computer is more than a few years old, even its built-in USB ports may not supply enough juice to recharge your iPad. It'll sync fine; it just won't recharge. If it says `Not Charging` next to the Battery icon at the top of the screen, use the included USB power adapter to recharge your iPad from an AC outlet rather than from a computer.

If you're in a hurry, charge your iPad for a minimum of 20 minutes. We think a full charge is a better idea, but a charge of 20 minutes or so is better than no charge at all. And for faster charging in any circumstances, turn off your iPad while it charges.

Restart

If you recharge your iPad and it still misbehaves, the next thing to try is restarting it. Just as restarting a computer often fixes problems, restarting your iPad sometimes works wonders.

Here's how to restart your iPad:

1. **Press and hold the Sleep/Wake button.**

2. **When the red slider appears, slide it to turn off the iPad and then wait a few seconds.**

3. **Press and hold the Sleep/Wake button again until the Apple logo appears on the screen.**

4. **If your iPad is still frozen or misbehaves or doesn't start, press and hold the Home button for six to ten seconds to force any frozen applications to quit.**

5. **Repeat Steps 1 to 3.**

If these steps don't get your iPad back up and running, move on to the third *R*, resetting your iPad.

Reset your iPad mini

To reset your iPad, merely press and hold the Sleep/Wake button and then press and hold the Home button, continuing to press both for at least ten seconds. When you see the Apple logo, release both buttons.

Resetting your iPad is like forcing your computer to restart after a crash. Your data shouldn't be affected by a reset — and in many cases, the reset cures whatever was ailing your iPad. So don't be shy about giving this technique a try. In many cases, your iPad goes back to normal after you reset it this way.

Sometimes you have to press and hold the Sleep/Wake button *before* you press and hold the Home button. If you press both at the same time, you might create a *screen shot* — a picture of whatever is on your screen at the time — rather than reset your iPad. This type of screen picture, by the way, is stored in the Photos app's Camera Roll album. Find out more about this feature at the end of Chapter 20. A screen shot *should* only happen if you press and release both buttons at the same time, but pressing and holding both buttons sometimes triggers the screen shot mechanism instead of restarting your iPad.

Unfortunately, sometimes resetting *doesn't* do the trick. When that's the case, you have to take stronger measures.

At this point, it's a good idea to back up your iPad's contents by right- or Control-clicking its name in the list on the left side of the iTunes window and choosing Back Up. Or look in the Backup section of the Summary pane in iTunes, which identifies when the last backup occurred.

Remove content

If you've been reading along in this chapter, nothing you've done should have taken more than a minute or two (or 20 if you tried the 20-minute recharge). We hate to tell you, but that's about to change because the next thing you should try is removing some or all of your data to see whether it's causing your troubles.

To do so, you need to sync your iPad and reconfigure it so that some or all of your files are *not* synchronized (which removes them from the iPad). The problem could be contacts, calendar data, songs, photos, videos, or pod-casts. You can apply one of two strategies to this troubleshooting task:

- ✔ **If you suspect a particular data type:** For example, you suspect your photos because whenever you tap the Photos icon on the Home screen, your iPad freezes — try removing that data first.

- ✔ **If you have no suspicions:** Deselect every item and then sync. When you're finished, your iPad should have no data on it.

    If that method fixes your iPad, try restoring your data, one type at a time. If the problem returns, you have to keep experimenting to determine which particular data type or file is causing the problem.

If you're still having problems, the next step is to reset your iPad's settings and content.

Reset settings and content

Resetting involves two steps. The first one, resetting your iPad settings, resets every iPad *setting* to its default — the way it was when you took it out of the box. Resetting the iPad's settings doesn't erase any of your data or media. The only downside is that you may have to go back and change some settings afterward — so you can try this step without trepidation. To reset your settings, tap the Settings icon on your Home screen and then tap General➪Reset➪Reset All Settings.

Do *not* tap Erase All Content and Settings, at least not yet. Erasing all content takes more time to recover from (because your next sync takes a long time), so try Reset All Settings first.

Now, if resetting all settings doesn't cure your iPad, you have to try Erase All Content and Settings. You find it in the same place as Reset All Settings. (Tap Settings➪General➪Reset➪Erase All Content and Settings.)

The Erase All Content strategy deletes everything from your iPad — all your data, media, and settings. Because all these items are stored on your computer — at least in theory — you should be able to put things back the way they were during your next sync. But you lose any photos you've taken or screen shots, as well as e-mail, apps purchased on your iPad, contacts, calendar events, playlists, and anything else you've created or modified on the iPad since your last sync.

After using Erase All Content and Settings, check to see whether your iPad works properly. If it doesn't cure what ails your iPad, the final *R,* restoring your iPad using iTunes, can help.

Restore

Before you give up the ghost on your poor, sick iPad, you can try one more thing. First, connect your iPad to your computer as though you're about to sync. But when the iPad appears in the iTunes sidebar, click the Restore button on the Summary tab. This action erases all your data and media and resets all your settings.

If your computer isn't available, you can also trigger this step from your iPad by tapping Settings⇨General⇨Reset ⇨Erase All Content and Settings.

Because all your data and media still exist on your computer (except for photos you've taken, contacts, calendar events, notes, and playlists you've created or modified on your iPad since your last sync, as noted previously), you shouldn't lose anything by restoring. Your next sync will take longer than usual, and you may have to reset settings you've changed since you got your iPad. But other than those inconveniences, restoring shouldn't cause you any additional trouble.

Performing a restore deletes everything on your iPad — all your data, media, and settings. You *should* be able to put things back the way they were with your next sync; if that doesn't happen, for whatever reason, you can't say we didn't warn you. That said, you may still be able to restore from an iTunes or iCloud backup, as described in this chapter's thrilling conclusion, the scintillating section "Dude, Where's My Stuff?"

Recovery mode

If you've tried all the other steps or you couldn't try some or all of them because your iPad is too messed up, you can try one last thing: Recovery mode. Here's how it works:

1. **Disconnect the Lightning connector cable from your iPad, but leave the other end of the cable connected to the USB port on your computer.**

2. **Turn off the iPad by pressing and holding the Sleep/Wake button for a few seconds, until the red slider appears onscreen, and then slide the slider.**

    Wait for the iPad to turn off.

3. **Press and hold the Home button while you reconnect the Lightning–to–USB cable to your iPad.**

    When you reconnect the USB cable, your iPad should power on.

If you see a Battery icon with a thin red band and an icon of a wall plug, an arrow, and a lightning bolt, let your iPad charge for at least 10 to 15 minutes. When the battery picture fades or turns green instead of red, go back to Step 2 and try again.

4. **Continue holding the Home button until you see the Connect to iTunes screen, and then release the Home button.**

   If you don't see the Connect to iTunes screen on your iPad, try Steps 1–4 again.

   If iTunes didn't open automatically already, launch it now. You should see a Recovery Mode alert on your computer screen, telling you that your iPad is in Recovery mode and that you must restore it before it can be used with iTunes.

5. **Use iTunes to restore the device, as we describe in the preceding section.**

Okay. So that's the gamut of things you can do when your iPad acts up. If you tried all this and none of it worked, skim the rest of this chapter to see whether anything else we recommend looks like it might help. If not, your iPad probably needs to go into the shop for repairs.

Never fear, gentle reader. Be sure to read the "If Nothing We Suggest Helps" section, later in this chapter. Your iPad may be quite sick, but we help ease the pain by sharing some tips on how to minimize the discomfort.

Problems with Networks

If you're having problems with Wi-Fi or your wireless carrier's data network (Wi-Fi + Cellular models only), this section may help. The techniques here are short and sweet — except for the last one, restore. Restore, which we describe in the previous section, is still inconvenient and time-consuming, and it still entails erasing all your data and media and then restoring it.

First, these simple steps that may help:

✔ **Make sure that you have sufficient Wi-Fi or cellular signal strength, as shown in Figure 16-1.**

Figure 16-1: Wi-Fi (top) and cellular (bottom) signal strength from best (left) to worst (right).

✔ **Move around.** Changing your location by as little as a few feet can sometimes mean the difference between great wireless reception and no wireless reception. If you're inside, try moving around even a step or two in one direction. If you're outside, try moving 10 or 20 paces in any direction. Keep an eye on the cell signal or Wi-Fi icon as you move around, and stop when you see more bars than you saw before.

✔ **Restart your iPad.** If you've forgotten how, refer to the "Restart" section, earlier in this chapter. As we mention, restarting your iPad is often all it takes to fix whatever is wrong.

If you have a Wi-Fi + Cellular iPad mini, try the following two bullet points.

✔ **Don't leave your iPad in Airplane mode, as we describe in Chapter 15.** In Airplane mode, all network-dependent features are disabled, so you can't send or receive messages or use any apps that require a Wi-Fi or data network connection (that is, Mail, Safari, Maps, Siri, or the iTunes and App Store apps).

✔ **Toggle Airplane mode on and off.** Turn on Airplane mode by tapping Settings on the Home screen and then tapping the Airplane mode On/Off switch to turn it on. Wait 15 or 20 seconds and then turn it off again.

Toggling Airplane mode on and off resets both the Wi-Fi and cellular data-network connections. If your network connection was the problem, toggling Airplane mode on and off may correct it.

Apple offers two very good articles that may help you with Wi-Fi issues. The first offers general troubleshooting tips and hints; the second discusses potential sources of interference for wireless devices and networks. You can find them here:

```
http://support.apple.com/kb/TS3237
http://support.apple.com/kb/HT1365
```

If none of the preceding suggestions fixes your network issues, try restoring your iPad, as we describe previously, in the "Restore" section.

Performing a restore deletes everything on your iPad — all your data, media, and settings. You should be able to put things back the way they were with your next sync. If that doesn't happen, well, consider yourself forewarned.

Sync, Computer, or iTunes Issues

The last category of troubleshooting techniques in this chapter applies to issues that involve synchronization and computer–iPad relations. If you're having problems syncing or your computer doesn't recognize your iPad when you connect it, here are some things to try.

Once again, we suggest that you try these procedures in the order they're presented here:

1. **Recharge your iPad.**

   If you didn't try it previously, try it now. Go to the "Resuscitating an iPad with Issues" section, earlier in this chapter, and read what we say about recharging your iPad. Every word there also applies here.

2. **Try a different USB port or a different cable if you have one available.**

   It doesn't happen often, but occasionally USB ports and cables go bad. When they do, they invariably cause sync and connection problems. Always make sure that a bad USB port or cable isn't to blame.

   If you don't remember what we said about using USB ports on your computer rather than the ones on your keyboard, monitor, or hub, we suggest that you reread the "Recharge" section, earlier in this chapter.

3. **Restart your iPad and try to sync again.**

   We describe restarting in full and loving detail in the "Restart" section, earlier in this chapter.

4. **Reinstall iTunes.**

   Even if you have an iTunes installer handy, you probably should visit the Apple website and download the latest-and-greatest version, just in case. You can find the latest version of iTunes at `www.apple.com/itunes/download`.

More Help on the Apple Website

If you try everything we suggest earlier in this chapter and still have problems, don't give up just yet. This section describes a few more places you may find help. We recommend that you check out some or all of them before you throw in the towel and smash your iPad into tiny little pieces (or ship it back to Apple for repairs, as we describe in the next section).

First, Apple offers an excellent set of support resources on its website at `www.apple.com/support/ipad/getstarted`. You can browse support issues by category, search for a problem by keyword, read or download technical manuals, and skim Apple Support Communities.

Speaking of the communities, you can go directly to them at `http://discussions.apple.com`. They're chock-full of useful questions and answers from other iPad users, and our experience has been that if you can't find an answer to a support question elsewhere, you can often find it in these forums. You can browse by category or search by keyword (Sync iPad, for example, as shown in Figure 16-2).

Figure 16-2: Search for *Sync iPad* and you'll see something like this.

Either way, you find thousands of discussions about almost every aspect of using your iPad. Better still, you can frequently find the answer to your question or a helpful suggestion.

Now for the best part: If you can't find a solution by browsing or searching, you can post your question in the appropriate Apple discussion forum. Check back in a few days (or even in a few hours), and some helpful iPad user may well have replied with the answer. If you've never tried this fabulous tool, you're missing out on one of the greatest support resources available anywhere.

Last, but certainly not least, before you throw in the towel, you might want to try a carefully worded Google search. It couldn't hurt, and you might just find the solution you've spent hours searching for.

If Nothing We Suggest Helps

If you tried every trick in the book (this one) and still have a malfunctioning iPad, consider shipping it off to the iPad hospital (better known as Apple, Inc.). The repair is free if your iPad is still under its one-year limited warranty.

You can extend your warranty for as long as one years from the original purchase date, if you want. To do so, you need to buy an AppleCare+ Protection Plan for your iPad. You don't have to do it when you buy your iPad, but you must buy it within 30 days of purchase. The retail price is $99 but it covers your iPad against almost every possible eventuality for two years. Without it, your warranty provides 90 days of phone support and a year of repair or replacement coverage.

Another benefit of AppleCare+ is that you're covered for up to two incidents of accidental damage from handling of your iPad. Though each incident is subject to a $49 service fee, we still think it's a good deal.

Here are a few things you need to know before you take your iPad in to be repaired:

> ✔ *Your iPad may be erased during its repair,* so you should sync your iPad with iTunes before you take it in, if you can. If you can't and you entered data on the iPad since your last sync, such as a contact or an appointment, the data may not be there when you restore your iPad upon its return.

> ✔ Remove any accessories, such as a case or screen protector.

Although you may be able to get your iPad serviced by Best Buy or another authorized Apple reseller, we recommend that you take or ship it to your nearest Apple Store, for two reasons:

> ✔ **No one knows your iPad like Apple.** One of the geniuses at the Apple Store may be able to fix whatever is wrong without sending your iPad away for repairs.

> ✔ **The Apple Store will, in some cases, swap out your wonky iPad for a brand-new one on the spot.** You can't win if you don't play, which is why we always visit our local Apple Store when something goes wrong (with our iPads, iPhones, iPods, and even laptops and iMacs).

If you've done everything we've suggested, we're relatively certain that you're now holding an iPad that works flawlessly. Again.

That said, some or all of your stuff may not be on it. If that's the case, the following section offers a two-trick solution that usually works.

Dude, Where's My Stuff?

If you've performed a restore or had your iPad replaced or repaired, you have one more task to accomplish. Your iPad may work flawlessly at this point, but some or all of your stuff — your music, movies, contacts, iMessages, or whatever — is missing. You're not sunk, at least not yet. You still have a couple of tricks up your sleeve:

Figure 16-3: Select the appropriate backup and click the Restore button.

- ✔ **Trick 1: Sync your iPad with iTunes and then sync it again.** That's right — sync and sync again. Why? Because sometimes stuff doesn't get synced properly on the first try. Just do it.

- ✔ **Trick 2: Restore from backup.** Right-click your iPad in iTunes sidebar and choose Restore from Backup. The Restore from Backup dialog appears and offers you a choice of backups, as shown in Figure 16-3. Select the one you want, click the Restore button, and let the iPad work some magic.

If you have more than one backup for a device, as Bob has for his iPad mini, try the most recent (undated) one first (refer to Figure 16-3). If it doesn't work or you're still missing files, try restoring from any other backups before you throw in the towel.

These backups include photos in Camera Roll, text messages, notes, contact favorites, sound settings, and more, but not media you've synced, such as music, videos, or photos. If media is what's missing, try performing Trick 1 again.

If you aren't holding an iPad that works flawlessly and has most (if not all) of your stuff, it's time to make an appointment with a Genius at your local Apple Store, call the support hotline (800-275-2273), or visit the support web page at www.apple.com/support/ipad.

Accessorizing Your iPad mini

In This Chapter

▶ Apple cases, keyboards, and chargers

▶ Apple connection options (camera, TV, and projector)

▶ Earphones, headphones, and headsets

▶ Speakers

▶ Third-party cases

▶ Other protection products

▶ Miscellaneous other accessories

*A*nyone who has purchased a new car in recent years is aware that it's not always a picnic trying to escape the showroom without the salesperson trying to get you to part with a few extra bucks. You can only imagine what the markup is on roof racks, navigation systems, and rear-seat DVD players.

We don't suppose you'll get a hard sell when you snap up a new iPad at an Apple Store (or elsewhere). But Apple and many other companies are happy to outfit your iPad mini with extra doodads, from wireless keyboards and stands to battery chargers and carrying cases. So just as your car might benefit from dealer (or third-party) options, so too might your iPad mini benefit from a variety of spare parts.

One thing is certain: If you see a Made for iPad label on the package, the developer is certifying that an electronic accessory has been designed to connect specifically to the iPad and meets performance standards established by Apple.

Lightning connector versus Dock connector

Your iPad mini uses Apple's latest and greatest connector, dubbed the *Lightning connector.* (In the photo, the Lightning connector is on the left and the Dock connector is on the right.) It's smaller but more capable than the old-school 30-pin Dock connector in first- through third-generation iPads and iPhones other than the iPhone 5.

The point is that your iPad mini requires accessories with Lightning connectors. If you have older accessories with Dock connectors you can still use many of them if you have one of the myriad of Lightning-to-Dock Connector Adapters from Apple and third-parties.

We start this accessories chapter with the options that carry the Apple logo and conclude with worthwhile extras from other companies.

Accessories from Apple

You've come to expect a certain level of excellence from Apple hardware and software, so you should expect no differently when it comes to various Apple-branded accessories. That said, you can find a variety of opinions on some of these products, so we recommend a visit to `http://store.apple.com`, where you can read mini-reviews and pore over ratings from real people just like you. They're not shy about telling it like it is.

Casing the iPad

The thing about accessories is that half the time, you wish they weren't accessories at all. You wish they came in the box. Among the things we would have liked to have seen included with the iPad was a protective case.

Alas, it wasn't to be — no iPad has ever come with a case though you can find cases aplenty just the same. You read about Apple's here and other cases a bit later in this chapter.

Apple's case-like offering for the iPad mini (and second, third, and fourth-generation iPads), shown in Figure 17-1, is more cover than case, which is probably why it's called a *Smart Cover* instead of a *Smart Case.* Made specifically for the iPad mini, it's ultra-thin and attaches magnetically. Flip the cover open (even just a little), and your iPad wakes instantly; flip it shut, and your iPad goes right to sleep. It's available in numerous bright colors in polyurethane for $39. Bob really likes his PRODUCT RED Smart Cover, as shown in figure 17-1.

Apple's newest entry is the iPad Smart Case, which combines a Smart Cover and a case to protect the back of your iPad. Like the Smart Cover and iPad Case, it too folds into a stand for reading, typing, or watching video. And because it's "smart," it automatically wakes and sleeps your iPad when you open and close it. Smart Cases are all constructed of polyurethane (sorry, no leather this time), and are available in six bright colors for $49.

Courtesy of Apple

Figure 17-1: Apple's Smart Cover for the iPad mini.

Exploring virtual keyboard alternatives

We think the various virtual keyboards that pop up just as you need them on the iPad are perfectly fine for shorter typing tasks, whether it's composing e-mails or tapping a few notes. For most longer assignments, however, we writers are more comfortable pounding away on a real-deal physical keyboard, and we suspect you feel the same way.

The Apple Wireless Keyboard

Fortunately, a physical keyboard for the iPad mini is an easy addition, and Apple offers a good one for $69.

The Apple Wireless Keyboard, as shown in Figure 17-2, is a way to use a decent-enough aluminum physical keyboard without tethering it to the iPad. It operates from up to 30 feet away from the iPad via Bluetooth, the wireless technology we discuss in Chapter 15. Which leads us to ask, can you see the iPad screen from 30 feet away?

Courtesy of Apple

Figure 17-2: The Apple Wireless Keyboard.

If you have an Apple TV connected to your HDTV, you can stream the screen of your iPad to the HDTV by using AirPlay. (See Chapter 8 for the details.) And although you probably can't see it from 30 feet, we've found the Apple Wireless Keyboard is great for using on the couch, where we can easily see the screen.

As with any Bluetooth device that the iPad makes nice with, you have to pair it to your tablet. Pairing is also discussed in Chapter 15.

The Bluetooth keyboard takes two AA batteries. It's smart about power management, too; it powers itself down when you stop using it to avoid draining those batteries. It wakes up when you start typing.

The Wireless Keyboard is very thin, so it's easy to take with you. If you use a backpack, briefcase, messenger bag, or even a large purse, you almost certainly have room for the Apple Wireless Keyboard.

And if your native tongue isn't English, Apple sells versions of the Wireless Keyboard in numerous languages, each still $69.

Not all the function keys on the Wireless Keyboard, will, um, function on your iPad. They're there, though, because you can use the same keyboard with a Mac.

Though we have tested only a few third-party Bluetooth keyboards, the iPad ought to work fine with any keyboard that supports Bluetooth 2.1 + EDR technology.

Connecting a camera

The iPad mini doesn't include a USB port or an SD memory card slot, which happen to be the most popular methods for getting pictures (and videos) from a digital camera onto a computer.

All the same, the iPad delivers a marvelous photo viewer. That's why if you take a lot of pictures, you'll probably need either Apple's Lightning–to–USB–Camera Adapter or Lightning–to–SD–Card Camera Reader ($29 each), which we also discuss in Chapter 9. As a reminder, these two components, shown in Figure 17-3, either of which plugs into the Lightning connector at the bottom of the iPad. One sports a USB interface that you can use with the USB cable that came with your camera to download pictures. The other is an SD Card Reader that lets you insert the memory card that stores your pictures.

Though the official line from Apple is that this USB adapter is meant to work with the USB cable from your digital camera, we've seen old USB keyboards work with it — and even USB speakers, MIDI keyboards, and more. But don't expect every USB device to be compatible: The power requirements of those devices (and their requisite software drivers) aren't loaded on the iPad.

We only hope that despite this helpful accessory, Apple will get around to adding a USB and an SD slot, but it hasn't happened yet.

Courtesy of Apple

Figure 17-3: The Lightning–to–USB–Camera Adapter (left) and the Lightning–to–SD–Card Camera Reader (right).

Connecting an iPad to a TV or projector

The iPad mini has a decent screen for what it is, a small tablet computer. But its display is nowhere near the size of a living room TV or even a computer monitor that you might find in a conference room or an auditorium. To send iPad content to a bigger screen, you can choose from these connectors:

✔ **Lightning–to–VGA Adapter:** Projecting what's on the iPad's screen to a larger display is the very reason behind the iPad Lightning–to–VGA Adapter that Apple is selling for $49. You can use it to connect your iPad to TVs, projectors, and VGA displays. What for? To watch videos, slide shows, and presentations on the big screen.

VGA (video graphics array) delivers, by today's standards, low-resolution video output, compared, say to the more advanced HDMI (High-Definition Multimedia Interface).

✔ **Lightning Digital AV Adapter:** The newest addition to the Apple adapter family is the $49 Apple Digital AV Adapter, which connects to your big screen TV via HDMI, which is pretty much the standard for HDTVs and other modern A/V gear. It lets you mirror the display on your iPad on a big screen TV, which is great for demos and presentations. Ed has used this adapter to, among other things, play *Angry Birds* on the bigger TV screen. Bob uses it to watch HD movies in hotel rooms. Both of us think it rocks.

Speaking of mirroring the display of your iPad onto a large-screen TV, you can do that wirelessly as long as you're streaming to another Apple accessory, Apple TV. It's all accomplished through AirPlay. Apple TV provides a lot of niceties in its own right, even if you don't own an iPad. (But if you don't, why are you reading this book?) For example, you can watch 1080p high-definition TV shows and movies; watch videos on Netflix, Hulu Plus, and Vimeo; listen to music from your iTunes library on a PC or Mac; and admire photos through iCloud, all for $99.

Keeping a spare charger

With roughly ten hours of battery life on the Wi-Fi–only iPad and nine hours on models with cellular access, a single charge can more than get you through a typical workday with your iPad. But why chance it? Having a spare charger at the office can spare you (!) from having to commute with one. The Apple iPad 10W USB Power Adapter sells for $29 and includes a lengthy six-foot cord.

And if you're traveling abroad, consider the Apple World Travel Adapter Kit. The $39 kit includes the proper prongs and adapters for numerous countries around the globe, and it lets you juice up not only your iPad, but also iPhones, iPod touches, and Macs.

Finally, if you have an old iPhone or iPod USB power adapter, or almost any other power adapter with a USB port, chances are good it'll work, though it may take longer to charge your iPad.

If you try to charge your iPad with an adapter that doesn't provide enough power, nothing bad will happen. Your iPad will merely display a Not Charging message instead of the battery-with-a-lightning-bolt icon you see when your iPad is connected to a charger with sufficient juice.

If you want the iPad mini to work with accessories that plug into the 30-pin dock connector on older iPads or iPods, consider the $29 or $39 Lightning to 30-pin adapters. And if you need an extra Lightning–to–USB cable, you can purchase extras for $19 each.

Listening and Talking with Earphones, Headphones, and Headsets

You've surely noticed that your iPad didn't include earphones or a headset. That's probably a blessing because the earphones and headsets Apple has included with iPods and iPhones since time immemorial aren't all that good. In fact, Bob refers to them as "mediocre and somewhat uncomfortable" in almost every article he's written about the iPod or iPhone. Ed agrees.

For what it's worth, Apple's new EarPods with Remote and Mic, which are included with the iPhone 5, are a million times better than the old Apple Earphones with Remote and Mic. But you won't find them in the box with your iPad mini, either.

When a pair of earphones isn't included, you can select a pair of headphones or earphones or a headset that suits your needs and your budget.

Though the new Apple headset is much better than the previous version, if you're shopping for earphones, you may find third-party options that sound better or that are more comfortable, or both, for around the same price ($29).

Earphones? Headphones? Headsets?

We refer to headphones and headsets several times and thought you might be wondering whether a difference exists, and if so, what it is. When we talk about *headphones* or *earphones,* we're talking about the things you use to listen to music. A *headset* adds a microphone so that you can use it for voice chatting, schmoozing with Siri, FaceTime video chatting, and (in the case of the iPhone or Internet VoIP services such as Skype) for phone calls. So headphones and earphones are for listening, and headsets are for both talking and listening.

Now you may be wondering whether earphones and headphones are the same. To some people, they may be, but to us, headphones have a band across the top (or back) of your head, and the listening apparatus is big and covers the outside of your ears. Think of the big fat things

you see covering a radio disk jockey's ears. Earphones (sometimes referred to as *earbuds*), on the other hand, are smaller, fit entirely in your ear, and have no band across the top or back of your head.

Headsets can be earphone style or, less commonly, headphone style. The distinguishing factor is that headsets always include a microphone. And some headsets are designed specifically for use with Apple i-products (iPhone, iPod, iPad) and have integrated Play/Pause and volume control buttons.

One last thing: Some companies refer to their earbud products as headphones, but we think that's confusing and wrong. So in this book, headphones are those bulky, outside-the-ear things, and earphones are teeny-tiny things that fit entirely in your ear canal.

Wired headphones, earphones, and headsets

Search Amazon for *headphones, earphones,* or *headsets,* and you'll find thousands of each are available at prices ranging from around $10 to more than $1,000. Or, if you prefer to shop in a brick-and-mortar store, Target, Best Buy, and the Apple Store all have decent selections, with prices starting at less than $20.

Much as we love the shopping experience at Apple Stores, you won't find any bargains there. Bargain-hunting doesn't matter that much for Apple-branded products because they're rarely discounted. However, you can almost always find widely available non-Apple items such as headphones, earphones, and headsets cheaper somewhere else.

With so many brands and models of earphones, headphones, and headsets available from so many manufacturers at so many price points, we can't possibly test even a fraction of the ones available today. That said, we've probably tested more of them than most people, and we have our favorites.

When it comes to headphones, Bob is partial to his Grado SR60i's, which are legendary for offering astonishingly accurate audio at an affordable price (around $80). He's tried headphones that cost twice, thrice, or even more times as much that he didn't think sounded nearly as good. Find out more at www.gradolabs.com.

Ed goes with sweet-sounding, albeit pricey (about $350) Bose QuietComfort 3 acoustic noise-canceling headphones.

For earphones and earphone-style headsets, Bob likes the Klipsch Image S4 Headphones and S4i In-Ear Headset with Mic and 3-Button Remote. At around $79 and $99, respectively, they sound better than many similarly priced products and better than many more-expensive offerings.

Bluetooth stereo headphones, earphones, and headsets

Neither of us has much experience with Bluetooth (wireless) stereo headphones and headsets, but we thought we'd at least plant the seed. The idea is that with Bluetooth stereo headphones/earphones/headsets, you can listen to music wirelessly up to 33 feet away from your iPad. If this sounds good to you, we suggest that you look for reviews of such products on the web before you decide which one to buy. A search of Amazon for *stereo Bluetooth headset* brought up more than 300 items, with prices starting as low as $15.

Listening with Speakers

You can connect just about any speakers to your iPad, but if you want decent sound, we suggest you look only at *powered* speakers and not *passive* (unpowered) ones. The difference is that powered speakers contain their own amplification circuitry and can deliver much better (and louder) sound than unpowered speakers.

Prices range from well under $100 to hundreds (or even thousands) of dollars. Most speaker systems designed for use with your computer, iPod, or iPhone work well as long as they have an auxiliary input or a dock connector that can accommodate your iPad.

Desktop speakers

Logitech (www.logitech.com) makes a range of desktop speaker systems priced from less than $25 to more than $300. But that $300 system is the Z5500 THX-certified 505-watt 5.1 digital surround system — surely overkill for listening to music or video on your iPad, which doesn't support surround sound anyway. The point is that Logitech makes a variety of decent systems at a wide range of price points. If you're looking for something inexpensive, you can't go wrong with most Logitech-powered speaker systems.

Bob is a big fan of Audioengine (www.audioengineusa.com) desktop speakers. They deliver superior audio at prices that are quite reasonable for speakers that sound this good. Audioengine 5 is the premium product priced at $349 a pair; Audioengine 2 is its smaller but still excellent-sounding sibling priced at $199 a pair. They're available only direct from the manufacturer, but the company is so confident that you'll love them that it offers a free audition for the speaker systems. If you order a pair and don't love them, return them within 30 days for a full refund. Bob knows a lot of people who have ordered them, and so far no one has sent them back.

Bluetooth speakers

Like Bluetooth headsets, Bluetooth speakers let you listen to music up to 33 feet away from your iPad. They're great for listening by the pool or hot tub or anywhere else you might not want to take your iPad.

Both of us have written favorable reviews of the $199.99 wireless JAMBOX by Jawbone, a rechargeable speaker that offers very good sound despite being able to fit into the palm of your hand. You can connect via Bluetooth or its auxiliary stereo jack. An added bonus: JAMBOX doubles as a decent-enough speakerphone.

More recently, Jawbone introduced the BIG JAMBOX. Quick quiz: What do you think that means? Right, a bigger version of the JAMBOX with bigger sound. Of course, at $299.99, it also carries a bigger price, and it's a bit less portable than its diminutive sibling.

Ed also likes a big rival to the BIG JAMBOX, the Bose SoundLink Wireless Mobile Speaker, which fetches a similar price.

Both of us travel with a Jawbone JAMBOX, and we both really like it. A lot.

AirPlay speakers

The newest type of speakers you might choose for your iPad feature Apple's proprietary AirPlay protocol, which takes advantage of your existing Wi-Fi network to stream audio and/or video from your iPad (or other compatible i-device or a Mac or PC running iTunes) to a single AirPlay-enabled speaker or audio/video receiver.

The biggest differences between AirPlay and Bluetooth speakers are described in this list:

✔ Bluetooth can stream music only in compressed form; AirPlay can stream music (and video) uncompressed. So a speaker with AirPlay should sound better than a similar speaker with Bluetooth.

✔ Bluetooth's range is roughly 30 feet; AirPlay's range is up to 300 feet. There's no way to extend Bluetooth's range; Wi-Fi range can easily be extended with inexpensive routers such as Apple's AirPort Express ($99).

✔ iTunes (on your computer) can use AirPlay to stream audio or video to multiple speakers or audio/video receivers, with individual volume controls for each device; Bluetooth only streams to one device at a time.

Wrapping Your iPad in Third-Party Cases

Much as we like the Apple Smart Cover, other vendors offer some excellent— and different — options:

✔ **Targus:** Targus (www.targus.com) has a full line of iPad cases in a variety of materials and prices. The nice part is that none of them, including the leather portfolio, costs more than $60.

✔ **Griffin Technology:** Griffin Technology (www.griffintechnology.com) also has a pretty good selection of iPad cases at reasonable prices (that is, none more than $50).

✔ **iLuv:** iLuv (www.i-luv.com) is yet another case maker with a range of affordable cases fabricated from leather, fabric, and silicone, none of which costs more than $40.

> ✔ **The iPad Bubble Sleeve:** From Hard Candy Cases (which is at www.
> hardcandycases.com), the Shockdrop ($49.95) offers significantly
> better protection against bumps and scratches than many other
> cases we've seen. If we expected our iPads to be exposed to moderate
> impacts, this case's rigid exterior and additional shock-absorbing rubber
> bumpers for the screen make it the case we'd choose (at least, Bob
> adds, until LifeProof comes out with a case for the mini).

But Wait . . . There's More!

Before we leave the topic of accessories, we think you should know about a
few more products, namely, film protection products that guard your iPad's
exterior (or screen) without adding a bit of bulk: the Griffin Technology
A-Frame tabletop stand for your iPad, and 2-into-1 stereo adapters.

Protecting the screen with film

Some people prefer not to use a case with their iPad, and that's okay, too.
But if you're one of those people (or even if you're not), you might want to
consider protective film for the iPad screen or even the whole device. We've
tried these products on our iPhones in the past and have found them to perform as promised. If you apply them properly, they're nearly invisible, and
they protect your iPad from scratches and scrapes without adding any bulk.

Bob recently discovered the joys of iVisor AG Screen Protector for iPad ($30)
from Moshi (www.moshimonde.com) and says it's the best screen cover he's
tested to date. It's easy to apply, resists fingerprints better than Apple's oleo-
phobic screen coating, and features patented technology for a bubble-free
installation every time. The best feature, Bob believes, is that if it gets dirty,
you just wash it under a faucet, and then air-dry and reapply it (bubble-free,
of course).

Another option is from the aforementioned RadTech (www.radtech.us),
which offers two types of Mylar screen protectors — clear transparent and
antiglare. These screen protectors are somewhat stiffer than the film products, and unlike film, they can be cleaned and reapplied multiple times with
no reduction in performance. They effectively hide minor scratches, surface
defects, and abrasions, and the hard Mylar surface not only resists scratches
and abrasions, but is also optically correct. Finally, they're reasonably priced
at $19.95 for a pair of protectors of the same type.

Bob has also tested more traditional film products from invisibleShield by
ZAGG (www.zagg.com), BodyGuardz (www.bodyguardz.com), and Best
Skins Ever (www.bestskinsever.com) and says, in a nutshell, they're more
similar than they are different. invisibleShield is the most expensive and
possibly the best-quality film. BodyGuardz products are roughly 25 percent

cheaper than invisibleShield and of comparable quality. Both invisibleShield and BodyGuardz offer free lifetime replacement of their products. Best Skins Ever products are 25–55 percent less expensive than invisibleShield or BodyGuardz, yet the product is, if not just as good, darn close to it. The difference is that Best Skins Ever has minimal packaging, and rather than including the "special liquid" you need to apply it (like invisibleShield and BodyGuardz), Best Skins Ever includes instructions for making it yourself. And unlike the others, Best Skins Ever has no free replacement policy, though it does offer a 30-day money-back guarantee. Finally, all three offer total protection (front, back, and sides) as well as separate products for the front or back.

Which one to choose? If you think you might take advantage of the lifetime replacement policy, you want either invisibleShield or BodyGuardz. If you want a good product at the lowest price but with a 30-day money-back guarantee instead of lifetime replacement, look at Best Skins Ever.

Any or all of these so-called skins (including the iVisor AG, which is the easiest of all to install) can be tricky to apply. Follow the instructions closely, watch videos on the vendors' websites and YouTube, and take your time. If you do, you'll be rewarded with clear film protection that's nearly invisible yet protects your iPad from scratches, nicks, and cuts.

The last time we checked, Best Buy will apply these skins for you for a small (under $10) fee, which may be a bargain compared to messing things up and having to buy another skin. Ask your favorite electronics retailer if it provides a similar service.

Sharing your iPad with a 2-into-1 stereo adapter

A *2-into-1 stereo adapter* is a handy little device that lets two people plug their headphones/earphones/headsets into one iPad (or iPod or iPhone, for that matter). They're quite inexpensive (less than $10) and extremely useful if you're traveling with a friend by air, sea, rail, or bus. They're also great when you want to watch a movie with your BFF but don't want to risk waking the neighbors or roommates.

We call 'em *2-into-1 stereo adapters,* but that's not the only name they go by. Other names you might see for the same device are as follows:

- 3.5mm stereo Y-splitter
- ⅛-inch stereo 1-plug-to-2-jacks adapter
- ⅛-inch stereo Y-adapter
- 3.5mm dual stereo headphone jack splitter
- And many others

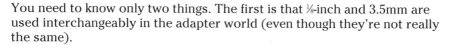

You need to know only two things. The first is that ⅛-inch and 3.5mm are used interchangeably in the adapter world (even though they're not really the same).

Some measurements to keep in mind: ⅛ inch = 0.125 inch, whereas 3.5mm = 0.1378 inch. Not the same, but close enough for rock 'n' roll.

The second is that you want to make sure that you get a *stereo* adapter. Some monaural adapters work but pump exactly the same sound into both ears, instead of sending the audio information for the left stereo channel to your left ear and the right stereo channel to your right.

In other words, you need a ⅛-inch or 3.5mm stereo adapter that has a single stereo plug on one end (to plug into your iPad) and two stereo jacks on the other (to accommodate two sets of headphones/earphones/headsets).

Test it before you travel. Bob recently discovered that the one he had packed made it much louder for one person than the other.

Part VI
The Part of Tens

The 5th Wave   By Rich Tennant

©RICHTENNANT

Accessories

iPadPad

"It's a docking system for the iPad mini that comes with 3 bedrooms, 2 baths, and a car port."

1 t's written in stone somewhere at Wiley world headquarters that we *For Dummies* authors must include a Part of Tens in every single *For Dummies* book we write. It is a duty we take quite seriously. So in this part, you'll find a list of ten of our favorite free applications plucked from the iPad App Store. These include a couple of really addictive games and even an app to help you find a recipe for your favorite dish. We then move on to our diverse collection of ten fabulous apps every user should consider buying, including an art studio, a database, and a piano for your iPad mini.

We close the show with one of our favorite topics: hints, tips, and shortcuts that make life with your iPad mini even better. Among the ten, you discover how to look at the capacity of your newly favored device in different ways, find out how to share web pages, and pick up another trick or two on using the iPad's virtual keyboard.

18

Ten Appetizing (And Free) Apps

....

*K*iller app is familiar jargon to anyone who has spent any time around computers. The term refers to an application so sweet or so useful that just about everybody wants it or must have it.

You could make the argument that the most compelling killer app on the iPad is the very App Store we expound on in Chapter 11. This online emporium has an abundance of splendid programs — dare we say killer apps in their own right? — many of which are free. They cover everything from food (hey, you gotta eat) to show biz. Okay, so some rotten apples (aren't we clever?) are in the bunch, too. But we're here to accentuate the positive.

With that in mind, in this chapter, we offer ten of our favorite free iPad apps. In Chapter 19, we tell you about our favorite iPad apps that aren't free but are worth every penny.

We show you ours, and we encourage you to show us yours. If you discover your own killer iPad apps, by all means let us know — our e-mail addresses are at the end of the introduction to this book — so that we can check them out.

Pocket Legends

If you're a fan of MMORPG-style gaming, we're happy to inform you that Pocket Legends for iPad is an incredibly cool 3D MMO game that doesn't (or at least doesn't have to) cost you a cent.

In case you aren't already a fan of the genre, MMORPG is the acronym for Massively Multiplayer Online Role-Playing Game. You may skip to the next section now if you're not a fan.

What that means is that you can join thousands of players from all over the world when you play. In Pocket Legends, you begin by choosing one of three character classes to play as: an archer, an enchantress, or a warrior. Then you (and, optionally, other players) wander around dungeons, forests, and castles, killing zombies, skeletons, demons, and other bad guys and collecting gold pieces. Every so often, your character finds weapons, armor, and shields, or you can buy them with the gold you find. The longer you play, the more powerful your character becomes and the more powerful the weapons, armor, and shields you can use.

Figure 18-1 shows Bob's character (Doc) in a forest, missing a bad guy with a hurled lightning bolt.

Figure 18-1: Pocket Legends is fun, easy to play, and — best of all — free (mostly).

Did you notice, in the first paragraph of this section, that we say "doesn't have to cost you money" rather than the more absolute "doesn't cost you money"? Here's the reason: If you enjoy playing (as we do), you'll probably want to purchase additional dungeon campaigns ($1.99 each), platinum (30 pieces for $4.99), additional characters (only $0.99 each), or one of the other goodies available for in-app purchase. You can have a lot of fun for a good long time without laying out a dime — but if you like playing, you'll probably find yourself considering a purchase or two.

Here is one last thing: Bob's character is an archer named Doc. So, if you happen to run into him in a dungeon or forest, use the chat system to give him a shout-out.

Shazam

Ever heard a song on the radio or television, in a store, or at a club and wondered what it was called or who was singing it? With the Shazam app, you may never wonder again. Just launch Shazam and point your iPad's microphone at the source of the music. In a few seconds, the song title and artist's name magically appear on your iPad screen.

In Shazam parlance, that song has been *tagged*. Now, if tagging were all Shazam could do, that would surely be enough. But wait, there's more. After Shazam tags a song, you can

- Buy the song at the iTunes Store.
- Watch related videos on YouTube.
- Tweet the song on Twitter, if you set up Twitter in Settings.
- Read a biography, a discography, or lyrics.
- Take a photo and attach it to the tagged item in Shazam.
- E-mail a tag to a friend.

Shazam isn't great at identifying classical music, jazz, show tunes, or opera, nor is it adept at identifying obscure indie bands. But if you use it primarily to identify popular music, it rocks (pun intended). It has worked for us in noisy airport terminals, crowded shopping malls, and even once at a wedding ceremony.

ABC Player

Do you watch any ABC TV shows such as *Grey's Anatomy; Dancing with the Stars;* Bob's favorite, the recently canceled *GCB;* or Ed's favorite, *Modern Family?* If so, grab your copy of the free ABC Player now. Go ahead; we'll wait.

With this app and a Wi-Fi connection, you can watch complete episodes of your favorite ABC-TV shows anytime you like. Just browse or search to find the shows and episodes you want to watch.

And (not to repeat ourselves) it's *all free!* Yes, the shows have commercials, but would you rather pay $1.99 (a typical cost of an episode of a TV show in the iTunes Store) for the commercial-free version?

We thought not.

Movies by Flixster

We like movies, so we both use the Flixster app a lot. Feed it your zip code, and then browse local theaters by movie, showtime, rating, or distance from your current location. Or browse to find a movie you like, and then tap to find theaters, showtimes, and other info, as shown in Figure 18-2. Another nice feature is the capability to buy tickets to most movies from your iPad with just a few additional taps.

Figure 18-2: Find out showtimes, watch the trailer, or get more info on the director or cast with a single tap.

We appreciate that we can read reviews, play movie trailers, and e-mail movie listings to others with a single tap. We also enjoy the movie trailers for soon-to-be-released films and DVDs. Other free movie showtime apps are out there, but we like Flixster the best.

IMDb Movies & TV

While we're on the subject of the silver screen, we couldn't resist opening IMDb, shorthand for Internet Movie Database (now owned by Amazon.com). And what a database it is, especially for the avid filmgoer. This vast and delightful repository of all things cinema is the place to go for complete cast and crew listings, actor and filmmaker bios, plot summaries, movie trailers, critics' reviews, user ratings, parental guidance, famous quotations, and all kinds of trivia.

You can always search for movies, TV shows, actors, and so on by typing a name in the search box in the upper-right corner of the screen. Or tap Browse at the lower left to find current movies by showtime, what's coming soon, or box office results. You can browse TV recaps, too, or find people born on the day you happen to be looking and poking around the app. It's also fun to check out the most-viewed stars on IMDb. The recent roster included Jennifer Lawrence, Channing Tatum, Kristen Stewart, Marion Cotillard, Tom Hardy, Johnny Depp, and Mila Kunis.

One piece of advice to movie buffs: Avoid the IMDb if you have a lot of work to do. You'll have a hard time closing the curtain on this marvelous app.

Netflix

Flixster, IMDb, and now Netflix — you've no doubt detected a real trend by now, and that trend is indeed our affection for movies and TV shows. If you love TV and movies, too, you're sure to be a fan of the Netflix app. Over time, Netflix, the company that built its reputation by sending DVDs to subscribers through the mail, started streaming movies over the Internet to computers, TVs, and other consumer electronics gear. You can now add the iPad to that list.

From the iPad, you have more or less instant access to thousands of movies on demand. And although these titles aren't exactly current blockbusters, we know you'll find plenty of films worth seeing. You can search by *genre* (classics, comedy, drama, and so on) and *subgenre* (courtroom dramas, political dramas, romantic dramas, and so on).

Although the app is free, as are the movies you choose to watch on the fly, you have to pay Netflix streaming subscription fees that start at $7.99 a month. You also need an Internet connection, preferably through Wi-Fi, though Netflix works on cellular models as well.

Remember what we've told you about streaming movies over 3G or 4G, and be mindful of your data plan.

DVD Netflix subscribers might also quibble about the fact that you can't manage your DVD queue inside the app.

Comics

Comics is three apps rolled into one. First and foremost, it's a fantastic way to read comic books on a 7.9-inch touchscreen. Second, it's a comic bookstore with hundreds of comics and comic series from dozens of publishers, including Arcana, Archie, Marvel, Devil's Due, Digital Webbing, Red 5, Zenescope, and many more (see Figure 18-3).

Figure 18-3: Comics lets you shop for and read (d'oh!) comics on your iPad.

Finally, this app provides a great way to organize comics on your iPad, so you can find the one you want quickly and easily.

The free Comics app gives you access to hundreds of free comics, or you can use the built-in store to purchase comics, usually 99 cents to $2.99 per issue.

New releases are available every Wednesday, so visit the store often to check out the latest and greatest offerings. Both the store and your personal comic collection are well organized and easy to use. And reading comics in Comics is a pleasure you won't want to miss if you're a fan of comics or graphic novels.

Epicurious Recipes & Shopping List

We love to eat. But we're writers, not gourmet chefs, so we'll take all the help we can get when it comes to preparing a great meal. And we get a lot of that culinary assistance from Epicurious, which easily lives up to its billing as the "cook's companion." This tasty recipe app comes courtesy of Condé Nast Digital.

Tap the Control Panel button in the upper-left corner of the screen to get started, and you can find a yummy recipe in no time. Tap Featured inside the Control Panel (if it's not already highlighted) to find recipes that have been lumped into categories, often timed to the season. Around the time we were writing this book, recipe collection categories included Summer Dinners, Summer Cocktails, Picnic Ideas, Family Reunions, and Grilled Mains. Some recipes carry reviews.

If you tap Search inside the Control Panel instead, you can fine-tune your search for a recipe by food or drink, by main ingredient (banana, chicken, pasta), by cuisine type, and by dietary consideration (low-carb, vegan, kosher, and so on), among other parameters.

When you discover a recipe you like, you can add it to a collection of favorites, e-mail it to a friend, pass along the ingredients to your shopping list, summon nutritional information, or share it on Facebook and Twitter.

If you want to sync favorite recipes on your iPhone and iPad through a personal Recipe Box on Epicurious.com, that'll cost you $1.99 as an in-app purchase.

Bon appétit.

Flipboard

The media stars of today aren't necessarily those employed by old-fashioned publications. Nope. The stars of today are you and all your buddies and contacts on Twitter, Facebook, Flickr, LinkedIn, and lots of other places. Flipboard transforms the social web into a gorgeous digital magazine. And you're the editor who gets to customize the content. Add Facebook pals, the folks you follow on Twitter, stuff from your Google Reader account, Instagram photos, and photos uploaded to Flickr. You can request nuggets from more traditional media too, including outlets *CNN, The Economist, The Huffington Post, Fox News, BBC World News, NPR, USA TODAY,* and many more. Figure 18-4 provides a glimpse of what your tweets and feeds can look like through Flipboard.

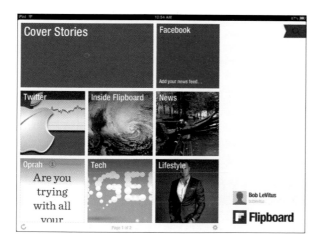

Figure 18-4: We think you'll flip over Flipboard.

Pandora Radio

We've long been fans of Pandora on other computers and mobile devices. So we're practically delirious that this custom Internet radio service is available *gratis* on the iPad. And you can play Pandora music in the background while doing other stuff.

Pandora works on the iPad in much the same way that it does on a Mac or PC. In the box at the upper left, type the name of a favorite artist, song title, or composer via the iPad keyboard, and Pandora creates an instant personalized radio station with selections that exemplify the style you chose. Along the left panel of Figure 18-5, you see some of the eclectic stations Bob created. Tapping QuickMix at the top of the list plays musical selections across all your stations.

Suppose that you type **Beatles**. Pandora's instant Beatles station includes performances from John, Paul, George, and Ringo as well as tunes from other acts.

Search for artist, song or composer

Station list   Bookmark or buy a song

Figure 18-5: Have we told you lately how much we like Pandora?

And say that you type a song title, such as **Have I Told You Lately**. Pandora constructs a station with similar music after you tell it whether to base tunes on the Van Morrison, Rod Stewart, or another rendition.

Pandora comes out of the *Music Genome Project,* an organization of musicians and technologists who analyze music according to hundreds of attributes (such as melody, harmony, and vocal performances).

You can help fine-tune the music Pandora plays by tapping the Thumbs Up or Thumbs Down icon at the top of the screen, above the album covers associated with the music you've been listening to during the current session.

If you tap the Menu button below an album cover of the song that's playing, you can bookmark the song or the artist who's playing or head to iTunes to purchase the song or other material from the artist directly on the iPad (if the song is available digitally).

Pandora also takes advantage of the iPad to deliver artist profiles (refer to Figure 18-5). You may see ads, too, unless you subscribe to the premium Pandora One service for $36 a year.

Bob says it's worth every penny to him because Pandora One adds significant benefits:

- **High-quality streaming:** When listening on the web, you experience audio at 192 Kbps. That's the highest-quality streaming experience on the Internet. More bits means better-sounding music.

- **Pandora One desktop:** Listen to Pandora from a dedicated desktop application; no need to keep a browser window open. Control playback from the Windows taskbar or the Macintosh Dock. Get pop-up alerts when a new song starts to play. It's the ultimate Pandora experience: simple, efficient, pure.

- **No ads:** Pandora One is completely free of any sort of advertising: no audio ads, no visual ads. It's just you and your music.

- **Personalization:** Surround the Pandora player with one of eight custom "skins" that make the look of Pandora as personalized as the music.

- **Mini player:** When you minimize Pandora One into the smallest possible browser window, the web version of Pandora can easily live side by side with other websites and applications.

- **Unlimited skipping:** With the standard ad-supported version of Pandora, you're limited to 12 total skips per day. With Pandora One, you can skip as many times per day as you'd like (*and,* thanks to licensing constraints, to six skips per hour).

- **Extended-interaction time-out:** Listen for up to five hours in a row without interacting with Pandora. Simply turn it on and let it go. Every time you interact, the timer is reset, so a single click around lunchtime can get you through an entire workday.

Before we leave the realm of the free apps, we'd like to remind you of one more freebie — a free app so wonderful that we wrote a whole chapter (Chapter 10) about it. The app is iBooks.

19

Ten Apps Worth Paying For

*I*f you read Chapter 18, you know that lots of great free apps are available for your iPad. But as the old cliché goes, some things are worth paying for. Still, none of the ten for-pay apps we've chosen as some of our favorites are likely to break the bank. As you're about to discover, some apps in this list are practical, and some are downright silly. The common theme? We think you'll like carrying these apps around on your iPad.

Bill Atkinson PhotoCard

Who is Bill Atkinson? He had a hand (or both hands) in the first Macintosh computer as well as the MacPaint and HyperCard Mac applications. Today he's a world-renowned nature photographer, which brings us to his app. Bill Atkinson PhotoCard is a free app that lets you create gorgeous high-resolution postcards and send them via either e-mail or the U.S. Postal Service. Sending postcards by e-mail is free, and so is the app.

But the reason we love it is that you can have printed postcards sent via USPS for $1.50 and $2.00 per postcard, depending on how many print-and-mail credits you purchase. The 8.25-x-5.5-inch postcards are, in a word, stunning. Printed on heavy glossy stock on a state-of-the-art HP Indigo Digital Press, then laminated for protection, they're as beautiful as any postcard you've ever seen.

You can use one of the 200 included Bill Atkinson nature photos, as shown in Figure 19-1, or you can use any picture in your Photos library. You can add stickers and stamps, as shown in Figure 19-1, and you can even add voice notes to e-mailed cards.

Figure 19-1: Your postcard can feature one of Bill Atkinson's gorgeous nature photos.

If you're still uncertain, download the app (it's free) and try it. Send an e-mail postcard or two to yourself. After you've seen how gorgeous these cards can be and how easy the app is to use, we think you'll spring for some print-and-mail credits and take your iPad on your next vacation.

Words with Friends HD

This brings us to perhaps the only time in this whole book that your authors had a disagreement. Both of us love word games and puzzles, but Bob loves Words with Friends HD whereas Ed prefers the real thing, namely,

SCRABBLE. Because neither of us wanted to eliminate our favorite word game from this chapter, we decided it would be best if each of us wrote about our fave. So the description of Words with Friends here was written by Bob, and the write-up of SCRABBLE that follows is all Ed.

Social media is all the rage these days, but most multiplayer iPad games are either boring or not particularly social. Words with Friends HD ($2.99), on the other hand, is the most social game I've found — and a ton of fun, too. It's kind of like playing SCRABBLE with a friend, but because it's turn-based, you can make a move and then quit the app and do other stuff. When your friend makes his next move, you can choose to be notified that it's your turn by sound, onscreen alert, and/or a number on the Words with Friends icon on your Home screen.

Try the free version (Words with Friends HD Free), and I'm sure you'll be hooked. Then challenge me if you like; my username is `boblevitus` (although I often have the maximum 20 games going, so keep trying if I don't accept your challenge right away).

SCRABBLE

You already know we work with words for a living — and that we have a (slight) disagreement about favorite apps for playing such games. Ed appreciates a good game of SCRABBLE, whereas Bob, as we told you earlier in this chapter, prefers the virtual knock-off, Words with Friends HD.

Playing the $9.99 iPad version of SCRABBLE (from Electronic Arts and Hasbro) is the closest thing yet to replicating the experience of the famous crossword board game on an electronic device. For starters, check out the gorgeous high-definition graphics. The sounds of tiles placed on the virtual board are realistic, too.

In fact, you can build a decent case that SCRABBLE on the iPad even beats the original board game. Consider the following:

- You can play up to 25 multiplayer games at a time. Challenge wordsmiths on Facebook or play over the same home network (as I have) against someone with another iPad, an iPod touch, or an iPhone. Or, play against the computer and choose your level of difficulty (easy, normal, hard).

- Through Party Play mode, you can manage your private tile rack on your iPhone or iPod touch and seamlessly place tiles onto the iPad SCRABBLE game board. It works with up to four devices. You have to download the Tile Rack app from the App Store, but it's free.

- You can play iTunes music in the background for inspiration.

- A SCRABBLE Teacher feature lets you see the best available word choice from your previous moves.

- Personal stats are kept on the iPad. You don't need to keep score. And you can play within Game Center.

- You won't lose any letter tiles or have to fret that your small child or pet will swallow any.

Though I'm an obvious fan of this app, I did experience one quandary while playing over a home network — I wanted to use the word *quandary* because the letter *Q* is worth ten points in SCRABBLE. The app crashed on that occasion.

ArtStudio for iPad

Do you fancy yourself an artist? We know our artistic talent is limited, but if we were talented, ArtStudio for iPad is the program we'd use to paint our masterpieces. Even if you have limited artistic talent, you can see that this app has everything you need to create awesome artwork.

We were embarrassed to show you our creations, so instead we whipped up a composite illustration (see Figure 19-2) that shows the contents of the Paint Brush Settings overlay and the Filters menu, to give you a sense of how much power is packed into this reasonably priced app.

Here are only a few of the outstanding ArtStudio for iPad features:

- It has 25 brushes, including pencils, a smudge tool, a bucket fill, an airbrush, and more. Brushes are resizable and simulate brush pressure.

Figure 19-2: ArtStudio for iPad has a comprehensive set of tools and menus for fine-tuning images.

- You can have as many as five layers with options, such as delete, reorder, duplicate, merge, and transparency.

- It has desktop-quality filters, as shown in Figure 19-2.

Don't believe us? AppSmile.com (www.appsmile.com) rated it 5 out of 5, saying, "This is what Photoshop Mobile wishes it had been." SlapApp.com (www.slapapp.com) also rated it 5 out of 5 and said, "I've dabbled in quite a few painting and drawing apps and this one has 'em all beat by a long shot." And by all means, check out what talented artists can do with ArtStudio for iPad at www.flickr.com/groups/artstudioimages and www.artistinvermont.com.

One last thing: The app was only 99 cents when we bought our copies — a "special launch sale" price. The price has gone up, but even at the new price, a whopping $5.99, it's still a heck of a deal for a thoughtfully designed and full-featured drawing and painting app.

Beware of ripoffs in the iTunes App Store, such as the similarly named Art Studio HD — For Your iPad. That one, a bad knock-off from developer Party Sub Productions, has garnered mostly 1-star ratings. Don't be fooled — the app you're looking for is ArtStudio for iPad, from Lucky Clan. Note that Art and Studio run together to form a single word; if you search for the single word *ArtStudio,* you'll find it.

Pinball Crystal Caliburn II

Good pinball games require supremely realistic physics, and Crystal Caliburn II ($3.99) nails it. The way the ball moves around the tables and interacts with bumpers and flippers is so realistic that you'll think you're at an arcade. It's so realistic, in fact, that you can shake the table to influence the ball's movement.

Another hallmark of a great pinball game is great sound effects, and this game doesn't disappoint. The sounds the ball makes when it bounces off a bumper, is hit with a flipper, or passes through a rollover are spot-on and totally authentic.

If you like pinball, we think you'll love Pinball Crystal Caliburn II on your iPad.

Art Authority for iPad

We've already admitted to being artistically challenged. But that only applies to making art. But we both appreciate good art as much as the next person, or even more. That's why we're so enthusiastic about Art Authority, only $4.99.

Art Authority is like an art museum you hold in your hand; it contains more than 50,000 paintings and sculptures by more than 1,000 of the world's greatest artists. The works are organized into eight period-specific rooms, such as Early (up to 1400s), Baroque, Romanticism, Modern, and American. In each room, the artworks are subdivided by movement. The Modern room, for example, has works of surrealism, cubism, Fauvism, Dadaism, sculpture, and several more.

You find period overviews, movement overviews, timelines, and slide shows, plus a searchable index of all more than 1,000 artists and separate indices for each room.

Since we first wrote about this app, developer Open Door Networks has added an Art Near Me feature that lets you search for art in your vicinity. It was already an excellent app, and now it's even better. If you love art, check it out.

Solar Walk — 3D Solar System

We like to gaze at the heavens, but we often have no clue what we're looking at. This handsome, animated, 99-cent guide to the night sky from Vito Technology (it was recently refreshed to take advantage of the Retina display) will delight astronomy students and anyone else who's fascinated by outer space, even if purists scoff that Pluto, no longer considered a planet, is included in the solar system model.

From the start, you're taken on a virtual tour through the galaxy to the Earth. You can search planets, satellites, stars, and more and travel through time and space with a Time Machine feature. Animated movies cover topics such as Earth's Cycles, Solar Eclipse, and The Moon Phases.

What's more, the app can exploit 3D, provided you supply your own *anaglyph*-style cyan-red 3D glasses. And if you hook the iPad mini up to a 3DTV using an HDMI adapter (see Chapter 17), you can get a true sense of the depth and sheer size of the solar system in 3D, while controlling what you see on the screen through the iPad.

Of course, without 3D, you can use AirPlay to mirror what's on the iPad screen on the bigger TV screen, provided you have an Apple TV.

Instapaper

Have you ever happened upon a web page with a long, interesting story you wanted to read but didn't have time? Or have you wished you could somehow stick the story in your pocket and read it during the train ride home, on the airplane, or on a submarine?

If you've ever wished any of those things, you're going to love Instapaper — a $4.99 iPad app that lets you save web pages from your computer or iPad web browser and read them later on your iPad whether or not you have an Internet connection. Yes, Safari's Reading List does the same thing, but Instapaper is still one of Bob's all-time favorite apps.

Here are only a few of his reasons:

- Instapaper lets you save articles from web pages, organize them into folders (if you care to), and then read them at your convenience, with or without an Internet connection.

- Saved articles are displayed in an easy-to-read, plain text format, as shown in Figure 19-3.

Figure 19-3: Instapaper saves articles from web pages so that you can read them later, with or without an Internet connection.

- You can visit the web page the article was saved from with its ads, banners, and other graphics by tapping Open in Browser (refer to Figure 19-3).

- Instapaper has advanced settings that let you customize features such as scrolling, what happens when you open a !link, and how your articles are sorted, to name a few.

Give the tilt-to-scroll option a chance. We hated it at first but now think it should be in every iPad app.

Bento 4 for iPad

Full-featured database programs have traditionally been the province for professionals and employees in a variety of job types and industries. FileMaker's Bento "personal database" programs for the Mac and iPhone, however, tend to be more inviting for mainstream consumers. The same goes for Bento 4 for the iPad, which, at $9.99, strikes a real bargain.

Indeed, Bento should appeal not only to salespeople, marketers, and field workers, but also to students and pretty much anyone who wants to keep on top of hobbies, projects, lists, events, and then some.

The newly redesigned (in version 4) simple-to-use app comes with a variety of free premade templates, covering exercise logs, vehicle maintenance, donations, diet log, time billing , and so on, with more available online. The app can handle more than 20 types of data, for such things as text, numbers, ratings, durations, currencies, and phone numbers. And Bento is tightly integrated with the iPad's Contacts program, Mail program, Safari (you can view web pages without leaving the app), and Google Maps. You can even record voice memos.

If you have a recent version of Bento for the Mac, you can sync the two programs so that any changes you make to a database on one machine are reflected in the corresponding database on the other machine. You need a Wi-Fi connection to sync the iPad version with the Mac version. However, because of memory constraints, Bento 4 for iPad may not be able to handle the largest databases that you created for Bento on the Mac.

Among the neat stunts made possible by using this app: text fields that expand and shrink when you tap them, visual check boxes, and the capabilities to admire photos, dispatch e-mails, and watch videos.

It's rather easy to get going with Bento. You can start out by tapping the Libraries button in the bottom-left corner of the screen. *Libraries* are groups of records you might want to track: Contacts, Event Planning, Products For Sale, and so on. You can tap a button that has a + hanging onto a square to add a record to your library, or tap the square with the minus sign to delete records.

Bento is particularly smart about the Contacts library. It lifts all the names in your iPad contacts and automatically prepopulates them in your Bento Contacts. (Don't worry; they remain in Contacts, too.)

It's a breeze to move from library to library or record to record inside the app. Down the left side of the screen are the libraries you've selected from the aforementioned templates. On the right, you'll see the actual records. Tap to move from one record to another.

Customizing records is also a cinch. You can add a new record, add new fields, add records to collections, delete records, and more.

If you need a full-featured database solution, check out Bento's big brother, FileMaker Go for iPad, a $39.99 app that runs most databases created with FileMaker Pro on a Mac or PC.

Quickoffice Pro HD

In case you haven't noticed, we love using our iPads for fun and amusement. But, heck — we have a serious side too. And when we have to don our work hats but don't feel like schlepping our laptops, we can turn to Quickoffice Pro.

This popular business app, which by App Store standards is a pricey $19.99, lets you create and edit Microsoft Office documents, including Word files, Excel spreadsheets, and PowerPoint presentations.

You can save files as Adobe PDFs, and print using AirPrint. You can even track changes, check your spelling, consult a dictionary, make comments, and do many of the basic tasks you've come to expect when using Office on a PC or Mac.

It's a flexible app for that most flexible of tablets.

20

Ten Hints, Tips, and Shortcuts

A fter spending a lot of quality time with many iPads, it's only natural that we've discovered more than a few helpful hints, tips, and shortcuts. In this chapter, we share our faves.

Saving Time and Keystrokes with Keyboard Shortcuts

A keyboard shortcut is a way to have your iPad mini automatically type a phrase when you type the shortcut. For example, when we type **vty** followed by pressing the spacebar, our iPads type **Very truly yours**. In other words, we type a 3-letter shortcut, and the iPad replaces it with a 14-letter phrase in the blink of an eye.

How long would it take you to type **Dictated to and scent from my iPad mini; please blame Siri for any type ohs** on your onscreen keyboard? And would you type it without mistakes? It took a fraction of a second to type our shortcut for this phrase (**dict**), and another fraction of a second for the iPad to expand it (to **Dictated to and scent from my iPad mini; please blame Siri for any type ohs**).

So shortcuts save you time and keystrokes.

Another advantage is that you'll always spell things correctly (as long as you spell them correctly when you create the shortcut and phrase).

You can even use shortcuts to automatically correct the spelling of words you commonly mistype. Say you often type **taht** when you mean to type **that**. Here's how to create, edit, and enjoy your iPad's convenient little keystroke savers. Start by creating a shortcut:

1. **Tap Settings⇨General⇨Keyboard.**

2. **Tap Add New Shortcut.**

3. **Type the phrase and the shortcut you want to trigger it.**

   For example, you want the phrase "I'll call or text you as soon as I'm free" to appear when you type the shortcut **cty**, as shown in Figure 20-1.

4. **Tap Save.**

Figure 20-1: Here are some shortcuts and phrases we've created.

After you create a shortcut, simply tap its name to change (edit) it.

After you create and edit 'em, here's how you use 'em:

To insert a phrase, type its keyboard shortcut. Say the shortcut is **cty**, as shown in Figure 20-1. If you stop after you type **y**, the phrase appears below the cursor, as shown in Figure 20-2. To insert the phrase, press the spacebar on your iPad keyboard; to ignore the phrase, tap the gray *x* to the right of it.

One last thing: You can use the same technique to create keyboard shortcuts like this on any iPad, iPhone, or iPod touch. Although you can't easily sync or share your shortcuts, you can create and use them on any device running iOS 5 or later.

Figure 20-2: Type a space to insert the phrase "I'll call or text you as soon as I'm free."

One more last thing (this time we mean it, but we just *had* to include this tip-within-a-chapter-full-of-tips): You can create keyboard shortcuts such as these in OS X since at least version 10.6 (Snow Leopard). Just launch the System Preferences app, click the Language and Text (Snow Leopard) or Keyboard (Lion or Mountain Lion) icon, and click the Text tab (Snow Leopard) or Keyboard Shortcuts tab (Lion or Mountain Lion).

Auto-Correction Is Your Friend

Here are three related tips about Auto-Correction that can also help you type faster and more accurately.

Auto-apostrophes are good for you

First, know that you can type **dont** to produce **don't** and type **ive** to produce **I've.** Also note that the letter *I* in contractions such as *I've* and *I'm* is properly capitalized, even if you type the shortcut in all lowercase letters.

We've told you to put some faith in the iPad's Auto-Correction software. And that applies to contractions. In other words, save time by letting the iPad's intelligent keyboard insert the apostrophes on your behalf for these and other common words.

We're aware of at least one exception: The iPad can't distinguish between *it's* and *its*. (*It's* is the contraction of *it is,* and *its* is the possessive adjective and possessive pronoun.) So if you need, say, e-mails to important business clients to be grammatically correct, remember that Auto-Correction doesn't get it (or *it's* or *its*) right all the time. We should also point out that the iPad forms contractions from words such as *cant* (clichéd or hypocritical talk) and *wont* (accustomed to something) — both valid words.

In a similar vein, if you ever *need* to type an apostrophe (for example, when you want to type *it's*), you don't need to visit the punctuation-and-numeric keyboard. Instead, press the Exclamation Point/Comma key for at least one second, and an apostrophe magically appears. Slide your finger onto it and then lift your finger, and — presto! — you've typed an apostrophe without touching the punctuation-and-numeric keyboard.

Make rejection work for you

When the Auto-Correction suggestion isn't the word you want, rather than ignore it, reject it. Finish typing the word, and then tap the *x* to reject the suggestion before you type another word. Doing so makes your iPad more likely to accept your word the next time you type it and less likely to make the same incorrect suggestion again.

If you're using a physical keyboard (for example, Apple's Keyboard Dock or any Bluetooth wireless one), you can reject an autosuggestion by pressing the Esc key.

(Here you thought you were buying a tech book, and you get grammar and typing lessons thrown in at no extra charge. Just think of us as full-service authors.)

If you hate auto-correct, turn it off

Some people (such as our fifth-edition editor, Rebecca) don't care for auto-correct and turn it off. If you don't like it, either, here's how to get rid of it:

Tap Settings➪General➪Keyboard and tap the Auto-Correction switch to Off.

Settings➪General➪Keyboard is also where you enable or disable other keyboard-related features, including Auto-Capitalization, Check Spelling, Enable Caps Lock, and the "double-tapping the spacebar will insert a period followed by a space" shortcut. See Chapter 15, where we dive into settings.

Viewing the iPad's Capacity

When your iPad is selected in the sidebar in iTunes, you see a colorful chart at the bottom of the screen that tells you how your media and other data use your iPad's capacity.

By default, the chart shows the amount of space, in megabytes (MB) or gigabytes (GB), that your audio, video, and photo files use on your iPad. But you knew that. What you probably don't know is that when you click the text below this colorful chart (Audio, Video, Photos, and so forth), it changes to a slightly different display. When you click, the amount of space that's used changes to show the number of items (audio, video, and photos) you have stored, as shown in Figure 20-3.

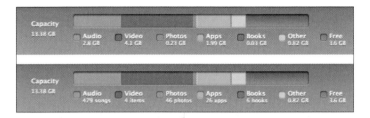

Figure 20-3: Click the colorful chart, and what's stored on your iPad is expressed in a different way.

Assault on batteries

Because this is a chapter of tips and hints, we'd be remiss if we didn't include some ways that you can extend your battery's life. First and foremost: If you use a carrying case, charging the iPad while it's in that case may generate more heat than is healthy. Overheating is bad for both battery capacity and battery life. So take the iPad out of the case before you charge it. The Smart Cover available for the iPad mini isn't actually a case, so if you use one, you're good to go.

If you're not using power-thirsty 3G, 4G, LTE, or Wi-Fi networks, or a Bluetooth device (such as a headset), consider turning off the features you don't need in Settings. Doing so could mean the difference between running out of juice and seeing the end of a movie.

Activate Auto-Brightness to enable the screen brightness to adjust based on current lighting conditions. Using this setting can be easier on your battery. Tap Settings⇨Brightness, and then tap the On/Off switch, if necessary, to turn it on.

Turn off Location Services (tap Settings⇨Location Services) globally or for individual apps with the On/Off switches. Figuring out your precise location takes its toll on your battery, so you may want to disable Location Services for apps you don't use often.

Push notifications are notorious juice-suckers as well. Disable them (tap Settings⇨Mail, Contacts, Calendars⇨Fetch New Data⇨Push On/Off switch) and watch the drain on your battery drop dramatically. You can disable push notifications for other apps via Settings⇨Notifications.

Finally, turning on EQ (see Chapter 7) when you listen to music can make it sound better, but it also uses more processing power. If you've selected an equalizer preset for a track in the iTunes Track Info window and you want to retain the EQ from iTunes when you listen on your iPad, set the EQ on your iPad to flat. Because you're not turning off EQ, the battery takes a slight hit, but your songs sound just the way you expect them to sound. Either way, to alter your EQ settings, tap Settings⇨iPod⇨EQ.

The Way-Cool, Hidden-in-the-Music-App Scrub Speed Tip

Here's the situation: You're listening to a podcast or an audiobook and trying to find the beginning of a specific segment by moving the Scrubber bar — the little red line representing the Playhead — left and right. The only problem is that the Scrubber bar isn't precise, so your fat finger keeps moving it too far one way or the other. Never fear — your iPad has a wonderful (albeit somewhat hidden) fix. Just press on the Scrubber, but rather than slide your finger to the left or right, slide it downward, toward the bottom of the screen (see Figure 20-4). As your finger slides downward, the scrubbing speed changes, like magic, and the Scrubber bar moves in increasingly finer increments. So, when you slide downward an inch or two, the speed changes to roughly half-speed scrubbing. Drag another inch or two, and the speed changes to quarter-speed scrubbing. Drag to near the bottom of the screen, and it changes to very fine scrubbing.

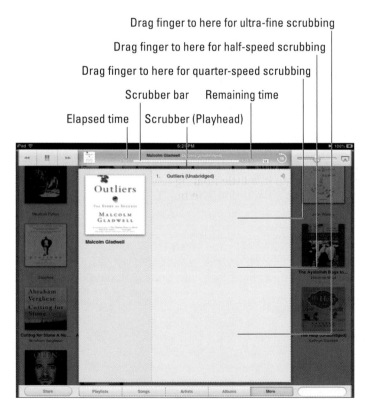

Drag finger to here for ultra-fine scrubbing

Drag finger to here for half-speed scrubbing

Drag finger to here for quarter-speed scrubbing

Scrubber bar   Remaining time

Elapsed time   Scrubber (Playhead)

Figure 20-4: Press the Scrubber bar and slide your finger downward to change the scrubbing rate.

While you're sliding, keep an eye on the elapsed-time and remaining-time indicators because they provide useful feedback on the current scrubbing speed.

The secret is to make sure that you've grabbed the Scrubber by pressing it and sliding your finger to the left or right. If the elapsed and remaining times change when you slide, you're good to go. Without lifting your finger, slide it downward on the screen to change the scrubbing speed, and then drag left or right to scrub.

This scrubbing trick is easier to do than to explain, so give it a try.

Tricks with Links and E-Mail Addresses

The iPad does something special when it encounters an e-mail address or a URL in e-mail messages: It interprets character sequences that look like web addresses (URLs), such as http://www.*websitename*.com or www.*websitename*.com, and any sequences that look like e-mail addresses, such as *yourname@yourmailhost*.com. When the iPad sees what it assumes to be a URL or an e-mail address, it appears as a blue link on your screen.

If you tap a URL or an e-mail address like the ones just shown, the iPad launches Safari, takes you to the appropriate web page for a URL, or starts a new e-mail message for an e-mail address. So don't bother with copy and paste if you don't have to — tap those blue links, and the right thing will happen every time.

Here's another cool Safari trick, this time with links. If you press and hold a link rather than tap it, a little floating text bubble appears and shows you the underlying URL. In addition, the bubble offers the following options, as shown in Figure 20-5:

- **Open:** Opens the page
- **Open in New Tab:** Opens the page while stashing the current page on one of the nine available tabs, as we describe in Chapter 4
- **Add to Reading List:** Adds the page to your Reading List, as we describe in Chapter 4
- **Copy:** Copies the URL to the Clipboard (so that you can paste it into an e-mail message, save it in Notes, or do whatever)

Figure 20-5: Press and hold a link to find additional actions you can take.

You also see the underlying URL if you press and hold a URL in Mail with buttons to open or copy it. Having this information in Mail is even more useful because it enables you to spot bogus (and potentially harmful) links without switching to Safari or visiting the URL.

Here's one last Safari trick: If you press and hold your finger on most images, a Save Image button appears in addition to the four other buttons (see Figure 20-6). Tap Save Image, and the picture is saved to the Camera Roll on the Albums tab of the Photos app. Tap Copy, and the picture is copied to the Clipboard so that you can paste it into an e-mail message or a document created in another app, such as Apple's Pages or Keynote.

Figure 20-6: Save images you want to find easily later.

Share the Love . . . and the Links

Ever stumble onto a web page that you just *have* to share with a buddy? The iPad makes sharing dead simple. From the site in question, tap the Action button, which looks like a little rectangle with an arrow sprouting from it. Just tap the Mail, Message, Twitter, or Facebook button to share the link via e-mail or iMessage or to post it to your Facebook wall or Twitter stream (see Figure 20-7).

Type a short message (or don't), supply your pal's e-mail or iMessage address if necessary, and then tap the Send or Post button.

Figure 20-7: Share links with your friends.

Choosing a Home Page for Safari

You may have noticed that there's no option to specify a home page in the iPad version of Safari, though this popular option exists on Mac and PC versions of the Safari (and, for that matter, on every other commonly used) web browser. Instead, when you tap the Safari icon, you return to the last site you visited.

The trick is to create an icon for the page you want to use as your home page. This technique is called *creating a web clip* of a web page. Here's how to do it:

1. **Open the web page you want to use as your home page, and tap the Action button. (It looks like a little rectangle with an arrow sprouting from it at the top of the screen.)**

2. **Tap the Add to Home Screen button.**

   An icon that will open this page appears on your Home screen (or on one of your Home screens if you have more than one).

3. **Tap this new Web Clip icon instead of the Safari icon, and Safari opens to your home page instead of to the last page you visited.**

You can even rearrange the icons so that your Home Page icon, instead of or in addition to the Safari icon, appears in the *Dock* (the bottom row that appears on every Home screen), as shown in Figure 20-8.

Figure 20-8: The B.L. Dot Com icon now appears to the left of Safari in the Dock.

Consider moving the Safari icon from the Dock to one of your Home screens so that you never tap it by accident. Finally, remember that the Dock has room for six icons, even though it has only four by default. If you like, place both Safari and your new Web Clip icon on the Dock so that you can tap either one, depending on your needs.

Storing Files

A tiny Massachusetts software company — Ecamm Network — sells an inexpensive ($29.95) piece of OS X software, PhoneView, which lets you copy files from your Mac to your iPad and copy files from the iPad to a Mac, as shown in Figure 20-9. (No Windows version is available.) Better still, you can try the program for a week before deciding whether you want to buy it. Go to www.ecamm.com to fetch the free demo.

The big deal here is that while automatic backups protect most of the files on your iPad, there's no way to manipulate them. They're backed up and restored, but heaven help you if you wish to extract one or more individual iMessages, specific songs, videos, notes, or other types of data from your iPad. The bottom line is that there's no easier way than PhoneView.

In a nutshell, here's how PhoneView works. After downloading the software to your Mac, double-click the program's icon to start it. Then do one of the following:

- **To transfer files and folders to the iPad** (assuming that you have room on the device), click the Copy to iPad button on the toolbar, and then select the files you want to copy. The files are copied into the appropriate places on the iPad. Alternatively, you can drag files and folders from the Mac Desktop or a folder into the PhoneView browser.

- **To go the other way and copy files from your iPad to your computer,** highlight the files or folders you want to be copied, and then click the

Copy from iPad button on the toolbar. Select the destination on your Mac where you want to store the files, and then click Save. You can also drag files and folders from the PhoneView file browser to the Mac Desktop or folder. Or you can double-click a file in the PhoneView browser to download it to your Mac's Documents folder.

If you need access to the files on your iPad or you want to use your iPad as a pseudo–hard drive, PhoneView is a bargain.

Bob says: I use Printopia, also from Ecamm ($19.95), to print from my iPad to several of our non-AirPrint printers. It works great and costs a lot less than a new AirPrint-enabled printer.

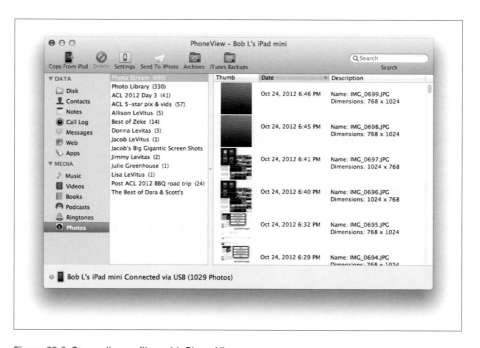

Figure 20-9: Store all your files with PhoneView.

Making Phone Calls on the iPad

Many people, including us, have compared the iPad to an iPhone on steroids — except that the iPad isn't actually a phone.

Don't let that stop you from making, or even receiving, phone calls on the tablet.

Come again?

You read it correctly. You *can* make (and even receive) phone calls on your iPad. After all, two of the key components to calling are built into the iPad: a speaker and microphone. Now all you have to do is head to the App Store to fetch a third component, an app that takes advantage of *VoIP,* or *Voice over Internet Protocol.* In plain-speak, that means turning the iPad into a giant iPhone. And yes, you can find more than one app to do the trick.

We've checked out Skype, Line2, and Truphone, all of which have a version specifically designed to take advantage of the large iPad screen. The apps themselves are free, although you have to pay for calls to non-Internet phones. Here are the details:

- ✔ **Line2:** We especially like Line2, although it costs $9.95 a month. It can receive calls through Wi-Fi or a cellular data network (if you have an iPad with 3G or 4G). Line2 boasts such features as visual voice mail (like the iPhone) and conference calling. And it taps right into your iPad contacts list.

- ✔ **Skype:** Skype's app permits free Skype-to-Skype calls, instant messages, and video chats; calls to regular phones around the world cost pennies per minute.

- ✔ **Truphone:** This app permits free Wi-Fi calls to Truphone and Google Talk users. Other rates are cheap.

Taking a Snapshot of the Screen

True confession: We threw in this tip because, well, it helps people like *us.*

Permit us to explain. We hope you admire the pictures of the iPad screens that are sprinkled throughout this book. We also secretly hope that you're thinking what marvelous photographers we must be.

Well, the fact is that we couldn't, even if we wanted to, take a blurry picture of the iPad using its built-in and little-known screen-grab feature.

Press the Sleep/Wake button, only for an instant, at the same time you press the Home button. The iPad grabs a snapshot of whatever is on the screen.

The picture lands in the Camera Roll on the Albums tab of the Photos app. From there, you can synchronize it with your Mac or PC, along with all your other pictures, or e-mail it to yourself or anyone else. And from there, the possibilities are endless. Why, your picture could wind up just about anywhere, including in a *For Dummies* book.

You can show what's happening on your iPad mini's screen on your high-def television in real time. All you need is a television that has at least one HDMI port and the $49 Lightning Digital AV Adapter or $99 Apple TV to connect your iPad to the HDTV.

Index

Notes